Telling It the Way It Was

Telling It the Way It Was

A Country Boy Survives Life in the City

DAVID JUSSERO

iUniverse, Inc.
Bloomington

TELLING IT THE WAY IT WAS
A Country Boy Survives Life in the City

iUniverse books may be ordered through booksellers or by contacting:

iUniverse
1663 Liberty Drive
Bloomington, IN 47403
www.iuniverse.com
1-800-Authors (1-800-288-4677)

ISBN: 978-1-4620-6665-0 (sc)
ISBN: 978-1-4620-6667-4 (hc)
ISBN: 978-1-4620-6666-7 (ebk)

Printed in the United States of America

iUniverse rev. date: 01/09/2012

Dedicated to

Caroleen and Charleen

If it weren't for you two, I wouldn't have had much to write about.

Acknowledgements

I WANT TO THANK THE PEOPLE who came before me to America to have a better life for themselves and the next generations. Without these brave, hardworking people life, as we know it, would not be possible.

I want to thank my wife, Caroleen, for the countless hours of typing, printing, sorting, and organizing the mountain of handwritten material that I've accumulated over the past couple of years. If she hadn't put up with me that past fifty years, there probably wouldn't be a book or it would be an entirely different story.

I've depended on the support of my friends, Bea and Jack Rawls, who kept encouraging me throughout this project. How could I be so fortunate as to have these fine people edit this thing and share their experience as authors. Bea's recent book *Stinkweed* inspired me to continue writing. *Stinkweed* is a book about growing up on the prairies of North Dakota that talks about one room school houses, the gift of childhood on a farm, and a way of life that is no more.

I also want to thank my friends who kept inquiring about the book hoping I would get it done before I expired. I had no intention of crapping out before it was done. It is my intention to stay around for a long time if for no other reason than to make life miserable for those of you who thought it would never be finished.

Thanks to my cousins Lucille and Vern Danes and David and Bernice Cadiuex for helping me sort out the history of Grandma and Grandpa Cadieux and my other relatives in Canada.

Thanks to Lillian Mitchell for helping me with the details of the history of our Grandma and Grandpa Jussero.

Thanks to Jason Nordmark for permission to use pictures and text from history books of Rolla, Hansboro, and Towner County that were published by his company.

Foreword

IF IT'S TRUE THAT A person lives their life forward and understands it backward, Dave Jussero has had a full and complete life. In his seventy plus years he has lived his life forward in an enviable style and he has spent that last couple of years understanding it backwards as he penned his book *Telling it the Way it Was.*

In the process of understanding it backward, he accomplished one of society's most significant mandates which is to pass along one's heritage and culture to the next generation. He has told his story as well as his parents' and grandparents' stories so that his children, grandchildren, and great-grandchildren can know about the sturdy and rugged people that preceded them.

Dave relates the hardships and successes of his Finnish and French ancestors who faced the demands of settling a new country. He tells of how they lived in sod houses and braved bitter winters on the prairies of both the US and Canada. He tells about the *mixed marriage* his French mother found herself in when she immigrated to the US to marry her Finnish sweetheart. He speaks to the closed culture of the Finnish community she faced and overcame. He writes with humor and ethos about the work ethic and perseverance that his Finnish ancestors modeled. He describes the way it was to grow up on a small wheat farm in North Dakota during the 30's, 40's, and 50's. He talks about one-room school houses, dropping out of school at age sixteen, and the dead-end farm jobs that spurred him into trading the life of a hired farm hand for city life. When he was still in his teens, he made his way to the west coast to seek his fortune.

Dave married his childhood sweetheart, Caroleen Messier, and together they managed to assemble a number of rental properties. They did it while Dave worked full time and Caroleen sold real estate. The work ethic of his ancestors paid off. They spent countless hours of hard work at night and on weekends remodeling and refitting their properties and before long, it began to pay off. Dave was able to retire from his 9 to 5 job to manage their investments when he was only in his 40's. Their judicious and timely real estate investments provided Dave the avenue to live the way he always knew he could . . . on his own terms and on his own schedule.

The last thirty years of doing it his way allowed Dave to travel extensively. He and Caroleen have toured the entire US and most of Canada by motorhome. Dave rode his Goldwing motorcycle on extended excursions and managed to cross the North America twice by bicycle. He has spent untold numbers of hours doing volunteer work for various service organizations and missions. He has helped build houses for the needy in the US with Habitat for Humanity and in Central America with World Vision.

Readers of Dave's book will enjoy a series of essays on subjects that he simply finds interesting. For his family in particular and other readers in general, Dave's backward glance at the life he lived forward, answers questions about him and a way of life that no longer exists. It answers questions that have yet to be asked.

Bea Rawls

Preface

Telling it the Way it Was

David Richard Jussero

I AM NOW 72 YEARS OLD. If you look at life as a tank full of gas, statistically I'm running somewhere between one quarter and empty, and, who knows how accurate the gauge is. I hope to run a long time on near-empty.

I am putting together a few pictures and stories from my past. Most of these stories are as I remember them which may or may not be the way they actually happened. I'm hoping these tales and photos will interest family and friends.

Life in North Dakota is much different now than it was when I grew up there. Looking back, times were not easy, but nobody realized it. It's just the way it was. My early years proved very helpful to me in my later life. We learned that hard work pays off, that in this life you work for what you get, and you always do your best at any job you have.

I've spent most of my life away from North Dakota. I never wanted to spend my life working for someone. I've had some good jobs, but they were all too structured. Start work at a certain time. Lunch at 12:00 noon. Back to work until quitting time. Wait for Friday and dread Monday. This didn't work for me although I enjoyed knowing the people I worked with. I had to try something else. Working 9 to 5 just didn't cut it. I began to question conventional wisdom years ago. I feel that there are few things that should not be questioned. Just because something has always been done a certain way, doesn't mean that there may not be a better way or at least a better way for a certain type of individual. I didn't mind the work, but I thought it would be nice to be able to work on my own terms.

Conventional wisdom is a guide that works for most people, but it is only a guide. Although it's necessary to live in such a way that is ethical, moral, and legal, you still have a lot of freedom to change the way you live to let the system work in your favor. Many people have not lived the way society would expect, and have made it work. I may be in this group.

When I say that I questioned conventional wisdom, I don't want to give the impression that at any time I considered myself smarter than the average person. It's quite the opposite—I went through many years with a lack of confidence. I tried many things and found some that worked and many that didn't. When I finally started to sort things out, I found that what worked for me wasn't necessarily what society expected. I tended to make adjustments to what fit my nature. I never considered myself among the most likely to succeed, but with lots of help along the way, I stumbled around until I found something that functioned for me.

Now I think of success as having resources enough to live comfortably on my own terms, enough to pay as I go, enough not to be a slave to excessive debt, and enough to be able to pay my way until they haul me away horizontally in that long, black limo. The key word is "enough."

There are ways to be happy
That don't depend on earning
More cash or buying more things.

Introduction

A True Sign of Wealth is Free Time

THE WAY I'VE LIVED HAS worked quite well and I wouldn't change very much of anything. I've had many years of setting my own schedule and hope to have many more. Life is good and getting better.

This "masterpiece" may answer some questions my friends and family have had over the years. I'm including many pictures from the past. I'll identify people for future reference. If my generation fails to document our way of life on the farm, it will be lost. Now I am the oldest in my immediate family so there is no one who came earlier to ask questions. My dad told me once that when you look around a crowd of people and realize you're the oldest, you know you're getting old. More and more I find myself in that situation. Growing older is my goal, but I have no intention of growing up. The kid in me keeps surfacing, and I wouldn't have it any other way. I try to think young, but each time I look in the mirror, I realize I'm not fooling anyone.

As you read this, it may sound as if I'm feeling sorry for myself having to work hard, but it's quite the opposite. I am thankful for the years I spent growing up in North Dakota. I wish more kids could have that experience. It wasn't easy, but who ever said life was supposed to be easy?

I had great parents and always had a good home. The houses weren't always great, but home is the closeness of family, and we had a great family. My brothers, Duane and Dwight, and I were born years apart and because of the age difference, we didn't have a lot in common when we were young, but we've become very close as we've aged. A few years difference in age is no longer important, and all three of us are growing older.

My parents got along better in the early years of their marriage. In later years they began to have heated discussions. Some may call them arguments. They stayed together as most people did in those days, and I think they loved and respected each other in their own way. My brothers and I always had Mom and Dad to support and love us.

I have had the joy of knowing my grandkids and my great-grandkids, and for this I am truly grateful. I am hoping that putting some of my life experiences on paper will answer questions for them about the way it was. Many times the questions don't come until we are older.

There are many things I would ask my mom, dad, and grandparents, but, unfortunately, it's too late. Dad died in 1980 at age seventy-two and Mother died in 1983 at the age of seventy-three. I am now the age they were when they died, and it's time to answer questions my grandchildren haven't yet asked.

WHERE IT ALL BEGAN

John and Anna Jussero, my grandparents. Possibly a wedding picture

Telling it the Way it Was

Anything worthwhile
is worth working for

John and Anna Jussero—my grandparents

JOHN JUSSERO WAS BORN IN IsoKyro, Finland on Oct. 8, 1869. He came to the US in 1888 at the age of nineteen. He lived in Rockport, Mass. where he met Anna Liisa Riikimaki, who was also born in IsoKyro. She was born Jan.1, 1871, and came to this country when she was twenty years old. They were married Sept. 17, 1892, a marriage that would last until Grandpa's death forty-six years later. They lived in Rockport until the spring of 1896 when they left for North Dakota to carve a life out of this new country. Grandpa and Grandma were among the first groups of Finnish settlers to homestead in what was to become Towner County.

We all need to be proud to be descendants of these very brave, courageous people who immigrated to the plains of ND to start a better life for themselves, their kids and future generations. I'm sure they didn't expect this venture to be easy and were undoubtedly prepared for a lot of hard work and sacrifice, but only extremely physically and emotionally strong people could have survived the challenges that lay ahead. They obviously knew that they weren't moving to a friendly climate, and the weather over the next years could only be described as severe with bone-chilling cold in the winter coupled with blinding snow storms. The summers were unpredictable as well with breathtaking heat, drought, hail storms and at times dust storms.

John Jussero arrived in ND on April1,1896, with Matt Juusala, Paul Juntunen, and John Luuko, four Finnish friends that planned to work together to develop their homesteads. As it turned out, only three of them stayed. John Luuko left the country and never returned. He probably figured there had to be an easier way to make a living. He wasn't up to building a home and converting 160 acres of grass, brush, trees and rocks into farm land.

The Homestead Act was an effort by the US Government to allow people to file claims on 160 acres of federal land. A homesteader paid $16.00 for a five year claim with the agreement that he would clear the land and construct buildings. By meeting these requirements he would own the land after five years. This was no small commitment. Much of this land was cleared with strong backs and teams of oxen or horses.

Naturally, the first order of business was to build a house. A house was a necessity before the family arrived, and the families would be arriving soon. As was common in those days, the building material used was what was available on site. The local trees and brush weren't suitable for lumber so the alternative was to use sod. The prairie sod was turned over with a walk-behind plow pulled by oxen. The strips of sod were cut into approximately two foot lengths hauled to the site on a wagon pulled by horses then stacked to the height needed for walls. Next the roof was installed. A cross beam was put up to support the roof. Some fairly substantial logs or beams were needed considering the weight of the tar paper and sod roof not to mention the snow load most winters. The home builders probably cut logs for the beams in the Turtle Mountains about twenty miles away. They certainly didn't pick up a phone and call the lumber yard to deliver the material they needed because there were no phones, no roads, and no delivery trucks—only wagons pulled by oxen or horses. Lumber must have been purchased in Rolla, a town with a population of a few hundred at that time. The building materials were hauled to the building site about five miles east and a little north of town. There were also windows and a door that would be needed to make the building complete. These were probably also acquired in Rolla along with other necessities such as ox teams, plows, and tools needed to start life on the plains of North Dakota.

There were a few things in their favor. There were no permits required and building inspectors weren't concerned with sod shelters miles from town. Electrical wiring and plumbing systems weren't a problem either. Oil lamps didn't require electricity and the only plumbing needed was an outhouse in the yard. Using an outhouse in below zero temperatures is very uncomfortable but I'm sure they had provisions in the house for emergencies. They did what they needed to do to survive.

The second sod house was to be built on Grandpa's land, but until the first house was completed on his neighbor's property, the only shelter the men had was their wagon box. That must have been a tough way to live because the temperatures in April can be quite cold especially at night and there was always the threat of rain or snow. According to the Towner County historical record, those Finnish immigrants who arrived in April built two sod houses by May 10, 1896. They were strong, highly motivated young men who needed shelter for their families who would be arriving soon.

This is a typical type of sod house my grandparents lived in from 1896 until 1903 when they built a conventional home with lumber. No actual picture of my grandparents' sod house is available. Four children were born while they lived in a sod house.

Grandma and her daughter, Lempi, and Mrs. Matt Juusala and her daughter, Emilia, arrived in Rolla on May 10, 1896. They were assisted by two Finnish gentlemen, John Palmi and Paavo Routsalainen. Grandma and Mrs. Juusala, the kids and their two assistants came from Massachusetts by boat and rail to Churches Ferry, ND, where they found a ride to Rolla. The plan was for the women to stay in Rolla and Matt Juusala would pick them up the next day with the wagon. Grandpa had walked to town to meet them but the women were so anxious to see their new homes that they convinced Grandpa they could walk the six miles to their homesteads. That turned out to be a serious challenge because they followed a muddy wagon trail and at one point had to wade through waist deep water. Mrs. Juusala and her one year old daughter had to be carried across the swollen stream. They finally arrived at the sod houses after dark only to find that the men had run out of oil for the lamps. It must have been a long evening in a cold, dark sod house.

The next order of business was to clear and break land for the first season's grain crops. Plowing rough, virgin sod with oxen was back breaking work. Many rocks had be dug out with an iron bar, muscle, and determination. Those men were not strangers to hard work.

There was some grain harvested in 1896, but in 1897 and 1898 the crops failed due to hot, dry growing seasons. Feed to winter the cattle was also a problem in 1898. Many of the men needed to find work out of the state in lumber camps, the railroad, or mining before returning in the spring for the next planting season.

The winter of 1896 was a tough winter. By Thanksgiving there was so much snow that the sod houses were completely covered with only the chimneys visible.

Religion was always important to the settlers and as early as 1897 they held services in private homes. The Apostolic Lutheran Church was established in 1899. In 1900 a church was built on an acre of land donated by Henry Simonson.

They hauled wood from the Turtle Mountain about twenty-two miles west of the homesteads for heat in the winter. That trip would take from three to seven days. Nothing was easy in those years and it would not get much better anytime soon. Although the Finns and the Indians got along fine most of the time, there were occasions when removing fire wood from Indian land caused controversies. All the wood for heating had to be hauled after the snow covered the frozen ground so the sleighs could travel across the lowlands.

Drinking water was another problem for the homesteaders. Plenty of water was available in the marshes for the livestock, but it was unfit for drinking or cooking. Sometimes they melted snow for drinking water. Some locations had natural springs that produced limited amounts of clean water. Eventually, they dug wells to depths of 200 to 400 feet that produced adequate water for human consumption and for the livestock. They installed wind mills or hand pumps to pull water up from those deep water wells

The Finnish people continued to migrate to the area around the same part of Towner County where our family settled. Even though there were other immigrants in the area, it became known as the Finnish settlement.

Unlike the tough years of 1897 and 1898, things improved in 1899, 1900, 1901, and 1902. The crops were good yielding 30 to 40 bushels of wheat to the acre. The settlers became prosperous. They began to think about building more comfortable homes and the sod houses were replaced with more conventional materials. A sod house was warm in the winter and cool in the summer, but there were some disadvantages. It was hard to keep a house built out of dirt very clean. The soil settled down on everything. The earthen floors became so hard packed that they could be swept like a wooden floor. Animal skins and furs were often used for rugs. An occasional spider or fly wasn't much of a problem when there were bigger pests such as mice, rats, gophers, and snakes tunneling through the walls. That would have been a good argument for a resident cat. Although the sod house was shelter for family for many years, a frame house was something everyone anticipated enthusiastically. Men had to learn to remove muddy boots in a wood frame house and the women could actually hang pictures on the wall.

Grandpa and Grandma had four children—Hilda, Hilja, Elsie and John Oscar—while they lived in the sod house. The youngest, John Oscar, died as a result of a lightening strike.

In 1903 Grandpa built a six room wood frame house with the help of his friend and neighbor, Matt Jussola. My grandparents had five more children after their new home was built. They were Oscar, Richard (my dad,) John, Ellen, and Elma.

Jussero farm in the early 1900's

About 1915 tractors started to replace horses for the farm work and it became possible to farm more land more efficiently. Automobiles also started to come on the scene. Things were changing. Roads began to be improved to accommodate the early autos. Some of the main roads were graveled in the late twenties. Many secondary roads were not improved with gravel until many years later. The wagon trail between Grandpa's claim and Rolla eventually became part of State Highway 5. The highway was well maintained and stretched from near the Montana border to the Minnesota border. The Jussero farm was about a third of a mile from this good road and gave Grandpa excellent access to Rolla.

By the 1920's, the kids of the family were getting big enough to be quite helpful on the farm. Grandma was very good at managing the chores and work around the farm so that gave Grandpa a chance to go to town and play cards with his buddies. This was a favorite pastime. Dad talked about going to town on Saturday night and Grandma patiently waiting in the car parked on Main Street for Grandpa to finish playing a game of cards with his friends.

There were some reasonably good years for these settlers in the 1920's. The 1918 flu season was in the past. The blizzards of the winter of 1919 and the massive snow banks were history. The good times wouldn't last, and the country would experience the hardest times in history beginning in 1929 when numerous banks closed, many fortunes were lost, people lost farms, and businesses folded. This was the beginning of the Great Depression. Times wouldn't improve much for a decade or more. The price of wheat went down to about 20 cents per bushel down from over $2.00 earlier in the decade. Unemployment went up to 15 to 20 percent. The fact that many of these years the crops failed due to droughts, grasshoppers, and dust storms added to the financial difficulties of the times. People on farms may have had some advantage as they were able to raise gardens. They had a few milk cows and raised chickens for eggs and meat. I'm sure these settlers didn't go hungry.

Grandpa and Grandma undoubtedly saved some money during the good years. Finns are known to be careful with their finances. As tough as many of those years were, there were good times on the way.

Unfortunately, my grandparents didn't experience the better times of the late 30's and 40's. Grandpa died June 30, 1938, of liver cancer. He was on his homestead surrounded by family. They held the funeral on the farm. Grandma continued to live in her home until her death June 25, 1941.They are both now buried in the Mount View Cemetery nine miles east and two miles south of Rolla.

After my grandparents passed away, the farm was sold. The house was moved off the property to a new location and the barn and outbuildings were eventually removed. It would have been great if this original homestead could have been maintained as part of Jussero history, but this was not possible at the time. The good news is that the old Jussero farm site is now a modern up-to-date farmstead owned by the John Halone family. John Jr. is the descendant of Finnish people who immigrated to the area in the early 1900's. John's house is built on almost the same location as the original Jussero home. While excavating for the new home, part of the foundation of Grandpa's house was uncovered. Hopefully this well maintained farmstead will be home to future generations. I'm sure Grandpa and Grandma would agree.

Modern home on original site of the Jussero farm.

Grandpa and Grandma Cadieux

Grandpa Dolphus Cadieux was born in Ontario, Canada, in 1876, and Grandma Anna Tetley was born in 1881, also in Ontario. When Dolphus was in his early 20's and Anna was in her late teens, they were married in Ontario. They moved from Ontario to Colinton, Alberta in 1909, then to Lac LaBiche in 1914.

Dora, my mother, was one of the youngest of their family when they arrived in Lac LaBiche. By 1915 there were nine kids in the family. If the family hadn't decided to move west, I wouldn't be writing this. Dora would have a screaming son about twenty-five years later and that would be me.

Grandpa was a businessman in Lac LaBiche. He ran a livery barn. According to my cousin, Lucille, he furnished shelter and feed for the horses that were in town while their owners shopped or took care of business. The livery barn was an early parking garage. People could *park* their transportation with Grandpa where they were fed and protected while the owners went about town. There were few cars so horses and the railroad were the major modes of transportation. Neither of those choices provided quick travel. Many trains didn't travel daily. Some were weekly or bi-weekly and horses were only a little faster than walking. Horses, like the automobiles that would come later, produced pollution, but with cars you don't have to be as careful where you step. There were no parking meters in those days, but if there had been, the meter maids would have to do more than pin a ticket on a horse; they would need to bring a shovel and a wheelbarrow along.

Grandpa started his livery barn business sometime before 1918. During the early years of his business, he helped new settlers build trails to their homesteads as another business venture. He also ran a delivery service hauling freight arriving by rail to the local businesses in Lac LaBiche. It was called a dray service. When autos became practical, he bought a couple of cars and started a taxi business in the area and homesteaded at the same time. Grandpa Cadieux was a resourceful man and he needed to support his big family. Grandpa's homestead is very close to the property where Uncle Edward filed his homestead claim. Edward's son, Gerry Cadieux and his wife, Mae, and their family continue to run a successful ranching operation at the location of Edward's original claim.

In 1919 a forest fire went through Lac LaBiche and destroyed almost everything in its path. Everything went up in smoke which meant everyone had to start all over again. About this time Grandpa ran a butcher shop.

The year 1919 was a particularly bad year. Grandma was pregnant with another child and the baby was stillborn. Grandma needed immediate medical care that was not readily available. Lac LaBiche had no hospital, Edmonton was about 130 miles away where they had medical facilities. Grandma became critically ill but the train only ran every two weeks. Unfortunately, she didn't get to the hospital in time to save her. There is a good chance that earlier medical attention could have saved her, but it wasn't available. Her body was shipped back to Lac LaBiche on the next train and she was buried at the Mission Cemetery. Grandma Cadieux was only thirty-eight years old.

Grandpa had a family to raise alone. Fortunately, the older kids, Edward, Bertha, Marie Anne, and Lillian, were old enough to take care of the younger kids. Grandpa had some serious adjustments to make trying to raise a family without Grandma. He decided to send the younger kids—Dora, my mother, Virginia, Albert, Omer, and Emile—to a Catholic convent school. Apparently, this wasn't a very popular plan with my mother who was about nine years old at the time. She had very little good to say about her years of school at the convent. She may have been a bit of a problem with the nuns, because she was known to have a bit of a stubborn streak and probably questioned the authority of the teachers.

Uncle Edward was old enough to farm the homestead so Grandpa decided to go north about 30 or 40 miles and start a ranching operation. This ranch was on leased land. He built a nice log cabin, barns, shelters and whatever he needed to survive this rugged country. In order to get some great hay land to feed his herd, he drained a lake called Cranberry Lake. That gave him an abundance of luscious grass that could be stacked or baled during haying season to get his cattle through long, severe winters.

Aunt Marie Anne and Uncle Mike and the kids went to the ranch in the summers to help Grandpa during haying season. Uncle Omer also spent some time on the ranch with Grandpa, but, according to family lore, they didn't agree on many things because they were both set in their ways. Could it be a little bit of a Cadieux stubborn streak? The ranching venture started in the early 1930's, and Grandpa spent many years on the ranch before moving back to Lac LaBiche. In his later years he spent time with Mike Perron and his family, Aunt Marie Anne, Uncle Mike and their family, and the other sons and daughters who lived in the area.

Unfortunately, I never met Grandpa or Grandma Cadieux. The information about them came from my mother years ago, and my cousins Lucille Danes and David, Bernice, and Paul Cadieux.

It seems Grandpa was a well-respected man with a great sense of humor. He loved to joke around and was somewhat of a prankster. He enjoyed partying and was known to have a few drinks from time to time. According to Mom and the cousins who knew him, he was a good father and grandfather who was great fun to be with. He was a man with many friends.

The word is that he was quite a horse trader. Horse trading was a bit like car trading today. Grandpa was considered an expert on horses and he was proud of the fact that he was able to come out the winner in most of those transactions. David Cadieux told me that when he was about six years old, he was sitting on Grandpa's lap when he said, "Gosh, Grandpa, you have big ears." Grandpa said "You're the guy with the big ears. We can tell when you kids are coming home from school because we can see those ears coming over the hill!"

While I was growing up in ND, we lived only two or three days drive from Lac LaBiche. Unfortunately, it wasn't common in those days to take a drive of that distance. It seems that farm work took priority over travel of any distance and vacations were unheard of. It was never possible for me or my brothers to take this trip to Alberta while Grandpa was alive. It would have been a pleasure to meet this great man, but that didn't happen. After writing this account of his life, I almost feel as if I knew him.

Grandpa died April 20, 1949, in Lac LaBiche. He was seventy-three years old. He is buried near Grandma in the Lac LaBiche Mission Cemetery.

A wasted day
Is a day without laughter.

Grandpa Cadieux

We are all dealt different hands.
How we play them is up to us.

Mom and Dad

Mother was born in Ontario, Canada, on June 9, 1910. The family eventually moved to Lac LaBiche, Alberta, where she attended a Catholic convent grade school. When she was nine years old, her mother died leaving the family to be raised by Grandpa Cadiuex and his older kids.

When she was sixteen, she came to North Dakota to live on a farm near Perth, ND, with Bertha and Carl Henrickson, an older sister and her husband. She got a job at the tuberculosis sanatorium near Dunseith which was about thirty-five miles from Perth. Later she worked for Dr. Verret, the local physician in Rolla, and she also worked as a waitress at the Vendome Hotel and Café in Rolla.

In 1933 she was still living in ND but had to return to Canada as she was still a Canadian citizen. She wasn't anxious to leave ND because she had met a young man she was quite interested in. He was a strong, handsome, young Finnish man named Richard Jussero born June 7, 1907, and the son of pioneers, John and Anna Jussero. Apparently Richard thought she was pretty special too, and he missed his pretty, witty, young friend when she went back to Canada. He missed her so much that he decided to go to Alberta and bring her back as his wife. She was agreeable and they were married Dec. 30, 1933, in Alberta. All of this was good for me because I ended up with a great mother and dad.

In those days it wasn't easy to get a permanent resident status in the US. Although being married to a US citizen made it somewhat easier, it wasn't without complications. It was during the Great Depression and the US government wanted to be sure that anyone crossing the border from another country would not become dependent on the US public for assistance. My grandfather, John Jussero, had to produce a financial report stating his net worth in addition to a letter agreeing to financial support of his daughter-in-law as long as she was married to his son. Two letters were required to gain residency. Mother's sister, Marie Anne, and her husband, Mike Perron, provided a similar document assuming responsibility for Mother's welfare, so Mother was in. Both Mother and Dad were very capable, hard-working people and made it through a lot of tough times on their own.

Rolla, North Dakota, December 21st. 1933.

TO WHOME IT MAY CONCERN.

STATE OF NORTH DAKOTA,)
)SS:
COUNTY OF ROLETTE   )

Before me the undersigned personall appeared John O. Jussero of Towner County, North Dakota ,and being first duly sworn deposes and says, I am a freeholder in Towner County, State of North Dakota,and make this affidavit in behalf of my son Richard J.Jussero, who intending to marry Dora M.Cadieux ofLac La Biche, Alberta Canada,and if this marriage takes place between my son Richard J. Jussero, of Rolla, North Dakota and Miss Dora M. Cadieux of Lac La Biche, Alberta Canada, I will take care of her and promise she will not become a public charge as long as she is my sons wife.

I am the owner of the following personal and real property and value the same as follows to-wit:

Assets		Libilities	
30 head of cattle	$ 500.00	Mortgage on chattles	$ 1300.00
7 horses	$ 700.00		
2000. bu. wheat	1400.00	Net worth	$12300.00
Farm Machinery.	2000.00		
Other personal property. .	1000.00		
320 acre farm	8000.00		
	13600.00		$ 13600.00

I also state that my dependents are my wife and two children,who live with me.

John O. Jussero

Subscribed and sworn to before me this 21st day of December 1933.

Mike J. Coghlan
County Judge, Rolette County, N.Dak.

STATE OF NORTH DAKOTA,)
)SS:
COUNTY OF ROLETTE   )

I, Mike J.Coghlan, the duly elected qualified and acting County Judge, in and for the County of Rolette and State of North Dakota, hereby certify that I am personally acquainted with John O. Jussero and his son Richard J. Jussero, of the Post Office of Rolla, North Dakota, and I further certify that their repution for honesty and good citinship is good and they are know as good citizens and reliable residents of the Vicienty of Rolla, N.Dak.

IN TESTIMONY WHEREOF, I have hereto signed my name and affixed the seal of the County Court of Rolette County, State of North Dakota on this 21st day of December, 1933.

Mike J. Coghlan
County Judge, Rolette County, N.Dak.

I, Oscar Hjelt, Cashier of the First National Bank of Rolla, No. Dak. certify that the above statements are true to the best of my knowledge.

Oscar Hjelt

Dec. 21,1933

This is the financial report my grandfather had to produce to prove that my mother would not be a financial burden on the US when she left Canada to marry my father.

During those times, Finns usually married Finns. The Finnish community was very tight-knit and it wasn't common to have another nationality introduced to this group. Mother was accepted by Dad's family, but she would have been better accepted in the community if she had been a Finnish woman. They survived any problems their *mixed marriage* may have caused by not being afraid to be a little different. After the marriage, they temporarily lived with Dad's parents and they also lived with friends for a short time before they rented a farm northeast of Rolla.

This is probably their wedding picture

In 1935 during the height of the depression things were tough especially for someone just getting started in farming when Mother informed Dad that he was going to be a father. In those days there was no way to know if it would be a boy or a girl, but I'm guessing Dad thought if they had a boy, he'd have some help on the farm. Little did he know that he would get a boy, but not a whole lot of help. I was that baby boy.

In 1936 they survived one of the coldest winters in North Dakota history. Temperatures reached 60 degrees below zero. That summer the temperature reached near 120 degrees in parts of ND. The crops burned up and the dust blew. There was little to harvest that year. 1936 holds the record for temperature extremes in ND.

In the latter part of June and the first part of July, I was getting ready to see the light of day and Mom was getting anxious for it to happen. Dad took Mom to Cando about forty miles away, where a midwife ran a maternity home. Few babies were born in hospitals at that time and I was no exception. A few days after Mom went to Cando, I was born. I don't know if Dad was with her when I was born, but it's quite possible that he needed to stay home and tend to the chores on the farm.

Apparently I was a pretty active kid and some of that energy got me in trouble. When I was about two years old, Mother and I were riding in the family car, a 1929 Model A Ford. She stopped to open the gate near the big stone barn so we could get into the yard. The first mistake she made was leaving the engine running when she got out of the car, but there was a good chance the engine might not start again. Those old cars weren't all that reliable. It didn't take me long to jump behind the wheel, somehow jam the car in gear, and smash it into the stone wall of the barn. Obviously it was better to hit the wall than to run over Mom, not that I had much control over the situation. I was better at shifting than steering it seems and that might be because I wasn't big enough to see over the steering wheel. Except for a broken windshield, the car wasn't damaged, but I still have a scar on my head from the broken glass. Those old cars were built to protect the car in the event of a crash not necessarily the passenger. Even after the barn incident, Mother let me ride in the car, but I wasn't allowed to drive until I was much older.

This is the barn I drove the car into when I was two years old. It was my first car crash.

Mom took me to town with her when she went grocery shopping. At three years old, I had graduated out of diapers, but my bathroom habits were not up to city speed. On the farm we had freedom when it came to bathroom issues but nobody told me that I should use discretion when we were in town. As Mother was loading the groceries in the car, she saw me sprinkling the street. She probably felt like whipping me on the spot, but there were too many witnesses. Poor Mother was so embarrassed. We had a good talk on the way home and for the most part I've improved a lot concerning such things.

Mother and me when I was one year old.

In March, 1941 my brother, Duane was born at home. In this case the midwife, Mrs. Phelps, came to our house. She was well known for delivering babies around the area. She stayed for a few days after Duane was born to help Mother medically as well as with routine household duties. When all was under control, she left for the next delivery. On March 28, 1941, the night Duane was born, Mrs. Phelps had already been staying with us for a few days. I remember it well because I had to give up my bed and sleep on a roll-away bed in the living room. She heated water on the coal-fired cook stove in a big copper boiler for Duane's first bath. The bedrooms had no heat and even in the spring of the year they could be uncomfortably cold, especially for a guy's very first bath. Dad may or may not have been in the house at the time of the birth. He hired Mrs. Phelps for this job and probably had other things to do. All went well and I had a brother to torment.

This is the house where Duane was born. The photo was taken after years of being vacant.

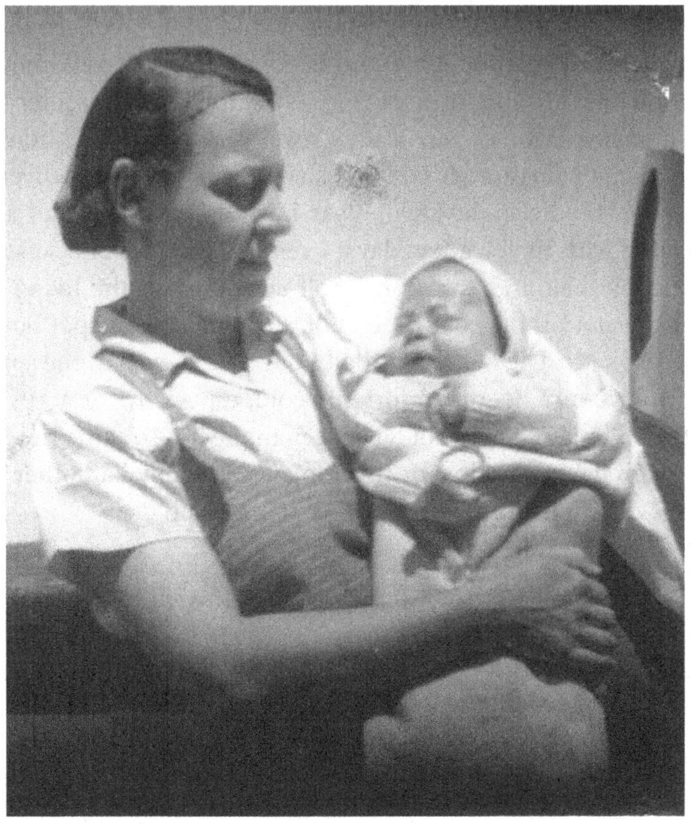

Mother and Duane.

Duane was the only one of us boys that my folks called by his first name. My other brother, Dwight, and I were each called by our second or third names. I could never figure out why I wasn't on a first name basis with my parents. My folks called me Dickie. Actually, I didn't mind being called Dick because that was also my dad's name—short for Richard. My birth name is Delphis David Richard Jussero. Who needs all those names? I settled for David after I left home, but seventy years later when I go back to ND, people still call me Dick. I'm glad I changed it. I wouldn't want to be called Grandpa Dickie. It just doesn't have a good ring to it.

After Duane's birth, there were four of us in the family—Dick, Dora, Dickie, and Duane. Being five years older than Duane, he and I had very little in common. He was a screaming little dude wearing a diaper and drooling while I was about ready to go to school.

About the time I started school, we moved from the H.P. Juntunen farm, a rocky piece of land the folks had been renting, to the Bill Loughlin farm, a short distance northwest of the first rental. Bill bought a lot of land during the depression for back taxes. Many farmers lost their land because they weren't able to pay the taxes.

The fifth D

In February 1948 my brother Don was born. It still doesn't seem right to call him Don because we always called him Dwight and I guess that is what I'll always call him. He was born in Cando at the same maternity home where I was born. The winter of 1948 was a really severe winter and the roads were really dangerous. The roads had been plowed many times which created huge snow-banks on both sides of the road. When a blizzard filled up the roads with several feet of snow, travel was impossible. Mom stayed in Cando for several days expecting the baby to arrive soon. When this didn't happen, she caught a ride back home with a neighbor. Dad wasn't very happy about that. He was hoping she would stay there until the baby was born. It was a forty mile drive each way. We didn't know if we would have a brother or a sister so Mom had a name for either one. A girl would have been named Dianne, and if it was a boy she would name him Donald and call him Dwight. I never did figure that one out. Mother finally went back to Cando and delivered another boy and she named him Donald Dwight. Now there were five of us: Dick, Dora, Dickie, Duane, and Dwight. The 5 D's.

As I write this, my baby brother has turned sixty-one years old. He plans to retire soon. I can't believe how quickly time goes by.

Dwight and Duane

Memories of Mom and Dad

Some of my favorite times with Dad were sitting at the kitchen table in the morning each with a cup of fresh, hot coffee, discussing all sorts of topics. Dad drank his coffee from a saucer because by pouring the boiled brew into the saucer it cooled faster. Most of the time he had a growth of whiskers on his chin that was several days old. His theory was that there wasn't a lot of need to shave if you weren't going anywhere. Shaving was a major task with a straight razor. There was always a chance of a serious wound if that super sharp shaving tool happened to cut more than whiskers. It was common to see Dad with little pieces of toilet paper stuck to his face and neck to stop the bleeding from the nicks from the razor. As he grew older and less steady, he moved to an electric razor which cut whiskers and not skin, but that had to wait until we got electricity on the farm to power such a modern convenience.

After downing several cups of coffee and discussing everything from farming and politics to school issues, we would work our way toward the barn to milk the cows and tend to the chores. While Dad and I were drinking coffee and doing chores, Mother was tending to the chickens and gathering eggs. Mom was constantly moving from morning till night so she rarely sat down. She even ate standing up most of the time. Mother ran a chicken and egg business. She had an established route in town for people who depended on her for farm fresh eggs and fryers. Dad was more laid back. It was common for him to lie down on the floor for a nap after he ate lunch and before he started the afternoon's work.

In the early years we went to town as a family. Saturday was usually the big day to go to town. We all changed from our work clothes into our town attire. Dad shaved and combed his hair and Mom primped in front of the mirror as she prepared to meet her friends and neighbors who also went to town on Saturday. I thought my parents were an attractive couple.

After we became a two car family, Mother claimed the car and the pickup was Dad's. Dad was pretty much encouraged not to use the car—a better word may be *forbidden* to use the car because Mom wanted it tidy for her to use. Dad wasn't the most meticulous person with a vehicle. He had the reputation of getting in the car with manure on his boots or grease on his overalls. Mother's claim on the family car didn't seem to bother Dad very much because the pickup was about all he needed for transportation. Most of the time it didn't look very great because some parts had fallen off, but nothing that kept it from working. My parents didn't find it necessary to make a statement with the vehicles they drove. Cars were transportation and not status symbols. This was, no doubt, a result of going through the depression.

In our house cash was king and, until the later years, cash was hard to come by. I was taught from an early age the value of a dollar and I really consider myself fortunate to be raised by people with great work ethics and common sense in financial affairs as well as practical matters.

Throughout my life I've tried to apply the lessons my parents taught me. I found that even though the times are different, the approach they used still works surprisingly well. I think of how very lucky I was to be raised by such sensible people.

My parents, Dick and Dora, in the 1970's

Change is inevitable.
Progress is questionable.

School Years

It was the summer of 1942, I was six years old, and my life was about to change. Mother informed me that I would be starting school in the fall. I imagine the conversation went something like:

"Son, you'll be starting school soon."

"Why do I need to go to school?"

"People who don't go to school could end up being stupid."

Being a smart aleck kind of kid I probably said, "Did you and Dad go to school?" That was the wrong thing to ask.

"That's not funny. Of course we went to school. Now go outside and play."

I gave that conversation a lot of thought. It was serious stuff for a kid my age. I would no longer be free to roam around the farm with the freedom to do as I pleased. I would be on a schedule for five days a week. Life would be different for sure. I'd need to carry a lunch bucket with a peanut butter and jelly sandwich, an apple and a cookie for the next several years. I would have to go to bed early so I could be up early for the trip to school.

After much consideration I decided that this was as good a time as any to get an education. I was big enough to be a pain in the butt to Mom and Dad, but not big enough to be much help on the farm, and I certainly didn't want to be stupid. Nobody told me that, with some people, this school business did very little good.

A few days before school started, Mother loaded me in the Model A Ford and we drove on ten miles of dirt roads to Rolla to shop. I got a new pair of bib overalls, a new pair of shoes, a few pencils, and a haircut. I was ready for school.

I started the first grade at Picton Grade School which was only a few miles from home. Many of the schools in the area were one-room schools located throughout the township so kids could walk to school. I was one of the lucky ones. Picton was the most modern schools in the area. It was used as a community center for public meetings and entertainment. There were lots of parties, picnics, and dances with live music at the school. It had four rooms, a small library, and indoor toilets, but they didn't flush. That came much later. They were pit toilets and had to be pumped periodically. They smelled bad but were better than outdoor toilets in the winter when there was lots of snow and the temperatures could dip to 40 degrees below zero. We didn't include the wind chill factor then. The thermometer reading was cold enough without a measurement that made it sound even colder. The winter conditions made you appreciate the indoor conveniences in spite of the smell.

The school had no running water, but there was a hand pump right outside the building where we got water for hand washing and drinking. The building was heated with coal and each room had a big coal-fired stove. Some of the kids brought potatoes that they put on the big old, cast iron stove to cook for lunch. It's hard to forget that wonderful smell of those baked potatoes,

Hauling coal to fire the stoves was the teacher's job, but she would sometimes ask some of the older kids to help with the heavy buckets of coal and water. As farm kids, we were used to heavy work. The teachers often lived in one of the four rooms called a teacherage.

The one-room schools such as Fairview, where my wife, Caroleen, started school, were like many in the farm communities. They were built close to existing farms so kids could get there on their own mostly by walking. These schools had all eight grades in one room with one teacher responsible for all eight grades. Although the total number of students was often only 20 or 30 kids, this was a lot of subjects for the teacher to cover on eight different levels. Teachers were usually women and they were also expected to get to school early enough to fire up the coal burning stove, haul the water, and be the janitor, on top of all the teaching duties. Some of the teachers lived in these one room school buildings in the winter, sleeping on a cot in the corner of the room. There were no cooking facilities and the bathrooms were outside pit toilets filled with snow and ice in the winter. Sometimes a teacher would board with a local family. Many times the teacher was a local person who had grown up in the community. Everybody did what was necessary to educate the kids. The teachers were very devoted to their jobs. They had no unions to protect them and there were no strikes for better conditions. Everyone just did their job, and we received a good, basic education in those first eight grades. Most kids went on to high school, but some didn't and still were able to function. Some even did quite well. Not many farm kids went to college.

This is one of the tiny schools that Caroleen attended. The photo was taken after several decades of being vacant and neglected.

From the time they were nine or ten years old, many farm kids were needed in the fields during the planting and harvest seasons. That meant that school wasn't the number one priority. The crops needed to be planted and they had to be harvested when the time was right. There was a lot of school work to catch up on or they couldn't go on to the next grade. The pressure was on for the seventh and eighth graders because they had to takes exams that the County Superintendent administered. Students couldn't go to high school without passing them. There was serious preparation and a lot of tension around those exams.

I had a dependable ride to school unlike lots of kids in other schools who had to walk or ride a horse. People from the neighborhood contracted with the school district to haul kids to school. I was on the route that Vivian and Nestor Juntunen ran. They had kids in school and they picked me up in their Model A Ford.

In the winter they traded the Model A for horse-drawn transportation. Horses pulled the *school rig* or *hack*. It was a home-built structure on a sleigh that had a little wood or coal fired stove and wooden benches around the edges. A door opened out the back or the side. The driver sat in the front looking through a frost covered window and guided the horses with reins that came through a small hole in the front of the cab. The hack could haul six to eight kids and the first ones on board got to sit next to the stove. Some kids toasted cheese sandwiches on the stove on the way to school.

The *hack*. It was a great way to get to school in the winter.

The hack was more reliable than cars when there was heavy snow that blocked the roads, but they weren't regulated by any government safety agency, and weren't especially safe going over snow banks. They were top heavy and could tip over easily, but I don't know of any serious mishaps. A ride to school in a hack was not only fun it was an adventure. Many times the journey is more special than the destination.

Some kids rode horses to school. When the school was built in the early 1900's, horses were the main mode of transportation so they built a barn at the school to accommodate the horses. Behind the barn was a good place to experiment with cigarettes so I'm told.

The first day of school I was so nervous that I slammed the car door on my thumb. Those early cars didn't have any rubber padding between the door and the frame of the car so it was metal to metal with my thumb in between. They wrapped gauze around my thumb and off I went to the first grade.

The first day of school had something in common with the next several decades of my life—the dreaded *schedule.* The atmosphere was different than anything I had known in my life. We were told to sit still and pay attention. My throbbing thumb distracted me from the story about Dick, Jane, and their dog, Spot. I looked around and saw all those kids. It was my first experience of being in a crowd and it wasn't comfortable even though I knew almost everyone in the room. Such a structured environment was a major adjustment in my life and I probably wouldn't have gone back the next day if I'd had a choice. This school business didn't seem to be working for me.

The next days became easier and school got a little more interesting as I began to apply myself. I was probably a challenge to my teachers when I wasn't as attentive as I should have been, but they were prepared to deal with me. They managed to provide a good basic education that prepared me for grade nine and has served me well over the years.

I didn't do very well in school the first year or two. I had trouble reading. One day I borrowed glasses from my friend, Eugene, and experienced a totally new world. I told my parents about this and they took me in to get glasses right away. I started doing well in school and I've been wearing glasses now for nearly seventy years. It helps to be able to see.

School served me well, even though I didn't get much of it, but I have spent my entire life learning new things both on my own and in classes. I am a strong supporter of schools and learning.

Picton School served the community well from when it was built 1923 until 1961 when the school closed. The family farms were becoming vacant as small farms were swallowed by bigger farms so there were fewer kids. The schools consolidated and kids were sent to school in town.

Helen Peterson, a long time friend, neighbor and former teacher said that in 1936 there were fifty students in Picton Grade School but by 2010 there were only three school age kids in the entire township.

I feel extremely fortunate to have experienced life in Picton township and at Picton Grade School in the 1940's and 50's, but it is sad to drive through the area where I was born and raised and remember where all the missing farmsteads and the school once stood.

Everything cannot be measured by the bottom line.

Picton School was built in 1923. It was the pride of the community

The last day of school in 1961. The building was no longer needed. The rural population had decreased so much they closed the school and sent the kids to schools in town. My youngest brother, Don (Dwight) is in the back row the third from the left.

After more than twenty years of disuse, the weather and vandals destroyed the building. Many of the windows were broken, the beautiful hardwood floors were warped, the roof leaked, and mice and birds had moved in. What was once a stately part of the community became a liability.

The Old School

By
David Jussero

There it sits in disrepair
As solid as a rock.
There's some stories it would tell
If only it could talk.

It would tell of times
When it was bright and new;
The pride of the community
With a great big job to do.

It would tell of schools hacks pulling up
With horses breathing loud
And drivers who could hardly wait
To unload their noisy crowd.

It would surely tell of parties
After the setting sun
Where music, fun and frolic
Was enjoyed by everyone.

It would tell about the school board
Who was proud to keep her strong;
Then all of a sudden
Redistricting came along.

It would tell of being vacant
On this North Dakota range.
This surely isn't progress
At best it's only change.

It may even tell some things
That would be such a shock!
It may be best for some
That this old school can't talk.

It would tell of coal stove's heat
Filling up the room,
And kids sitting safe and warm
In the cold winter's gloom.

It would tell of recess time
When kids thought it a joke
To go behinds the barn
And maybe sneak a smoke.
It would tell of some
Too mischievous to learn
And teachers who worked their hearts out
And got little in return.

It would tell of no gymnasium
And had no swimming pool.
Good basic education
Was the only rule.

# # #

One night the neglected remains of Picton School burned to the ground. Whether vandals were responsible for the blaze or someone from the school district decided to put the old building out of its misery we'll never know for sure. The only evidence that the school ever occupied the site is the old swing set that sits in the tall grass. That lonesome swing set brings back many memories to anyone who ever attended Picton School as a student or came to a dance at the school.

A Bird Worth Crowing About

THE FOLLOWING STORY WAS TAKEN from the *History of Rolla Centennial Book* written in 1988. No history of the years in Picton School would be complete without the story of a very smart, noisy bird named Mike.

Many people think of crows as obnoxious, noisy, scavengers that are not very exciting to look at. They definitely are not the most colorful of our feathered friends. What this bird lacked in beauty, he made up for in other ways and anyone who knew him would never have the same impression of crows again.

I was one of the fortunate kids going to Picton School where the Hoerer family and Mike were next door neighbors to the school. The bird entertained the kids at Picton until sometime in the late 1940's.

Mike the Talking Crow

Many people who lived in the Picton School area in the 1930's remember the Hoerer family's unusual pet, a talking crow named Mike.

Mike really belonged to Floyd Hoerer. When Floyd was about 11 years old, he caught a baby crow that was too young to fly. He brought it home, made a cage for it and named it Mike.

Mike took well to captivity and soon became a part of the family. He would go outside with the children but was always ready to come in when called, and they always brought him in at night for his own protection.

Although they left him loose once in a while in the house, he spent most of his time in his cage when he was indoors and he was indoors most of the winter.

During the warmer months, Mike stayed outside all day perched on the roof of the house enjoying the shade of a nearby tree. He was no problem to feed because he loved table scraps like fried potatoes and eggs, milk, and bread.

No one tried to teach Mike to talk. He was a noisy little fellow and soon after they found him, they began to realize that he was saying words. He was a natural born imitator. One of the first phrases he learned to say was "Sic'em, Pal." Pal was the family dog whose job was to keep the pigs from coming up to the house. Any time they ventured too close, someone in the family would yell, Sic'em, Pal," and he would put the pigs on the run.

While reminiscing about their pet, Reginald Hoerer said that Mike learned to say about 25 or 30 phrases including "Where's Floyd?" and "Shut the door."

The Hoerer family lived right next to Picton School and Mike followed the children to school each day were he would sit, perched on the school house or in a nearby tree until the children came out to play. Baseball was the favorite outdoor pastime for the students and it didn't take Mike long to learn this. As soon as the children came out of the door, he would start to holler, "Play ball! Play ball!" Then he would sit and laugh so realistically that anyone listening would think it was a person.

Although he seldom got into trouble, he did have one bad habit. He loved ripe tomatoes. So when the tomatoes began to ripen, he would poke holes in the ripest ones. To prevent this from happening, the children were armed with a fly swatter with orders to go chase Mike out of the garden. It only took a few swats for Mike to devise his own plan of action. When he saw them coming, he would scramble down under the leaves of the plants and run to the end of the row where upon he would step out where he could be seen and say, "Here's Mike! Here's Mike!"

Another humorous incident concerning Mike occurred one day when a salesman came to the house at a time when all the family members were outside. He had knocked on the door several times when someone at the barn saw him and came to the house. They informed him there was no one in the house. The salesman replied angrily, "Oh yes there is, I heard him talking and laughing at me but he wouldn't open the door." He had to meet Mike before he could be convinced that what he heard was only a talking crow.

Reginald also recalls the embarrassment Mike caused the family when they entered him in an amateur contest in Rolla and he refused to say a word.

Mike lived to be at least 15 years of age before he died of seemingly natural causes. He has been gone a long time, but for those who knew him, he is still very well remembered.

Eagles soar and Crows are very smart birds
But turkeys don't get sucked into jet engines.

North Dakota people have a work ethic
And a survival ethic as well.

Life in the Country

LIFE ON THE FARM WAS a good life. I consider myself lucky to be raised in the country. We always had something to do. The kids were expected to do their share of the work starting quite young. I fed the chickens, gathered the eggs and brought the cows in for milking, along with other duties, but still had time to play.

Toys

My favorite toy was an old wooden wheelbarrow that had a steel wheel with wooden spokes. I must have pushed that thing for miles. When we got a wheelbarrow with a rubber tire, that was progress, but it wasn't nearly as much fun to play with. Another favorite toy was an old worn out car tire that I rolled around.

Some of the toys we played with we made ourselves. Slingshots were a good example. We found a tree branch shaped like a "Y", cut a piece of discarded inner tube for the elastic part and a piece of old shoe leather for the pocket that held the stones. The ammunition rocks were plentiful and free, so it was a low budget toy but one that could easily break a window if you weren't careful. The only real expense was repairing the damage we did with these weapons. Some kids got pretty accurate with them and could knock a bird out of a tree.

We also played with discarded wooden thread spools. In those days women did lots of sewing so this provided a good supply of wooden spools. We used a rubber band threaded through the spool anchored on one end. We put a wooden match stick through the rubber band then wound it up. When you set it down, it scampered across the floor like crazy using the spring energy of the rubber band. It was a self propelled toy that didn't require batteries like so many of today's toys. The toys we built ourselves probably meant more to us than the cheap plastic variety the kids have today or maybe it just didn't take as much to entertain us.

Roads

We lived about a half mile from the main road and the path to it was two tire tracks with grass growing between them. What we called the main road was a dirt road maintained by the county. It was wide enough to meet another car if you were careful. It had ditches on both sides that were deep enough to do serious damage if you slipped off the road. In the early days the road wasn't graveled. The dirt road turned to mud when it rained and the mud would build up on the tires of the car to the extent that the wheels wouldn't turn in the wheel wells. We didn't go very far under those conditions. We waited until the roads dried up leaving deep ruts to deal with.

Better times were ahead. The county put gravel on many of the roads and that was a huge improvement. A person could actually go places when the roads were wet. It was kind of a status symbol to live near a road that had gravel on it. Paved roads were unheard of. You had to go great distances from the farm to experience the luxury of pavement.

Town

Our nearest town, Hansboro, a town of about 100 residents, was about five or six miles east of our farm. Dad went there to buy tobacco and other small items from Olson's store. Ralph Olson and Dad had serious discussions about politics and other topics and Ralph chewed Dad out for not buying more goods in Hansboro. He said that if people didn't patronize the businesses in Hansboro, the town wouldn't survive. How right he was. The barber shop was down the street from Ralph's general store. Bert Johnston was the barber and all the kids called him Uncle Bert. He was everyone's friend.

Hansboro also had a post office and a bar. Penny Orton owned and operated the bar which was in the basement of the big dance hall also owned by Penny. The dance hall really hummed on the nights when Penny hired a local band to play for a dance.

Kids were allowed to go into the bar to eat hamburgers. We could sit on the tall bar stools and watch our hamburgers sizzle on the grill. Penny was a special friend who bought bottles that I found around the farm. They refilled beer bottles, so most of the bottles had some value, but Penny bought whatever I brought him which sometimes included catsup bottles. There were some people who considered Penny's bar a sinful place. I picked up on this and one day I told Penny that I thought he might not go to heaven when he died. He asked why. I told him it was because he sold liquor. Penny was my friend and I thought I should warn him.

Hansboro also had grain elevators right beside the railroad tracks where the farmers could sell their grain. Penny's was a good place to stop and have a nice cold beverage before heading home after selling a load of grain.

Hansboro, like many small farm towns, lost almost all of its population and most of its business over the years, but the bar in Hansboro is still operating. Penny left us years ago and the bar has changed ownership several times, but many still call it Penny's bar. It is currently owned and operated by my friend, Jack Seghers, a guy who never gave up on the town of Hansboro.

Hansboro now has a population of about twenty people. A new business started in Hansboro in the last few years. Jack built a new motel on the site of the old lumber yard. Much of the building is built from salvaged lumber from the site. It's always nice to see positive things happening in Hansboro.

Olson's Store

By
David Jussero

I fondly remember
As I ramble around
This man who lived
In our little farm town.

He owned the general store
Not too far from the school
Where us kids would hang out
Thinking we were real cool.

I remember one day
I told him a lie
When a sack of tobacco
I tried to buy.

He said, "Kid,
Is that tobacco for you?"
I said, "No, it's for Dad."
He said, "That's not true."

Then as he took
The sack from my hand,
He said "You could have at least
Picked the right brand.

Your dad Smokes Prince Albert
And this is no joke,
Just stick with candy, Son,
You're too young to smoke.

Ralph, you weren't only
A business man then
To many a kid.
You were truly a friend.

We'll always remember
And we're better off cause we
Know this man who owned the
Store in our town, Hansboro.

He wouldn't sell me tobacco
There was no such luck
He wouldn't ruin a kid's health
Just to make a buck.

I speak for the kids
Who walked through that door
With mud on their shoes
And probably manure.

For us kids in school
We couldn't ask for more.
We had no McDonalds
But we had Olson's store.

The view of the inside of Ralph Olson's store as you entered from the street. The young woman in the picture is Ralph's daughter, Helen. The store was a family enterprise run by Ralph, his wife, Ruth, his son, Ralph Jr. and daughter, Helen. Although the store was small, there were many necessities available including groceries, shoes, clothing and numerous miscellaneous items.

Hansboro

By
David Jussero

The grass is now growing
Where buildings once stood.
The population went down
Much more than it should

The streets are not paved
And there's no traffic light
But they are not needed
There's no traffic in sight.

The grain elevators stand
Like monuments to the past,
When times were much different
And the best times don't last.

Wihelmina and Hubert stayed
Through good times and bad.
They raised their kids there
A great family they had.

If it weren't for them
We pretty well know
There would not be the town
Of old Hansboro.

The town may never be
What it once was back then.
But there's no doubt
It's growing again.

Friends of the town
Though far they may roam,
Are proud to say Hansboro
Once was their home.

Now people are coming
From both near and far
To visit Jack's Old Lumber Yard,
Motel and the Bar.

Aerial view of Hansboro in the 1950's.

Main street of Hansboro in the 1950's.

The high school I attended for two years is at the end of the street.

Winters on the Farm

SOME WINTERS IN NORTH DAKOTA were tough. There were times when we'd be snowed in for long periods of time. Sometimes it lasted weeks, but there were always enough groceries. We ate lots of canned food that we grew ourselves and the women preserved. Occasionally a person froze to death after getting caught in a blizzard that came up with little notice. Weather forecasting wasn't as accurate as it is today. You were pretty much on your own if you got caught in a blizzard. There were no cell phones to call for help. There weren't even land line telephones until the 40's and 50's and a severe storm could disable them. I have seen 40 degrees below zero and a 40 MPH wind. There's not much hope of surviving that kind of weather without shelter.

Dad told stories about tying a rope between the barn and house so they could do chores during a snow storm. During a blizzard, the snow was so heavy it was easy to get disoriented in the distance of a just a few feet. Most of the time it wasn't that cold. If it got above zero and the sun came out, it felt warm.

We didn't have snow days at school. Either you showed up or you didn't. I'm sure the teachers welcomed days when there were no children. They probably considered those days as vacation. Winters tended to be long. Some years it started snowing in October and the snow stayed all winter. One of the worst snow storms I remember was in May, but most years weren't that bad. The main roads got plowed out and cars were back on the move then another blizzard would come and fill in the plowed area with hard snow sometimes as deep as 10 or 15 feet.

The Snowstorm of 1941

The snow storm of March 5, 1941, is an example of how quickly a beautiful winter day can turn into a deadly blizzard.

My cousin, Anne, has vivid memories of this day that will be remembered as one of the most tragic weather phenomena in ND history. That March day began as a beautiful winter morning with the temperature in the comfort range for ND in the winter. The sun was bright reflecting off the massive snow banks that had been building up over months of winter snow and wind.

My aunt and uncle, Bertha and Carl Henrickson, decided that this would be a great day to hitch the team of horses up to the sleigh and go to Perth, a town a few miles from the farm. Although they had an automobile, it was of little use with the roads blocked with drifted snow. It could be a month or more before the snow melted enough to use the car.

They had a nice trip to town. They did their shopping and tended to business they needed to deal with before heading for home. They intended to get home in time for evening chores and see to the three kids they left there when they went to town. Anne was 10 years old, John was 11 and Donald was 14.

A short distance from town the weather changed. The sky clouded over and the snow began to fall. The wind started to blow and it wasn't long before visibility was near zero. The blowing snow felt like sand hitting their faces and the wind penetrated their clothes.

The horses were well trained and always obeyed commands, but this time they refused to go against the strong north wind. They took the sleigh in a different direction that wasn't going to take them home.

Horses are very smart animals and have been known to take their masters home in blinding blizzards, but this team had a different plan and probably saved Aunt Bertha and Uncle Carl's lives. Either the horses knew where they were going or were very lucky because they took them to the door of a neighbor's house. If the horses had continued north, the wind and snow would, no doubt, have been disabling and Carl and Bertha would have been added to the death toll of that fierce storm.

The neighbors were surprised to have company in the middle of that storm but happily shared their warm home with Carl and Bertha and the warm barn with their horses until the storm was over.

It was a frightening experience for the kids left at home as well for their parents. They worried about their folks, and Carl and Bertha worried about the safety of their kids at home alone, but the kids were resourceful. When Carl and Bertha weren't home in time to do chores, they decided it would be their responsibility to do them. They had helped with the chores so many times, it wasn't a problem, but the storm was.

John and Don probably didn't realize how severe the storm was as they left the house and headed for the barn. In a blinding storm it is easy to become disoriented and the wind and snow can blow a person off course. Although the barn was only a short distance from the house and would only take a minute or two in normal weather, they couldn't make it and were forced to go back to the house. In trying to get back to the house, Donald, the older of the two boys, had a severe asthma attack. He struggled with asthma normally, but the wind and cold made it even worse. John was an unusually strong kid for his age and managed to physically drag him to safety.

Carl and Bertha spent the night worrying about the kids. Even though they knew they were responsible young people, anyone could be overcome with that kind of weather, and the kids knew it was very possible that their parents could die in the storm. A telephone call would have made the situation much less stressful for everyone, but few rural people had reliable phone service in 1941.

Bertha and Carl were able to get home the next day and were relieved to find the kids safe at home. That blizzard, one of the worst in ND history, killed 38 people.

I was almost five years old at the time and have no memory of it. To me it was probably just another storm. I do remember as I grew older, we were very aware that March could be a very dangerous month for storms and March definitely wasn't the end of winter. Sometimes storms extended into April and occasionally even into May.

Winter Fun on the Farm

THERE WERE TIMES WHEN A person could drive a car on some hard-packed snow banks, but if the car fell through, it could be there until the spring thaw. Spinning donuts on a frozen pond was a lot of fun. Cars sometimes flipped over during these maneuvers if they hit a rough edge of a slough. My friend, Larry, had a beautiful lake near their farm where we could get pretty crazy with my '48 Dodge always hoping the ice was thick enough to hold us. Fortunately, we never tipped it over and we never fell through the ice.

Winters were a great time to hunt rabbits at night with a spot light. My friend, Gerald and his brothers did their best to hold the rabbit population down. They borrowed their dad's new Ford that was equipped with a spot light, then race across frozen plowed fields. They went over rocks, ruts, and dead furrows shooting at jack rabbits in the spot light. It took a toll on the car but their dad traded cars often.

Another dangerous sport that was considered acceptable was tying a toboggan behind a car and riding it on the snow in the ditches. Caroleen got twisted up riding one of those things when one leg hit the side of the road. There were no broken bones, but it caused a very serious sprain.

Skiing behind cars was also accepted by the younger generation, although it was extremely dangerous, and might be one of the reasons life expectancy in those days wasn't all that long. It wasn't unknown for the driver to be slightly impaired so anyone on the toboggan or skis was at the driver's mercy. When a toboggan hit a mail box post or skis got lodged in a culvert, it was not a good situation. Those winter sports were pretty crazy, but we had a good survival rate which is pretty amazing.

Most of the time we were working and tending to business, but everyone needs to have fun once in a while. Halloween provided another opportunity for some fun at other people's expense. There wasn't any trick or treat business. It was pretty much all tricks. While one farmer was tipping over his neighbor's outhouse, someone else was hoisting a piece of his machinery on top of the barn. We had one neighbor who protected himself by standing on his front porch with a shot gun. A couple of shots in the air proved to be a great deterrent to anyone coming near his farm with any cute ideas. His time with the shot gun was probably time well spent.

There were stories about people moving their outdoor toilets forward about three feet so the perpetrators of mischief would fall in the hole. This made tricksters very careful when approaching an outhouse in the dark, but it didn't deter the activity.

One year someone hid Dad's hay rake in the bushes a short distance from where it was parked in the yard. We didn't find it for months. It was the first time Dad lost anything the size of a piece of machinery.

Another devious activity was painting the neighbor's cows. That was downright destructive and dangerous. This went on for years until someone burned his neighbor's barn and livestock. That was Halloween gone bad. I don't know of anyone ever being convicted of the crime.

The morning after Halloween there was major clean up in town as well. There were large wagons and trucks blocking the streets, bales of hay in store entrances and equipment tipped over. I'm sure everyone was glad Halloween happened only once a year.

Feeding the Cattle

In the winter the cattle stayed in the barn. There was no grazing with the pastures covered with snow. The cows had to eat so that meant hauling hay all winter. The haystacks were always out in the hay field covered with snow. Dad hooked his horses to a sleigh and hayrack and hauled hay when the weather permitted. During some of the bad winters, we had to dig the hay out of the snow with shovels and pitchforks. There must have been an easier way to feed the livestock such as moving the hay closer to the barn during the summer. That makes sense now, but sixty years later is a darn poor time to think of it.

Times changed and loose hay in stacks wasn't the trend anymore. Baling became common. The bales were hauled in close to the buildings and stacked near the barn. There was still a lot of hand work since the bales weighed from 60 to 100 pounds and they had to be moved by hand. Dad and my future father-in-law, Napoleon Messier, tried to outdo each other stacking the bales with a pitchfork. A pitchfork isn't designed for pitching bales, but neither is the human body. They broke many pitchfork handles and both men ended up with hernias. Dad and Napoleon were the strongest men I knew. Imagine lifting an 80 pound bale on the end of a pitchfork handle. Years later bales were handled mechanically and there wasn't nearly as much competition with pitchforks. There were also fewer hernias.

The Snow Machine

Albani Perron who never married was a neighbor who lived with his parents. When I was a kid, he was a young farmer and an extremely hard worker. When he wasn't running his tractor, he was working in his shop maintaining his machinery. Being very frugal, he saw no real reason to trade in equipment and buy new stuff the way many of his neighbors did. He repaired his old machines and kept them running. Many thought he was a mechanical genius.

We often saw him driving his decades old Model A Ford. There is no doubt he could afford to drive anything he wanted. He was actually a very wealthy man, but he took great pride in living beneath his means. Maybe we could learn something from that guy.

One winter he was heading out to do some shopping in his trusty Model A. The roads were blocked with banks of drifted snow, but it was common practice to take a run at these snow banks and many times a car was able to plow through the drifted snow. Sometimes it didn't work and it was time to retrieve the shovel that was always close by and dig the hopelessly disabled car out of the snow. Seeing this huge drift ahead of him, Albani stopped and backed up a good distance to get up some speed to plow through the snow drift, but he wasn't aware that this huge snow bank was hard packed snow.

Rather than going through the snow bank, his car went over it, became airborne and landed on its top on the other side of the snow bank with Albani still in the car. This was several decades before seat belts were introduced, so it's a miracle that he survived this incident. The Model A was not great in the deep snow and Albani must have been thinking there must be a better way to travel as he walked back home.

It wasn't long before this ingenious man invented a snow machine. He took the grain box off his ancient International truck, mounted tractor wheels and tires on the back from one of his tractors and mounted a fabricated ski on the front axle to keep the wheels on top of the snow. The snow machine was ready for a road test. He had a snow mobile and it worked. He took me to town in it one day over hopelessly blocked roads. It was an adventure.

From grain truck to . . .

Albani's snow machine

In the 1940's and 50's farmers did what needed to be done with what they had available on the farm. It made sense to take the old grain truck that was sitting idle in the winter and get some use out of it.

As busy as Albani was, he always had time to help his neighbors. He also took care of his parents when they became disabled in their later years. They lived to be quite old and when they died, Albani lived alone of the farm until he was in his 80's. As I write this in 2010, he lives in a nursing home and is in his 90's.

Electric Lights

I fondly remember following my dad to the barn in the evening in the short days of winter. He carried his trusty kerosene lantern which was a type of lamp with a glass globe that would deflect the wind so the flame wouldn't blow out. When we got to the barn, he hung the dim light somewhere in the middle of the building. The cows were lined up on either side of the barn waiting patiently for Dad to begin milking. The light from the lantern was about what a fifteen watt electric bulb would show.

Many of the houses were illuminated by either kerosene lamps or gas lanterns. The lanterns were similar to the ones we use camping. The tank was pressurized by a small hand pump attached to the lantern. The fragile mantles lit up and provided a fair amount of light. As a night light, Mom had a very small kerosene lamp. It was about the size of a small coke bottle. She put it near a window on a cabinet. Our closest neighbors were about a mile away and they could see this tiny light in our window on a clear night when the snow wasn't blowing. Many nights when there were no clouds, the stars and moon were so bright that no light was needed to play outside. It was almost like daylight.

Eventually the gas lanterns gave way to electricity. First we had six volt, then 32 volt, and in about 1950 we were connected to the public power system. We enjoyed the 120-240 volt power that energized modern appliances and provided bright lights in the house and barn. The old lanterns and lamps were still handy in the event a storm knocked out power.

The Mail

In the very early days before there was rail service to Rolla, the mail was delivered from Churches Ferry, a town about fifty miles south of Rolla. It arrived there by train and they brought it to Rolla with teams of horses. After the railroad came to Rolla, horses were still used for many years because rail service was irregular. Often the trains couldn't get through for days or even weeks at a time when snow covered the tracks in the winter. The rural route service started in the early 1900's. The first mail carriers used horses for delivery three days a week. As cars became available and the roads improved daily delivery was possible.

When I was growing up, George Mitchell was our mailman and he spent most of his life delivering mail on Rural Route #2. He started working on that route in the 1920's and was still on the same route over three decades later in the 1950's. He delivered the mail through muddy roads and snow banks. He had a job to do and he took it seriously.

The rig George drove during the winter of 1932 was a Model A Ford with skis mounted between the front wheels and tandem wheels with tracks on the back and he was able to deliver the mail in the winter in spite of the challenges of the road and weather conditions.

The US mail was an important means of communication on the farms before telephones. When I was growing up in the 40's and 50's, a first class stamp was three cents and a post card cost a penny which included the card and the stamp. Our address in those days was Rural Route # 2, Rolla, ND. We had no house numbers, named streets, or area codes.

George Mitchell on his mail route in the winter of 1932 using a Model A Ford which had skis on the front and tracks over the tandem wheels on the back. Fred Gailfus used a similar vehicle on his mail route.

Christmas in the 40's

Christmas in the 1940's was always a great time. I don't remember having a Christmas tree when I was young, but a little cardboard nativity scene was a big part of our Christmas decoration. My parents focused more on the religious aspect of the holiday. After all, that is what Christmas is supposed to be about.

In those days there wasn't a lot of extra money to spend on toys. In fact, during World War II, there weren't a lot of toys available. I think we appreciated the few things we did get more than the kids appreciate the bounty they get now days. Santa Claus was also part of the picture. We hung our Christmas stockings and couldn't wait to find what the jolly old elf left for us. Most of the time it was an orange or an apple, a few nuts, and some Christmas candy.

One year when Duane was about two or three years old, Dad dressed up in a Santa Claus suit and paid us a visit. Duane heard stomping on the porch and then a loud knock on the door. He opened the door and saw Santa Claus and it scared the living heck out of him. He headed for the bedroom and hid under the bed. Santa left us a small gift then left. For months after that, Dad stomped on the porch when he came in from the barn and Duane would dive under the bed. He had no love for Santa and Dad thought it was really funny.

I don't think the merchants in small towns depended on the Christmas season for their yearly profit like businesses do today. Most of the gifts were necessary items like clothing. I found that Christmas in the city was much different. It seemed as if people had everything they needed, but the marketing system sent a message that obligated everyone to give gifts even if it wasn't something anyone needed. This certainly was different from the laid back Christmas seasons I experienced as a kid in ND.

Our school always put on a Christmas program. We practiced for this special night for several weeks before the holiday. This was a big deal. It seemed as if the whole community attended the performances. All the kids had some part in the programs. That meant being on stage in front of all the parents and many other people we didn't recognize. That part of the Christmas season terrified me. I hated being on stage in front of such a large crowd of possibly fifty people. It wasn't until the Christmas program was over that I could kick back and really enjoy the rest of the holiday season.

In ND there was about a 99 percent chance that Christmas would be white. We pretty much took this for granted. Christmas was always white just like Santa was always dressed in red. How could it be any other way?

Now after being in the Seattle area for over fifty years, I still remember fondly all the white Christmases I spent in ND.

Christmas in the Cities

By
David Jussero

It starts in mid fall
They start stocking their shelves
And talk about
Santa Claus and Elves.

They put out lots of things
That I'm sure there's no doubt
That most of us
Could well live without.

Then we all get caught up
In a holiday glow
And we start buying presents
For everybody we know.

He buys things for her
Just to do a good deed
And it either don't fit
Or there's probably no need.

They charge all these things
On their credit card
Because paying cash
Would just be too hard.

Then she says to him
Just don't worry, my dear.
We'll just pay for this stuff for
Most of next year.

The kids get some gifts
And it's fine for a while
Then most of this stuff
Just ends up in a pile.

I would say that most
Of these things without fail
Will probably end up
In next summer's garage sale.

Now some of this Santa Claus
Hype is OK
But it's really not all that
Is meant for the day.

Something many forget
In This commercial heist
Is that it is the birthday
Of our Lord Jesus Christ.

When Christmas is over
Everyone's kind of sad
But the shopping is over
Of this I am glad.

If you've learned anything
From all of these tales,
You'll just do next year's shopping
At the local garage sales!

I gripe and complain
Till the season is thru
But I still want to wish
A Merry Christmas to you.

Doctors and Dentists

Medical attention wasn't high on the list of priorities when I was young. When we did consult a physician, it was likely because of an illness that had progressed to the point of becoming an emergency or some sort of accident that resulted in broken bones or other severe injuries. Serious accidents happened occasionally in the country. Farming is among the most hazardous of occupations. Kids often got injured or killed working and playing around farm equipment or animals. Adults had their share of mishaps as well. The hazards of working around machinery are not to be taken lightly. Just one lapse in judgment or careless act can disable someone for life or even be fatal.

Dental care was another area that didn't get its share of attention. People in the country tended to neglect their teeth. Many times a simple filling could have saved a tooth. This condition however, after weeks of tooth aches often progressed to a point of requiring extraction of the tooth. It was common practice to have teeth pulled rather than filled. After all, once the tooth was pulled, it couldn't give any more problems. This practice was extremely unfortunate as many people only thirty or forty years old already had dentures. I've known people to go in at a young age and have all their teeth pulled and be fitted for dentures thinking that would solve their dental problems for life. I'm sure part of the reason people avoided dentists was because a visit to the dentist could be extremely painful.

I don't remember any dental visits until I was in my teens. I did have some teeth filled and also a few pulled. The dentist used an anesthetic for extraction which eliminated much of the discomfort, but drilling and filling without novocain was painful beyond words.

Dentistry in the past was extremely crude compared to the standards of today. My dad told about an alcoholic dentist he knew when he was young. He said this tipsy dentist would take out of bottle of cheap whisky, take a good drink, then hand it to the patient before he got down to business. Dad did love a good story, but he claimed this story was true. I don't think that was a common problem, but the dentist I went to also had a reputation for drinking on the job. A drinking dentist wouldn't be among the top of the practitioners in that profession, but the small towns in the country didn't always attract the best in the medical fields.

Time to Till

After the long winter, spring was a very welcomed season. The black North Dakota soil began to show through the disappearing snow. It was time to service the tractor that may have been buried in a snow drift much of the winter.

Field work could start as early as April, but April wasn't always the end of the possibility of snow. Many times fields that were seeded would be covered by a fresh layer of snow. A late snow didn't last long and it didn't seem to affect the freshly seeded crops, although it would put a temporary end to field work.

Growing season was a busy time. First the crops which consisted mostly of wheat, oats, and barley were planted then it was time to summer fallow. That meant setting taking about one third of the acreage out of production and under cultivation. The purpose was to destroy weeds and preserve moisture. Working summer fallow was a chance for kids to run the tractor. I was about twelve or thirteen when Dad finally let me drive the tractor working the summer fallow. Actually, I was quite old by the standards of the time. My friend, Delmer, was driving his dad's tractor when he was only nine years old. My dad's explanation was that Delmer's dad had a much better tractor than we did. I didn't argue with him. I preferred riding my bike anyway. When I was finally allowed to run the old Model D John Deere, I felt pretty grownup. I did get into trouble a few times by getting too close to swampy areas where I occasionally got stuck or went through a fence. I didn't do too much damage and it was all a learning process. The main thing I learned was that I definitely didn't want to do that the rest of my life. Running a tractor isn't all that much fun. Time really goes slow going back and forth across a big field listening to the two cylinder engine popping for ten or twelve hours. The fascination and novelty didn't last long, and the fun soon became work. Mosquitoes were also a real problem. There were days when they would eat you alive. Just before a rain they were particularly bad. Some people called them the North Dakota state bird.

If I had been born a couple of decades earlier, I would have been driving horses instead of tractors in the fields. The tractor was a great improvement. Tractor farming was much more efficient. One man or kid could do the work of several men and many teams of horses. This was good news from a labor standpoint, but it wasn't all good news for the small family farm. In America it seems that everything gets larger and larger and tractors were no exception. As time went by, small tractors were replaced by bigger more powerful machines that made it possible to do even more work with the same amount of man power. As this happened, the farms became larger and more productive. Farms of 400 to 1,000 acres were common when I left the farm in the mid 50's, but quickly became a thing of the past. Now five to ten thousand acre farms are commonplace. Production per acre has increased as well. With improved farming methods fewer people live in the farming communities and small towns are disappearing.

Hard work has a future payoff.
Laziness pays off now.

Rolla in the 1940's and 50's in the summer.

Rolla during the winter.

Pets

Many time farm kids would bond with unusual pets like chickens. A chicken is probably one of the dumbest of birds, but they can become a loyal pet.

The pet chick I had was the runt of the flock. It would come when called and couldn't wait to be put in its small pen at night. My brother, Dwight, tells about a pet chicken he had that waited around each evening to have him pick up its cage and put it on top of the chicken. The chicken wouldn't leave its pen until the next morning when the cage was lifted up and it was free to roam.

Calves also made good pets. I had a calf that became my friend when it was quite small. It would follow me around like a dog and it loved to playfully butt me with its head. The calf grew up to become a full sized steer, but the problem was he still liked to play. One day when Dad bent over to pick something up, the calf butted him and Dad landed on his head. I thought it was quite funny, but Dad failed to see the humor in the situation. I don't remember what happened to my pet calf, but shortly after the incident with butting Dad, it was no longer around. I suspect that it may have become hamburger.

My friend, Delmer, had a favorite pet billy-goat. A goat can be quite unpredictable and stupid. Delmer and I would roll a large truck tire up a hill in the yard. The goat stood at the bottom of the hill waiting for us to let the tire roll down the hill so he could butt it with his head. The tire always won as the goat was no match for a heavy truck tire. We'd lug the tire back up the hill and play the game until Delmer, the goat, and I were exhausted.

There wasn't a lot of free time on the farm. We always had cows to milk and they had to be milked twice a day—no exceptions. We milked by hand which meant you sat on a stool and squirted milk into a bucket. Some of the cows didn't go along with the program and would kick or get their foot in the bucket, which wasn't the most sanitary situation, because you never knew where that foot had been. The calves got that milk. They didn't really care. Milking machines became more common later.

We usually had an abundance of barn cats that would sit in the middle of the barn and beg for milk. As we were milking we'd squirt milk at them across the aisle and they'd lick it off their faces. Cats had a purpose and that was to keep down the population of rats and mice on the farm. We seldom allowed cats in the house because that wasn't where the action was. Cats rarely became pets. Buying cat food was unheard of. They lived on what they could catch and if they didn't catch anything they'd go hungry. Most cats did fine just doing what cats do.

Dogs were more likely to become house pets, but they still had to work. Many times dogs were trained to help round up cattle and bring the cows in from the pasture at milking time. They usually lived on table scraps and what ever else they could find. They didn't get commercial dog food. They learned to eat what we ate.

Shep, the proud mother, shares her litter with Duane and me. Tippy, the pup I'm holding, was with us for many years. Duane still feels bad that he didn't get to keep his pup. I remind him that I had seniority and still do.

The Harvest

The summer season was busy. Working summer fallow took a lot of time and putting up hay for winter had to be done while the weather was good. Haying and summer fallow lasted until harvest time. Harvest was the farmer's payday. Many years during the 1930's the harvest was small and the times were extremely tough. Being born in 1936, I don't remember those lean years. I do remember that about 1940 farmers were still using threshing machines.

The threshing machines were towed from farm to farm and were usually owned by more than one farmer. This machine sat in the middle of a field and the threshing crew hauled the cut grain to the thresher in bundles in large hayracks pulled by horses. The threshing machine was powered by a steam engine or a gas powered tractor. The thresher separated the grain from the straw and they used the straw to fire the steam engines that powered the thresher. It took one man to fire the steam engine with straw and another man to haul water for the thirsty engine. The process was extremely labor intensive. It required a binder to cut the grain and tie it into bundles which were gathered by hand and piled into shocks which were bundles neatly stacked together in piles and stood upright to dry. The shocks were easier for the bundle haulers to pick up with pitchforks and throw into the hayrack.

Threshing crews followed the harvest from state to state and farm to farm where the men usually slept in the barn or in tents. The threshing crews took advantage of rainy days and often went to town to spend their hard earned money. The local bars did a land office business when it rained.

When the weather was good, working days were long. When the moon was bright, threshing continued until the straw became damp with dew and wouldn't go through the machine. During the harvest, the sun didn't set until about 9:30 so there was lots of daylight. A twelve hour workday was common but during harvest it could extend to fifteen or sixteen hours for both the men and the women.

Often there was a cook car on the threshing site where women prepared the meals on a coal or wood fired kitchen stove. The cook car was about eight feet wide and about twenty feet long. It was built on wheels so it could be towed to different locations. I can only imagine how hot it would be inside when the outside temperature was 80 or 90 degrees.

Farmers got up early, grabbed a cup of coffee, and headed for the barn to do chores and milk cows. After chores about 7 AM, it was time for a breakfast of more coffee, bacon and eggs—a lot of eggs—plus oatmeal, toast and maybe some fried potatoes. About 10 AM work paused for lunch—more coffee, sandwiches and goodies. At noon everything stopped and it was time for dinner which was usually potatoes and gravy, a vegetable, and lots of meat. We didn't worry about cholesterol because we had never heard of it. About 3:00 or 4:00 PM it was time for lunch again with more sandwiches, coffee and goodies. The big meal we called supper came after chores and milking were over. People didn't worry about extra pounds because the extra pounds were mostly muscle and a little extra fat was good insulation in the winter. Obesity wasn't a problem as most of the calories were burned just doing what had to be done. I can imagine what those farmers would say to people who ride stationary bikes today and work out with weights. "Get to work and you'll accomplish the same thing!"

When the threshing machine yielded to the combine in the early 40's, harvest time was still labor intensive, but it didn't require huge crews. A tractor pulled a combine that picked up grain that had been cut and left in swaths or windrows. The combine separated the grain from the straw much like the threshing machine did. Dad bought his first combine in the mid 40's.

An early threshing scene.

Meals were often prepared for the threshing crew in a cook car. The men could eat meals on the threshing site rather than waste time going to the farmstead. Cooking was accomplished on a wood or coal fired cook stove in the cook car. They pulled the cook car from field to field.

Dad with his new combine in about 1946 threshing wheat at the Loughlin farm. He pulled the combine with his D John Deere. The tractor is the same one that I operated a few years later after the steel lug-wheels were replaced with rubber tires in about 1949. Notice the wind charger and wind mill in the background. We used the wind charger to produce electricity. The windmill was for pumping water.

The Old John Deere

By
David Jussero

Few things in my memory
Are as vivid to me
As the days when I rode
The old John Deere "D."

I'd get up in the morning
And head for the yard
There it would sit
All dirty and scarred.

I'd fill it with fuel
Then check the oil
Add a few quarts
And it was ready to toil.

You'd turn on the flywheel
And it would hiss like a snake
Then it would start poppin
And you were really awake.

Grab a thermos of coffee
A can of water or two
The old John Deere
He'd get thirsty too.

Going straight was no problem
You would soon learn
But things started to happen
When you'd try to turn.

At thirteen years old
You didn't have lots of sense
But you would find out
You could wipe out the fence.

Out in the field
You'd keep watching for rain
When a storm would come up
It could be a real pain.

The old John Deere
Although it would last
One thing it wasn't
It wasn't real fast.

When it would start raining
It was a safe bet
That before you'd get home
You'd get your butt wet.

We go back to Dakota
But we no longer hear
The poppin sound
Of the Old John Deere!

Though fun became work
I'd still long to be
Back in the days
When I ran that old "D."

World War II

World War II began in 1939. The US entered the war Dec. 7, 1941, when Japan bombed Pearl Harbor. That war killed more people, destroyed more property, and cost more than any war in history. More than sixteen million military were killed including ten million allied troops. At least fifty countries were involved and the whole world was affected.

People living on the farms in ND also felt the effects of the war. Everyone was encouraged to buy War Bonds. Even kids were expected to buy savings stamps to help finance the war. Savings and sacrifice were accepted by all to help with the war effort, as opposed to the recent wars in Afghanistan and Iraq, where we were asked to spend freely. Even spending money that we didn't have was considered okay. Anything to keep our consumer-based economy rolling.

Many things were rationed during the war years including sugar, gas, and tires. The speed limit was reduced to 35 mph to save on gas and tires. Few cars and very little farm equipment were manufactured between 1941 and 1945. The factories were converted to building airplanes, Jeeps, tanks, and other war machinery.

We all had friends and relatives in the military, and we felt the grief when one of our own didn't return from combat. The people of this greatest generation made huge sacrifices so we could have the freedom we enjoy today. Many gave their lives for the cause.

Dad was the age where he could have been drafted, but farmers with families were not called to serve. I was about five years old in 1941, old enough to know that people were dying in the war and I worried that Dad might need to go.

The war ended in 1946 with the beginning of the Atomic Age when the allies bombed Hiroshima and Nagasaki, Japan.

The end of the war was the beginning of better times in the US. The factories started once again to build automobiles, farm machinery and appliances. Farm land wasn't expensive and grain was a good price. The Great Depression had ended in 1941. Many people believe that the large amount of money spent on the war effort ended the depression. The good times lasted for many decades interrupted only by an occasional recession.

Freedom comes with sacrifice.

Transportation

In 1946 my dad bought a 1941 Ford. Our neighbor bought a new 1946 model and we ended up with his old car which had nearly 100,000 miles on it, This was unusual in the 40's because the winters and road conditions really took a toll on cars.

The car was in fair shape and quite an improvement over the 1940 International pickup that dad bought new for $800. The pickup had provided for all our transportation needs. It was also used for hauling grain, hay, and other farm work. The fact that there were now four people in our family made the narrow pickup cab seem quite small. When the weather was good enough, I often preferred to ride in the box of the truck. By 1946 it didn't have a lot of miles but it was starting to show serious wear. Buying the used Ford gave the old truck a bit of rest. Bad things such as running over rocks and ending up in ditches, began to happen to it when I took the wheel. The old truck was around until 1949 when Dad traded it for a new model.

Cars and trucks were always considered strictly transportation. My parents didn't buy anything that was meant to impress anyone. If they bought a new vehicle, it was always a stripped down model. One accessory we always needed in ND was the heater. In the 1940's heaters were optional. Radios were available on most models, but weren't all that good and were strictly a luxury. Automatic transmissions were options in the 50's but most people could care less. It would be several decades before air conditioning, tape players, heated seats, sun roofs, and electric windows became common. I'm sure most people from my parent's generation would be amazed by the vehicles we drive today, but they probably still would buy a basic car. Cars, like many other conveniences in the past, were based on needs not wants.

The Ford car, Dad, Duane and me. Notice the snow packed in the wheels after plowing through snowbanks.

Shopping in the 40's

In the country during the 1940's shopping was a whole lot different than what we experience today in the city. Most of the things we needed were available in town where we usually shopped once a week. In the event of a breakdown of farm machinery, we would make a quick run to the local hardware or machinery implement dealer in Rolla for parts. This was considered a minor emergency. We needed to keep the equipment running. The seasons were short and time was critical, especially in the planting and harvest months.

Rolla, a town of about 2,000, was where we did most of our business and shopping. There were two or three hardware stores, several grocery stores, three or four car dealers, a lumber yard, two drug stores, a newspaper, three implement dealers selling tractors and other machinery, a movie theater, and several grain elevators.

Saturday night was a big night in Rolla. Most of the farmers in the area would quit work early, clean up, change clothes, and head for town. The town would rock as the kids say today. The bars and pool halls did a brisk business and there were three or four of them.

Many times on those trips for repairs, the farmers would end up in the local saloon to have a cold drink or two. After all the dust and heat, they deserved to relax for a few minutes before heading home. After a couple of beverages with their buddies, the machinery repair became less important. The farmers talked about crops and politics sometimes at great length. After a few hours of socializing, it was too late to go home and get anything accomplished so they might as well continue the party. If they stayed that long, they were already in trouble with their wives. The women were home milking the cows and tending to the kids with supper getting cold on the stove. How much more trouble could they get into if they just had another drink and a couple more games of pool? That was the typical reasoning of someone who stayed in town too long. When they got home there were problems. They had probably heard it all before, but, after a good night's sleep (often in the barn,) everything would be okay.

Now they were a day late getting the equipment repaired assuming they had remembered to pick up the necessary parts. It would have been more rational and productive for the wives to have gone to town for the repair parts.

I knew a guy named Steward who had some problems staying on the job. He had just started harvest and had gotten his first load of grain to mark the big event. He rushed the first load to town, sold it, and bought a pickup load of beer. He didn't go back to the farm for several days. Partying was much more important to Steward than farming and that was the way he did business. The work was accomplished on the farm in spite of his behavior. It's safe to say Stewart didn't end up being the farmer of the family. The farm survived and thrived due to the hard work and good management of his brother. I couldn't spend time with the older guys in the bars because the legal drinking age was 21 and the bartenders knew me. I had to go out of the area to do my partying.

Farmers are actually very responsible people with good work ethics. They are typically very disciplined self-starters who are very hard workers. An eight hour day is unheard of. It's more like twelve or fourteen hours or until the job is finished. On the farm the work was never totally done. When one job was finished, there was a backlog of jobs that needed to be started.

When I first began working in the city, I wasn't used to working only eight hours. Lots of times on the farm we would work eight or nine hours after lunch. I have found a great life away from the farm, but I still have a soft spot in my heart for my ND friends and rural life on the plains.

My dad for the most part behaved better than many of his buddies. He knew he'd better not come home smashed or it there would be hell to pay. Mom wouldn't put up with that behavior. I think Mom was the reason he quit drinking about the time they were married. He had been known to take a few drinks when he was younger—sometimes quite a few. Being the disciplined guy that he was, he gave it up to raise his family. He went twenty years without taking a drink of alcohol. I think I may have been the reason Dad had a few beers after so many years of abstinence.

This is how the events took place. I had my 48' Dodge parked in the yard when Dad ran out of tobacco. I was working in the field and Dad didn't want to drive to town to replenish his stash of nicotine. He knew I smoked even though I didn't smoke when I was with him. He checked out my car thinking he might find a pack of cigarettes or some pipe tobacco hidden away in there. He was thorough in his search. He even took out the back seat where he found several cans of beer stashed neatly in the space under the seat. My buddies and I had been partying in Canada the night before and thought it would be a good idea to hide the beer and get rid of the empties before we went back across the line. If my mother had known, she would have thought I was running with a bad crowd.

When I came in from the field that night, Dad came to where I parked the tractor next to the fuel tank. He said, "Son, I was looking for tobacco in your car and I came across some beer you had hidden. I didn't know you drank."

I said, "Dad, I've been known to have a beer," and he said it was okay as long as I didn't overdo it. Then he informed me that Mom was in town shopping and that he had put a few of the warm beers in her freezer to cool and thought we had better get them out of there before she got home. He knew that this could be serious trouble if Mom found the forbidden beverage in her freezer.

We took the nice cold cans of beer to the machine shop, drank two or three each, and had a great visit sitting on buckets on the dirt floor. Dad was a great sport. He knew he couldn't do anything about my drinking or smoking, so he might as well join me. This was the start of Dad and I having a social drink or two together occasionally. I don't remember him having more to drink that he could handle. He controlled it well so I don't think he ever had an alcohol problem.

As I said earlier, once a week shopping seemed to be the rule at our house. We actually had plenty of food stocked up to last for a long time. There was little chance we would starve. We grew most of our groceries on the farm. We could always butcher a chicken or two, dig up some potatoes, and maybe go into the basement to find a quart jar of canned vegetables. We always had plenty of eggs. Sometimes we ate eggs three times a day. Farmers needed to have plenty of food on hand because the winters were unpredictable and many times so severe that it was impossible to do shopping for extended periods of time.

Hansboro was closer in miles than Rolla, but Rolla was bigger and had a better selection of merchandise and groceries. Although our address was Rolla, Hansboro has a special place in my heart and I'm really sorry to see that it didn't survive as it once was. Due to changes in farming, the farms became larger and the population of the area wasn't able to support the great little village as it once was.

Hansboro was a town where young people could party and have fun without worrying about a lot of law enforcement interference. The county sheriff was the only police presence in the area and he was much too busy with the more populated areas to worry about a sleepy little town like Hansboro. As kids, we felt we could get by with more nonsense in Hansboro than in most other areas.

We did a lot of our shopping from home when peddlers stopped by periodically. Alec Hassen was the peddler who came most often and the one I remember most fondly. His headquarters were in Rolla, but he traveled with his merchandise covering a large territory. In the early days he travelled by horse and wagon. Alec wasn't just a very good businessman; he was a friend of his customers wherever he happened to be. The farmers fed his horses and if he stopped late in the day, he stayed for supper and sometimes over night. He eventually retired his horses and bought a Model A Ford and he was able to expand his territory. He sold dry goods—mostly clothing. Alec eventually opened a dry goods store in Rolla called the Golden Rule. He operated the store for many years with the help of his family and many devoted employees. His son, Ron, and his daughter-in-law, Freda, ran the store many years after Alec passed away. It is still a thriving business in Rolla.

There were other door to door salesmen who regularly called on the farms in the area. The McNess dealer handled spices, extracts, cleaning supplies and other kitchen necessities. The Fuller Brush man would stop with his selection of brushes, brooms, and other housekeeping necessities.

Today door to door salespeople have a reputation that isn't all that great, but the peddlers years ago were respected, honest people who provided a wonderful service for rural people. They provided a unique shopping experience that people used and appreciated.

Catalog shopping was also a flourishing business. The Sears & Roebuck and Montgomery Ward catalogs were in every rural home. When we ordered something from the catalog, we waited for the US Mail to deliver the goods sometimes weeks later. Both Sears and Wards had a variety of inventory from socks and diapers to entire houses. The houses came from Sears Roebuck as a kit consisting of precut lumber and all the necessary parts to construct a complete house. Those packages were delivered by rail.

Sears and Wards were great reference and dream books. They provided information about what was available if you had the money to spend. We called them the wish book and the ultimate wish book was the Christmas catalog that came out in late fall. Every toy and gadget you could imagine was included in the colorful pages of that masterpiece. The wish book was well worn in every family home by kids dreaming about what Santa might bring.

On a rare occasion we made a trip to Cando which was a slightly larger town than Rolla. Cando was also the Towner County seat. This didn't happen often because it was about an eighty mile round trip, so we only went when there was farm business to tend to. Dad usually had some land or farming details to tend to at the court house. It was a real shopping opportunity because Cando had one of the few J. C. Penney stores in the area. It was a huge treat to enter a store that in reality was quite small but seemed like a Super Wal-Mart to me when I was a kid. We didn't buy much but checking out the amazing inventory was an awesome experience.

When the time was right to trade cars, our local Chevrolet dealer, Bruce Theel, often brought a brand new shiny car to a potential customer.

He just left that beautiful set of wheels parked in the yard and gave the keys to the interested party. It proved to be a great temptation to buy, and I'm sure he sold many cars that way. It gave the customer a chance to see if a cream-can would fit on the floor of the back seat which was an absolute necessity in the farming community. There was no proof of insurance papers to sign, or copies of driver's licenses carefully put on file. He'd say, "Just drive it for a while and see how it works for you. If you decide you don't want it, Ill come and get it." Life was simple.

Most deals were not bound by a complicated contract. In those days people trusted each other because they could. Many times a man's handshake and his word were sufficient to clinch a deal. In the rare event that someone proved to be less than trustworthy, the word soon got around. In small communities news travels quickly and a person's good reputation was important if they wanted to do business in the area.

Few women admit their age
Few men act theirs

The Miller Farm

The Miller Farmstead

In 1948 we moved to the Miller farm. This was the first farm that my parents owned. We rented the previous two farms on a share crop basis. Half the crop went to the landlord. Dad paid cash for the Miller farm. He wrote a check for $6500. We found the cancelled check after he died. He was proud of the fact that he didn't owe any money on their farm. He and Mom sacrificed a lot be able to do this.

Our house was modern by the standards of those days, but the barn wasn't great. We still milked cows and Mom raised chickens. The cream, chickens and eggs were a good part of our income. It was pretty much an accepted fact that the proceeds from the chickens and eggs would pay for much of the groceries. Although, raising chickens and milking cows was a tedious task, this was a dependable source of extra money. Many families in those days would have had it much tougher financially had it not been for this income. Mom delivered eggs in Rolla where she had several customers who depended on her for both eggs and chickens. Her poultry business was a good part of her social life as most of her customers were friends.

After years of raising cattle and milking cows in the ramshackle barn, Dad decided to build a new, modern barn with a milking machine, electric lights and all the conveniences. This had been his dream for many years. They enjoyed this new barn for only a short time. They decided to quit raising cattle and keep their operation limited to small grain production.

If you are failing to plan
You're planning to fail.

The Early 50's

Our house on the Miller farm was heated by coal from the coal bin in the basement. Dad hauled coal in the pickup from Rolla then shoveled it in through an opening in the side of the house foundation. Even though the coal bin was in the basement and had a door, dust seemed to go everywhere. We had to tend the furnace twice a day. There was only a big register directly above the furnace on the main floor of the house and that part of the house stayed really warm.

The farm had an artesian well and it was our only source of water. It seemed like really good water but it was a shallow well near the barn so we were a little concerned about the safety of the water. We hauled our drinking water from a neighbor's well until we drilled a deep water well near the house. It had an electric pump which was different than the bucket and rope we used to access the water from the old well. We had to use that method to water the cattle. In winter ice accumulated around the well from the spilled water and it's a wonder someone didn't fall in. This method was a step backward from our previous farm where we had a windmill to pump the water.

For the first years in our new place, we had a 32 volt electric system. There were 16 two volt glass batteries in the basement which were charged by the wind charger. It provided enough electricity to run a refrigerator and a few light bulbs. Our house was wired for electricity when it was built in the 1920's. There was one light hanging from a wire in each room with just a bare bulb. No fancy light fixtures. It wasn't great but it was a whole lot better than a kerosene or gas lamp. There were times when the wind didn't blow enough to keep the batteries charged and we had to rely on a gas powered generator in the basement. It had a flexible exhaust pipe running through the wall to the outside.

It was quite acceptable to go outside and around the side of the house to relieve yourself. There was a terrible odor coming from the generator one time when Dad started it up. It didn't take him long to figure out that I had peed down the exhaust pipe of the generator. Not a good plan and it was one more time I was in trouble.

We caught rain water from the house roof and piped it to a several thousand gallon tank in the basement. There was a hand pump upstairs near the sink and we could pump water up to wash clothes and wash our hands. Mom used a wringer washer to do the laundry. It was an early model with a two cycle engine that ran on a liberal mixture of oil and gas. It put out a blue smoke that almost made us sick. Later Dad figured out a way to adapt a 32 volt motor to the wringer washer that was a terrific improvement. We didn't have an electric or gas water heater then, but that came later when we got 120 volt electricity.

Mom heated the water for washing on the kitchen stove in a boiler. Some of the wood fired kitchen stoves had a reservoir attached that could heat a few gallons of water but that wasn't nearly enough to wash clothes. She hung the clothes on the line outside both winter and summer and they froze stiff as a board in the winter. They were mostly dry when she brought them in to thaw. Some people dried their clothes on racks in the house during the coldest weather.

Electric Lights

Electricity came to the farm in the early 1950's and we could abandon our 32 volt system. We could finally replace many of the appliances with new ones that ran on REA power. Dad loved our new electric toaster because we didn't have a 32 volt toaster. The REA (Rural Electrical Association) was a federal program designed to electrify rural America. Many areas in the US received power before we did in ND.

The electric company encouraged people to buy new appliances. There were many cash incentives sponsored by the electric companies and the appliance dealers who sold a great number of new stoves and refrigerators. It also sold a lot of electricity. Now the farmers had a monthly electric bill. Rather than generating their own power and pumping their water with free wind energy, they now were dependent on the power companies, but it was a great improvement and did make life easier and more convenient.

Next came the telephone. Until the phone system came through our area, there was no means of communication except by mail or telegraph. There was rural mail delivery, but the telegraph was in town where there were also telephones. The first phones were not all that dependable because the lines were strung on poles along the main roads, and a good storm would put the system out of commission.

Even with telephone service, if there was a winter storm, people were on their own. Everyone knew it and was prepared with enough food and fuel to keep warm. There was no one to bail you out and you could die if you weren't prepared. There was no 911 to call in the event of sickness or accident. There would be help in town but with the roads blocked, people couldn't access it. There were many periods of weeks that we were unable to get to town except by horse and sleigh. Although the winters in ND are still rough, the climate has changed for the better. The winters haven't been as severe and farmers have snowmobiles and four wheel drive vehicles. Life is better.

Before Modern Plumbing

We had outdoor toilets on the farm when I was a kid. They were crude homemade affairs built over a hole dug in the ground similar to toilets in some primitive campgrounds today. Many of these toilets had two holes even though I don't know of many families that were close enough to use two seats at one time. The Sears or Wards catalog was available for toilet paper. The glossy paper didn't work very well unless you wrinkled it up and rolled it around in your hands to soften it up, but that still didn't make it like Charmin.

The unheated outdoor facility in below zero weather was not comfortable. It definitely was not a situation where you would linger and read the catalog. You could find yourself frozen to the seat.

One summer morning when I was about eleven or twelve years old, I was sitting in the outhouse reading the catalog and smoking a cigarette when Dad pulled the door open. He, no doubt, saw smoke coming out of the vents and knew what was going on. I quickly crushed the lit cigarette in the palm of my hand and held on until the fire went out. It burned like hell. Dad stood in the doorway and wanted to visit. Sitting there with a red hot cigarette in my hand and my pants down wasn't the ideal situation for a social call. He never said anything about the incident, but he certainly got his point across. Dad had his own way of dealing with things and his way usually worked quite well, but it wasn't the last time I experimented with cigarettes. I found other places to smoke.

My parents had a makeshift indoor toilet in the basement to use in the coldest part of the winter. It was just a glorified bucket with a toilet seat and a lid. As it filled up, it was my job to carry it out and empty it. About the worst thing that could happen would be to trip on the stairs. It was my worst nightmare, but, thank God, it never happened. All the time our friends in town were enjoying indoor plumbing. Some of our wealthier neighbors had indoor plumbing before we did. My folks eventually installed running water but not before I left home in the early 1950's. It might have been because I was no longer around to carry out the honey bucket!

While we were still living on the Loughlin farm, Dad built a sauna bath. Being a Finn, the sauna was part of his heritage. Many Finnish families had a wood fired bath house. Saturday night was the big bath night. Occasionally neighbors would drop by for a bath. It was understood that anybody visiting was welcome to take a bath whether they needed one or not.

The bathhouse consisted of two small rooms. The steam room had a stove built out of a steel barrel designed with a bin full of rocks on it that were heated by the fire. When the rocks were hot, we sprinkled water on them to produce steam. The stove also had a crude water tank attached that was also heated by the stove. The men would compete to see who could take the most heat. The temperature was over 150 degrees and people came out of the bathhouse and into the dressing room looking like lobsters. They usually sat around after a bath, drank a few beers and talked farming and politics with the neighbors.

When we moved to the Miller farm, we took the sauna with us. Dad jacked it up and put a couple of wooden beams under it and slid it across the country with the old D John Deere to its new location several miles away. My family used it even after they got modern plumbing in the 1950's.

Entertainment

In the early 40's the radio was our entertainment and source of news. We had a large cabinet type radio that was powered by a six volt car battery. The battery was charged by a small wind charger hooked up to a car generator. That arrangement also powered one or two light bulbs. We had this system before we had 32 volt power.

Dad sat by his radio and listened to the World War II news events. Mom listened to soap operas during the day. On Saturday night the Grand Ole Opry was the family entertainment for the evening. The radio was a big part of our lives much like TV is today, and the record player was sort of like CD players or IPods are today. My grandpa Jussero bought a record player when Dad was still living at home. When Grandpa and Grandma died, Dad inherited it. It was in a large cabinet with a crude speaker system and a 78 rpm turntable that ran by a wind-up system. We had a box of records many of which were Finnish songs because my grandparents spoke Finnish as their first language. I now have the phonograph and the records, and it still works just fine.

When I was young, it was a special event to crank up the record player. We gathered around and marveled at how it was possible to get music out of a flat black disc. A few songs were family favorites. Many were songs about hobos riding the rails. This wasn't long after the Great Depression and some of the songs were reminders of those hard times. One favorite was "*The Wreck of the Old '97.*" Another was "*I Don't Work for a Living.*"

I don't work for a living
I get along alright without
I don't toil all day
I suppose it's because I'm not built that way.

Some people work for love
And say its all sunshine and gain
But if I can't get sunshine
Without any work
I think I'll stay out of the rain.

Some of the songs depicted hobos as lazy, filthy beggars, but I think that might have been unfair. There's little doubt that most of the hobos were willing to work, but with unemployment over twenty percent with no unemployment insurance, they were just trying to survive. Probably there were some who made bumming a career. Not too different from today where some people living under bridges take simple living to an all new level.

If you think there's good in everybody,
You haven't met everybody!

Drivers Education

When I was about fourteen years old, I got my first driver's license. We didn't have to take a driver's test and there was no official driver's training class. Our training came from driving vehicles around the fields and pastures on the farm. The license was *supposed* to be limited to hauling grain and driving to school.

One day Dad and I got in the pickup and he said, "You can drive." I was about twelve or thirteen when. I got behind the wheel, started the truck, and away we went across the field. He said, "Where did you learn to shift gears like that?" I said, "I've been watching you." I had sat in the truck when it was parked in the yard and practiced shifting. After that, I was able to haul grain from the field during harvest and do other chores with the truck although I wasn't allowed to drive on country roads. That made sense because the first couple of times I drove, I found out it was a lot harder than driving in the pasture or in the field. The first time I had Mom as a passenger, we ended up in the ditch on a pile of rocks. Our neighbor, Clarence, pulled the truck back on the road with his tractor and we continued on home with Mom driving. We never told Dad about that incident, but he suspected something when the truck didn't handle all that well after that. I'm sure some of the steering mechanism under the truck was bent from landing on those boulders.

Make it idiot proof
And someone
Will make a better idiot.

Tractors

Some time in the mid 40's, Dad had rubber tires installed on the old John Deere. The tractor came from the factory with steel wheels with lugs for traction. On hard surface the lugs would shake the heck out of the driver, but on fields that were worked up, it wasn't so bad. The lugs could sink in the soft soil. When the lugs hit a submerged rock, it would be an unexpected jolt to your body as well as the tractor. The rubber tires made the old tractor a much more civilized machine.

After the tire conversion, I was allowed to run the tractor. It was fun for awhile, but soon it began to feel like work. It wasn't the most exciting piece of equipment. Top speed was about six mph and it had two slower gears that were used for heavier loads.

Dad used the John Deere until 1951 when he bought a new Minneapolis Moline. It was a big improvement with four or five speeds and a road speed of about 20 mph. It didn't take long to get home for lunch.

New Neighbors

In 1948 or 49 new neighbors moved to the farm directly across the road from us. Napoleon and Delphine Messier had two daughters. The oldest, Caroleen, and I were almost exactly the same age. Joyce was a few years younger. As I look back, I'm sure Caroleen couldn't wait to meet me!

Caroleen and I were both in the 8th grade and it would be our last year at Picton School. I made it a point to sit close enough to her to copy many of her papers. She wasn't all that much smarter than I, but she worked a lot harder. We usually got similar marks on our tests. We became close friends.

During the summer we rode bicycles together and sometimes we stayed out much later than my dad thought was appropriate. One night I heard Dad's pickup leave the yard and I had a pretty good idea about where he was going. He was on his way to find me, and he didn't have to go very far. We weren't far from home on those gravel roads, but it looked like serious trouble and that called for serious action. I jumped off my bike and let the air out of my rear tire. I was pushing my bike down the road when Dad came storming down the road in his truck. He said, "Son, I see you have a problem. Throw your bike in the truck and I'll run you home." Caroleen had to ride home by herself which served her right as it was pretty much her fault we were out so late.

Biking was fun, but I figured it was time to enjoy floating around on the pond between our two farms. I built a raft out of an old tractor inner tube and some lumber I found. It worked pretty well. We pushed ourselves around with a pole. We had our own personal water craft and it didn't cost a thing. Once again Dad was keeping a close watch on me as Caroleen and I floated around on the slough. When it got dark, he stood in the yard and called me to come in. I told him to come and get me. I don't know what he was worried about. How much trouble could we get into floating around on the water?

This is the raft we built and paddled around on a big slough.

When I turned fourteen, Dad let me use the pickup. It was a farm truck and it smelled like a farm truck. It needed a thorough cleaning each time we used it to go to town on a date. We went to MD's burger place or to a movie. At least we told our folks we went to a movie, but if they asked what the name was, we had to make up something. They were low budget dates. Dad furnished the gas for the truck. I don't remember having much money, but we didn't need a lot of cash.

Caroleen and I graduated from Picton School in 1950. We finished the eighth grade and it was time to advance to high school. That was when Caroleen and I went different directions. She went to school in Rolla where four years were available and I went to school in Hansboro for two years. We were still neighbors and continued to date and I'm sure we both suspected that a wedding in the future was possible, but we were only fourteen and much too young to make any serious commitment.

The two years in Hansboro High School were fun years. My good friend, Gerald Peterson and I were the only boys in our class. Gerald drove a Model A Ford and hauled his younger brothers and sisters to school. I drove myself in Dad's 1949 International pickup. At lunch time we were allowed to go downtown. It sounds exciting, but a town with fewer than one hundred residents doesn't have a whole lot happening. We cruised up and down Main Street and in the winter months, we went out by the grain elevators and spun a few doughnuts on the ice and snow.

Olson's general store was our hangout and we bought candy and goodies there. Ralph Olson was our friend, but I doubt he was overjoyed when the kids from school invaded his neat little store with snowy, muddy boots. We knew enough not to give him too much trouble because he knew us and he knew our parents. In a small town you had to behave or a least not get caught misbehaving. I got pretty good at the latter.

After two years at Hansboro, I figured it was enough. I thought formal schooling was interfering with my education so I didn't go back to school after the tenth grade. I was a drop out, but I later got my GED.

Earning a Living

When I was sixteen years old, Dad suggested that I should get a job or go to some kind of trade school. I went to work for our neighbor, Bill Henderson, in the fall of 1952. He lived a couple of miles north of our farm, and I really learned what work was all about. It was a family of extremely hard workers. A day was never long enough to accomplish what they expected of themselves or their employees. They set the pace and didn't ask anyone to do a job they wouldn't do themselves. I was well aware of the fact that I was going to work for some of the most ambitious people in the community.

The first morning the wake up call came about 5:30. We had breakfast and by seven o'clock we headed for the hayfield with two trucks to haul hay. We pitched hay all day and didn't get to bed until about 10 pm. At that point I should have had second thoughts about more education. Little did I realize at the time that this was a learning experience and things would only get better. One thing I learned was that I didn't want to do that the rest of my life. I made $5.00 per day plus room and board. The wages were OK because there was very little opportunity to spend the money anyway.

One day I was working in the field with the tractor. I started at 7 AM and pulled into the yard at 8 that night. In the summer in ND it was full daylight until about ten o'clock at night. The boss came running out and asked me if I'd had trouble with the machinery. I said everything was fine that I just thought it was quitting time. He thought that was fine, but I could go help the boys butcher a cow.

When it came time to butcher the pigs they raised for meat and for sale, Bill's sons, Howard and Fritz, and I headed for the pig pasture with a tractor and trailer armed with rifles. We were supposed to come back with several animals ready to butcher. We thought we could drive through the pasture and shoot the pigs then pick them up on the way back, but there weren't any dead pigs on the first trip through. Eventually we were successful and came back with the bacon, although there were some anxious moments in the pasture. That was the ultimate ND red necked hunting trip.

When winter came, I was still working at the same place. The winter hours were shorter but the wages dropped to $3.00 per day, and it was a seven day a week schedule. My job was to help with the cattle and pigs. I cleaned the barn and pig pens. It was all manual labor because there was little automation and labor was cheap.

I worked for Bill's son, Alvy, and his wife, Rita, the winter of 1952. We got along great and became close friends. During the short days of winter when the evenings were long, Alvy and I would sit around and play blackjack for small change. One day we decided to play a trick on Rita. Rather than the dimes and nickels we usually played with, we gathered up all the folding money we could find, then added a few checks written for huge sums and started to play a fake game of blackjack. When Rita saw what we were doing, she thought we both had gone crazy and began to chew us out. Alvy got the worst of it and I learned that women are gentle, loving creatures until you make them mad.

The first time away from home taught me a lot about the real world, but I was still happier cleaning up after pigs than going to school. My next job was working for Ed, Bill's son-in-law. He offered me $150 per month plus room and board and he only worked 12 hours a day six days a week. That made it a much easier job and we became good friends. His theory was that if we didn't get something done today, it would be there tomorrow and if tomorrow didn't happen, it wouldn't make any difference anyway. His wife, Sylvia, was a fun person and a great cook. They had two young daughters, Sharon and Dorothy.

I slept in the bunkhouse and during the busy season, Ed hired extra help. He hired a guy named Jerry from town to haul rocks in the field and work around the farm. Jerry and I stayed in the bunk house. He went to town every night and drank up his wages at Penny's bar. Then he'd come home and crawl into my bed. I wasn't really happy about this but there was only one bed. One morning I woke up and the bed was wet. I thought possibly the roof had leaked, but I quickly ruled that out when I discovered Jerry had wet the bed. I told Ed we needed to talk. He asked if there was a problem. I said, "I don't know how to tell you this, but your buddy, Jerry, peed the bed and this isn't working." Ed had a great laugh about that but he did let me move into the house. I failed to see the humor. Jerry didn't stick around long after that and I had my bunk house back.

The shower bath Ed had in the basement of his new modern house felt really good after a long, dusty day running the tractor. Today we take a shower for granted, but in those days it was a luxury.

When I turned seventeen, Dad and I decided to rent three more quarters of land and try farming together. I could use his equipment and farm the rented land and help farm the home acreage. We did this for one year and raised a good crop. The problem was the tractor and equipment we had wasn't large enough for that many acres. We could have bought larger machinery, but financially it just didn't work out. I was able to pay off the car I bought the previous year and had a few dollars left over after my one and only year of farming.

Farming is a risky business. A good crop depends on the weather. It is dry land farming which means that there is no irrigation, so everything depends on rainfall coming at just the right time. Some years there was too much moisture and others there was not enough.

I guess I wasn't cut out to be a farmer, but I knew I had to come up with a plan for my life. At that point I only knew what I didn't want to do the rest of my life.

Trade School

I decided to go to Fargo in the fall of 1953 to take a short course in auto mechanics. My cousin, Don, was living in Fargo at the time. He had gone to the same school and was doing well. I learned a lot from Don. He was a valued employee on the job servicing heavy equipment and was also very successful investing in rental property. He grew up on a farm not far from ours and was a really hard worker.

Don introduced me to the owner of the Iverson Hotel. Carl Iverson offered me a part time job painting, doing janitor work, and helping around the hotel. The job included a room and meals in the café. I also got fifty cents an hour for any extra hours I worked. That worked well. I was going to school, had a place to live, meals furnished, and spending money. Life was good. The Iverson Hotel wasn't an expensive place. Many of the residents had cheap rooms for the winter. The rest of the year some of the residents worked on nearby farms. There were even cheaper accommodations. There were cots lined up in the hallways where the homeless slept for fifty cents a night in the winter. North Dakota is not a good place to be homeless in the winter. During the day many of the men just hung out in the lobby. I enjoyed visiting with them because they all had a story.

One of the men brought his own slices of bread and a tea bag to the café. The waitress toasted the bread and gave him a cup of hot water. She didn't rely on tips from that low budget customer. When we knew Carl and his wife were out for awhile, the waitress, Tina, and I made milk shakes. She was a super sized woman who must have eaten too many hamburgers and milkshakes.

Trade school was fine, but I learned that I didn't enjoy auto mechanics as much as I thought I would. I did learn enough to do most of my own car maintenance, but I didn't feel confident enough to take a job as a mechanic so I went back to work for my friend, Ed. He always had a job for me. When I wasn't working for him in the warm seasons, I worked for his dad, Ed Sr., in the winter feeding cattle, milking cows, and other chores around the farm. My wages in the winter were $90 per month. We did chores seven days a week, but it wasn't a very tight schedule. There was plenty of time to kick back and relax.

Caroleen had worked the previous summer for Ed Sr. taking care of his invalid wife, cooking for the crew and cleaning house. She worked from 6:00 in the morning until 9:00 o'clock at night. The job paid $3.00 a day, but she got Sundays off—without pay, of course. There was no sick pay. Taking a half day off meant getting docked a dollar and a half. It was a good reason to head for the city where people were making big money.

Not one shred of evidence
Supports the notion that
Life is serious.

Heading for the Cities

.I was nineteen years old in the fall of 1955. I decided it was time to try something different. Dad and I discussed my future. He suggested that I go east to Detroit where his brother, Oscar, had worked for GM and had done well. My other uncle, John spent most of his life working for Ford, much of his time in management. John, unfortunately, didn't live until retirement. He died in his fifties.

Even though I didn't have a real plan for the rest of my life, I did have a vague idea of what I thought I wanted to do. I was certain I wasn't going to work for someone else, retire at 65, and die of boredom a few years later. I had a goal of working until I was about forty and at least partly retire by them. Those were ambitious dreams for someone with little education and no particular work experience except farm work, but dreams sometimes work out and there's nothing wrong with dreaming.

I decided in the fall of 1955 to head west to Montana rather than east to Detroit. As I look back, this was one of my better choices. I am forever thankful that I didn't head east. The economy in Detroit was OK at the time, but I know now that there were many more opportunities out west.

I told Ed about my plans and he was disappointed that I was leaving. He told me that he had heard that people were starving and times weren't good in that part of the country. He said if I kept working with him, he'd see that I would do OK. That could have been an opportunity. I told him I might be back, but for now I needed a change. I think he knew that my chances were better away from ND.

I talked to my friend, Roy, and asked him if he'd like to take a trip. He said, "Sure. I'm not doing much anyway." Roy had been a school mate and a neighbor. We had been friends all our lives.

We tuned up the old Dodge and headed toward Great Falls, Montana. We checked with the employment office and found there was absolutely nothing available in that area so we decided to keep heading west. We both had relatives in Oregon. We had enough money for gas, cheap motels and food. We drove in snow all the way from ND and it was snowing when we arrived in Portland, OR. We easily found my aunt and uncle in north Portland, but only because they happened to be near the road we were on, Highway 30.

Aunt Elsie and Uncle Reader had no idea we were coming. We really didn't have a plan; we just happened to end up in Portland. I had never been in a city bigger than Fargo and the traffic really made me nervous. Traffic lights didn't exist where I grew up. Ending up in a city with a half million people was intimidating to say the least.

We stayed with Elsie for a few days then Roy contacted his uncle and went to stay with him. When I told Elsie I planned to get a job, she said it would be impossible because the times weren't good and winter was usually a poor time to look for work. But after a few days, I decided to check out the job market for myself. I told Elsie that I planned to just walk around the area and talk to a few people. I really didn't feel confidant driving with all the snow on the streets and I was freaked out by the traffic.

The only big business I saw was Harbor Ford, a car dealership about four blocks from the house. I went in and talked to a salesman and asked for the man in charge. He said to talk to Larry, the head of sales and service. I introduced myself and said I needed a job and that I had some mechanical schooling, but I was willing to do anything. I told him I do a good job and I work hard. He said he needed someone to wash cars and I was ready to do that. He said he would pay me $225 per month for five and half days a week. His regular lot boy didn't show up that morning so I got the job. I don't remember ever filling out an application.

I went back and told Elsie about the job and she offered to rent me a room in her basement. The home they were living in had several rooms and apartments that she rented out to bring in some extra income. The room she had available was about 10 x 10 feet. It had a bed, a refrigerator and a hot plate. It also had a post supporting the floor above right in the middle that had a makeshift table built around it. There was a laundry sink near the washing machine just outside the door where I washed dishes and brushed my teeth. There was also a room with a shower and another room with a toilet in separate areas of the basement. I got all of that for only $25 per month.

Many times I ate dinner with Elsie and Reader because Elsie knew I wasn't the best cook. My utilities were furnished and life was good.

My job was washing the inventory of the 1956 Ford cars and trucks—rain or shine. That kept me busy most of the time. I could wash about four cars an hour. I also drove Ford cars and trucks between dealers in the area. I did that a lot and got lost a lot. A GPS would have been nice, but I was about fifty years too soon for that technology.

Success keeps you growing.
Failure keeps you humble.

Caroleen

I wrote to Caroleen and asked her come out west. She was working in Rolla at the courthouse, and in the spring of 1956 she decided to join me in Portland. I'm not sure my living accommodations impressed her all that much, but it worked fine for me.

Elsie made sure that she had a separate room in a totally different part of the house. We were both nineteen years old and had plans to get married. In May, 1956, Caroleen and I were married in the Catholic Church in north Portland. The reception was at Elsie and Reader's place. It was a low budget wedding. We ordered flowers that were never delivered and the honeymoon was the weekend off from work spent in a cheap motel near Portland because I had to be back to work on Monday. We were home by Sunday evening to our first apartment in the basement of Elsie's house. I didn't carry her over the threshold. I just kind of helped her down the stairs.

The first thing Caroleen did was clean up all the dust balls from the floor. It was a good thing I hadn't married someone accustomed to living in a mansion because our little 10 x 10 room with the bathroom in the hall was anything but a mansion.

Before she came out to Portland, I started a new job. My cousin, Julia's husband, Don, worked at Portland Chain Company where he got me a job as a welder's helper. We manufactured conveyor chains for sawmills. Oregon still had a healthy lumber industry in the 1950's. It was a pay raise to almost $300 per month and I only worked 40 hours a week. We were rich!

Caroleen got a job at Pacific Power and Light working in the office. Between the two of us we were making over $500 per month and our rent at Elsie's was still only $25 per month. We eventually moved into a different apartment, but it was still in Elsie's basement. She had three apartments down there and the sizes were small, smaller and medium. We eventually lived in all three units. The last one was the largest but we had to duck under the furnace pipes to get in the door. It was quite an improvement because there was a little room for furniture in that apartment. We did all that moving but didn't have to change our address. It was an easy move because we only had a few clothes and our toothbrushes. We didn't have a high consumption life style—we didn't have that kind of money.

While we were living in Elsie's basement apartment, we often had company. It's not easy to entertain friends with only a couple of kitchen chairs and a bed to sit on. We became friends with Reader's brother, Frank, and his wife, Jeannie. They actually had a house a few miles away, so we visited back and forth. In our little cave we usually had dinner and a few beers, but we had to be careful that Elsie didn't find any beer bottles around. Beer was strictly off limits in her house. Reader and Elsie hadn't always been against drinking. In their youth Reader made his own brew, but that was before they reformed and started going to church. That put an end to the home brew operation.

Jeannie kept after us to start looking for a house. She thought we should upgrade our standard of living and get into a house like normal people, and Caroleen agreed with her. I didn't care because I thought the little apartment worked fine. A house would complicate things. As I write this, we've been married 53 years and we have had several different houses. And I was right. Life became considerably more complicated but also considerably more comfortable.

Over the years we saw less and less of Jeannie and Frank because they were busy making a living and raising their four kids, Dennis, John, Dianna and Julie. Caroleen and I were also quite busy. Making a living required a lot of time. In retirement all four of us have had more time and we've spent several vacations together in Hawaii reminiscing and enjoying the sand and sun.

Charleen

It wasn't long before our life was about to change. We would be parents in a few months and I was hoping for a girl. I became a little frightened when I realized it could be a boy and I wasn't so old that I didn't remember what a pain in the butt I had been for my parents. It would be just my luck to have a son just like me, but we were happy to bring home a lovely, drooling baby daughter we named Charleen.

Before Charleen was born we were still living in our little apartment in Elsie's basement. Caroleen informed me that she didn't intend to raise a baby in that small, dark apartment. I said that a baby isn't very big and I was sure we could figure out somewhere to put a crib. My argument didn't work and we started checking out the housing market.

One day as I stood in Elsie's front window and looked across the street I noticed a really good looking home. I thought to myself that it would be nice to buy a home like that, but as far as I knew it wasn't for sale. I was just dreaming and I didn't mention it to anyone. A few days later Elsie told me that the house across the street was for sale. She knew the woman who owned it. Her husband had died recently and she needed to sell the house. I told her I would like to buy it, but didn't see how I could with no credit rating and not even being 21 years old, but we contacted the owner anyway. She agreed to sell the house for $7,000 with $500 down and $50 per month on a real estate contract. Elsie and Reader agreed to co-sign for us and we were instant homeowners.

Our house on Tyler Ave. in Portland.

Caroleen got her wish. It wasn't necessary to bring Charleen home to a small, dark basement apartment. We had more room in that house than we needed even with a new baby. There were bedrooms on the second floor that we never did use.

Charleen was a great baby. She didn't become a pain until much later. Not true. We are really proud of her. She did well in school and became a very capable adult. I regret that I didn't find more time to give to her when she was a child. It seems that I had my priorities mixed up.

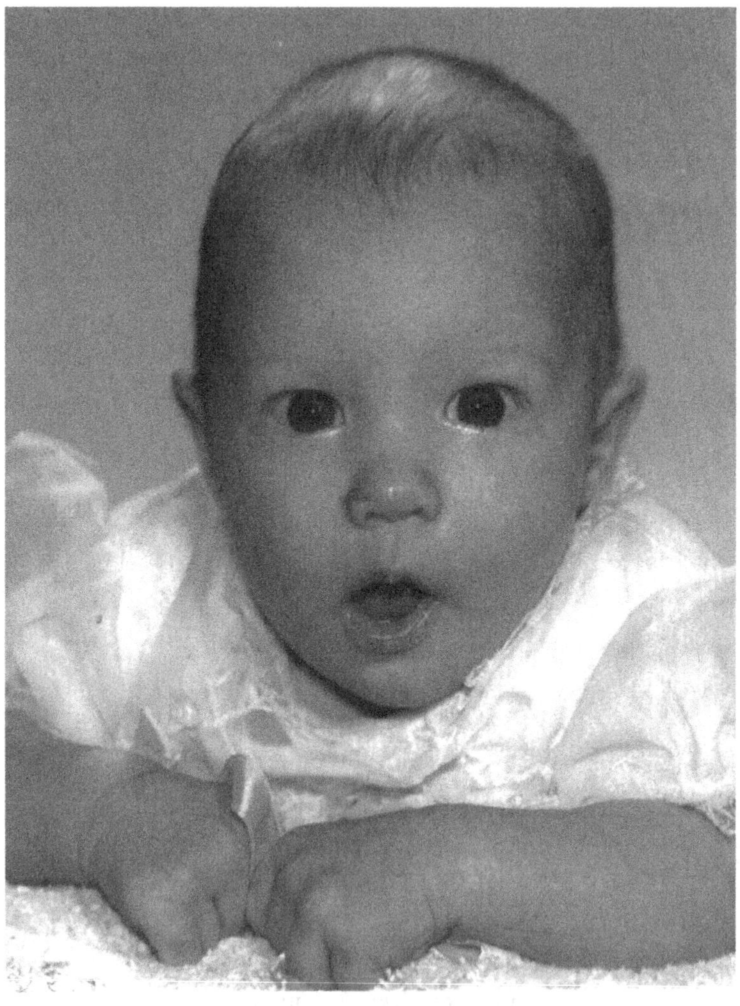

Charleen at six weeks old.

A privacy issue at six months

My girls, Caroleen and Charleen.

Moving to Seattle

We were only in our new home a few months when the work at Portland Chain began to slow down because of a lack of orders. Since I was at the bottom of the seniority list, I was the first one to be laid off. I was called back a few weeks later only to be laid off again. After looking for work in Portland, I soon learned that the Oregon economy wasn't all that great. There were no jobs available and our savings were disappearing quickly. I liked living in Portland, but decided to check things out in Seattle. I heard there were more opportunities up there.

My first stop was Boeing. I filled out an application, had a short interview and was hired. Boeing was working on a refueling tanker for the Air Force and they were also building the 707 airplane on the same frame for the airlines. They were hiring and I was available. I went to work while

Caroleen and Charleen were still in Portland. I stayed with Caroleen's uncle and aunt, Chuck and Delores Ducatt, in Renton. On weekends Chuck and I drove to Portland and moved a few things to Renton.

We sold our house in Portland to my former boss at Portland Chain. We hated to sell it because it was our first home and we had lived in it such a short time. We really didn't want to leave Portland. I didn't care much for Seattle, but we had to go where we could find work.

Caroleen's Grandpa agreed to let us stay with him temporarily. He was living in a small house by himself in Renton and needed a cook, but really didn't have room for three more people in his tiny home. It must have been a terrible inconvenience for him, but we appreciated his hospitality.

A few months after we moved to Seattle, I talked to Bill Reinholm, a family friend who had been raised in the same part of ND as my family. Bill, Elsie, and their daughter, Judy, often came back to ND from Seattle and visited us on the farm when I was growing up. They weren't related, but I thought of them like family and always looked forward to their visits. Bill worked for the American Laundry Machinery Co. servicing and installing laundry machinery in commercial laundries and hospitals. He thought I should go to work with him at American as an apprentice in the service department. That job was the beginning of better times for us. Caroleen was also working as she always had except for a short time after Charleen was born. Times would have been tough for us financially if it hadn't been for her contributions to the family budget.

When I went to work for American, we rented an apartment in Seattle for a short time. My aunt, Lempi, lived with us and babysat Charleen for a short time. Caroleen rode the bus to work when I was using the family car as a service vehicle on my job. There were times when I was able to take her to work in the morning when we both worked in the same general area of Seattle. I was only on the job for a short time when they started sending me on service installations jobs as far away as Montana. That left Caroleen without a car. It was a long time before we became a two car family.

I enjoyed working with Bill at American, but the wages were quite low. I told Bill I was thinking about applying for a job at one of the commercial laundries in the area. He said he would give me a good recommendation and even gave me the names of some laundry owners to contact. He knew I could make more money somewhere else.

I called a man named Mr. Hagen, who managed a laundry that employed several operating engineers who operated the steam boilers and provided mechanical maintenance on the equipment. I felt somewhat confidant about maintenance, but I didn't have the boiler experience. This was a problem. Seattle required a boiler license to operate boilers. To take the test to get the license, a person needed experience and there was no apprentice program in the operating engineers union. Mr. Hagen suggested I call Bill Weaver, another laundry owner in Seattle because he was always looking for help.

I lost no time calling Pantorium Laundry, one of the businesses Weaver owned. It was a problem not having a boiler operator's license, but his chief engineer hired me and I had a limited amount of time to get the license. The job filled the work experience requirement but I took classes to prepare for the test.

A short time after I started working at Pantorium, Weaver asked me if I knew how to weld. He had fired the only engineer who knew how to weld and he needed someone to take that job. I told him I wasn't a great welder, but I could do it and would take a welding class at the community college to get better. Welding was quite easy for me and with a few hours of instruction, I felt confident to fabricate whatever they needed.

I found myself going to boiler classes and welding school while I was working full time, but it was helping me hold a pretty good job. It was the first job that paid enough to live comfortable and possibly buy a house in Seattle.

Weaver always paid in cash. On payday he personally handed everyone a small brown envelope of cash. I had never worked for anyone who didn't pay by check. When I started taking home $100 a week, I told Caroleen that maybe she could quit work. Things were looking good. One hundred dollars a week was considered good wages in the 50's. It looked especially good to us after working for $90 per month. I really appreciated my job.

I took the test for a third grade City of Seattle Boiler License and passed with no trouble. I was qualified to fire the boiler and start up the plant in the morning. In order to have a full head of steam by 7:00 AM, the boiler needed to be fired by 5:30 AM.

I worked for several years as an operating engineer. Pantorium was bought out by New Richmond Laundry, so I worked there for a time. I liked the chief engineer at New Richmond. Lee was laid back and a great guy to work with. The chief at Pantorium was somewhat of a challenge to work with and it took serious effort to get along with him. Sometimes I talked when I should have been listening. I've learned over the years why we have two ears and only one mouth. The sooner we learn this, the better off we are.

Be smart enough to know what you don't know
And humble enough to ask.

1961 and 1962

In 1961 I was working for New Richmond laundry when the company bought a laundromat in another location. It was there I heard the news that President Kennedy had been shot. There are somethings that stay very vivid in my mind and that is one of them. I remember exactly what I was doing at the time. It's something I'll never forget. Kennedy was a very popular President. The entire United States and the world mourned his passing by such a senseless act of violence.

1961 was the final year of preparation for the Seattle World's Fair in 1962. A large part of the city was transformed into what is today the Seattle Center. From the top of the laundry where I often worked servicing equipment installed on the roof, I could see the construction of the Space Needle and other buildings that would become Seattle landmarks. People from all over the world visited the fair. It really put Seattle on the map.

Buying a House in Seattle

It was time to begin looking for a house. Our second floor apartment worked OK, but we really wanted a yard where Charleen could play and maybe have a pet. We knew we wouldn't find a house as nice as the one we briefly owned in Portland because the Seattle market was very different. I didn't want to commute long distances and we would need to be on a bus line so our choices were limited.

We found a small house in the Northgate area that was only about 25 years old. It needed serious cleaning and attention before we could be comfortable in it. You might call it distressed property. But that little house with a leaking roof turned out to be a great investment.

After we moved to Seattle, we had a lot of relatives from ND visiting us. One winter when we were living on Stone Ave. in Seattle, my cousin John, and my brother, Duane, came out for a few months. John liked to party and one day he went out for a few beers and came home with a 15 foot camp trailer. I asked him what he was planning to do with it and he said he planned to live in it if we could figure out a way to get in our back yard. That wasn't a problem and he and Duane set up housekeeping in the little trailer.

We enjoyed having them as neighbors. They helped around the house and occasionally babysat Charleen, but John did like to party and so did I. Sometimes John and I pushed the limits and got in trouble, but Caroleen liked John so that helped. He was fun to be around. Duane was only eighteen and didn't care to party so he behaved himself and stayed home with Caroleen and Charleen. Duane spent part of the winter working with a contractor building a duplex down the street.

One day I stopped by the trailer and when I opened the door, it was clear they were cooking. I could tell by the smell that it definitely wasn't something I wanted to eat. They said they were shopping and bought some beef kidneys. I told them I thought they should have emptied them out before cooking. I don't know if they actually ate them, but I suspect they made other choices for their protein requirements after that.

John did a lot of living in his short life. He died a few years later of a heart attack at a very young age. He was doing one of the things he loved most. He was fishing.

Caroleen's sister, Joyce, also came out to visit when we lived in Seattle and in Mountlake Terrace. She babysat Charleen and helped around the house while Caroleen was working. On one of those trips she met Joe, a young man from Minneapolis who came west to try his luck. They later married and had two great kids, Janelle and Matt. Janelle and Dominic are the proud parents of Blixa, a delightful little girl who is five years old.

Caroleen's parents, Napoleon and Delphine, and her youngest sister, Linda, also came out in the winters to visit, usually during the holidays. When they quit farming, Napoleon and Delphine moved near our home in the Martha Lake area. For many years they lived in a mobile home they owned in the neighborhood. They eventually built a house on an adjoining lot where they lived for many years. We enjoyed having

Napoleon and Delphine living near us. They were great neighbors. Don't believe the negative things about mothers-in-laws. I couldn't have had a better one. Napoleon and I had been friends for a long time and I always had his encouragement and support. They have been gone for a long time. I think of them often and they are missed by all who knew these fine people. There is more about Napoleon and Delphine in the family section of this book. He was a survivor of some really hard times. I encourage everyone to read more about Napoleon and the years of the flu epidemic of 1918.

Linda often came out during the summer to spend time with us as she grew older. When she was in her teens, she met Vic on one of her summer visits. Vic, a refugee from Denver, was staying with some friends in the neighborhood. I never did figure out if leaving Denver was Vic's idea or if he was staying one step ahead of the law! Linda and Vic eventually got married and Vic and I became very good friends. He and my brother, Dwight, were also good buddies and most of the time those two were up to no good.

Before they were married, Vic rented an apartment from us. He was a good tenant, but I can't say the same for his painting skills or his choice of paint colors. Evidence of his handy work kept surfacing for years after he left the apartment. After Linda and Vic were married, they rented a different apartment in the same building. I felt better having Linda around to maintain some control over that Denver fugitive. All BS aside, Vic is a good man and a good friend.

They had a daughter, Paulette, while they were still living in the apartment. Eventually they moved to Monroe and years later they retired in Oregon. Paulette is now married and has two kids, Tabitha and Jay.

The Rental Business

The apartments that Linda and Vic rented were in the building we purchased a few years earlier when we repossessed the house in Seattle the buyer had quit paying on. We resold it and invested the equity in an old triplex on 164th Street about twenty miles north of Seattle. At that time we were living in our house in Mount Lake Terrace.

It was a long commute to Seattle from 164th because I-5 hadn't been built. It was a narrow two lane road with deep ditches and no traffic lights.

The Mill Creek area was woods, brush, and pastures and investments in the area were considered risky. There wasn't much happening in Everett. This was years before Boeing built the 747 plant in Snohomish County and the Everett Navel base wouldn't become a reality anytime soon. The triplex had a negative cash flow when we bought it. We could absorb some negative income from the property, but we needed to get it paying for itself quickly. There were only two units rented when we took over, but it had a third unit that needed to be finished. It took a few months of Saturdays and evenings to make a cute, little one bedroom apartment. We were both working so spare time was limited. Finally it was paying for itself and generating a few extra dollars per month. We had very few vacancies in the triplex over the years and it sometimes even covered some temporary negative cash flow from other investments we made in the Everett area.

We were beginning to see possibilities in the rental business. If we could purchase a few more properties and pay them off, it could potentially lead to a comfortable early retirement.

While working on the triplex on 164th, we spotted what we thought looked like a desirable building lot a few blocks from the triplex. We bought it and had a new house built on 161st Place.

Service Vehicle

We were both still working but starting to get into the rental business and found we needed another car. We still had the Pontiac, but I needed something to use as a service vehicle. New Richmond Laundry had company vehicles for a few sales people and executives. One was a 1956 Ford station wagon the boss's brother had driven. He had too much to drink and drove it into the rear end of a truck. The dented sides indicated it had other mishaps too, but I knew the car had a new engine and transmission and was OK mechanically. I offered him $100 for it and he said that would be fine if I would just get it the hell out of there. I opened the hood with a wrecking bar, pried the radiator away from the fan, and checked the water level. It still had water. I charged the battery and the engine started right up. It ran like a new car. I wired the hood shut and drove it home with the help of my friend, Cy. The car looked so bad that Charleen laid down on the floor boards when we met another car. She didn't want to be seen riding in my pride and joy.

I even used that car to haul oversized furniture such as the living room couch that would only fit on the top. I put it on the roof and tied it down, but that left four big dents where the couch legs rested on the roof. When I got it home, I asked my neighbor to help me get the couch into the house. He looked at my car and called me a damn hillbilly. He and his family had just moved into the community and already had me pegged as the neighborhood redneck.

A Seattle cop stopped me for speeding and walked around the car with his ticket book. Finally he said, "What the heck is this thing?" I told him it was a 1956 Ford and he said, "No kidding?" then only wrote me a warning ticket.

When we were building the house on 161st Place, I drove the car to the job site where the builder and a sub-contractor were discussing something. The contractor wanted to know who the hell was driving that old car and thought our builder was kidding when he told him it was the owner of the house they were building.

'When we built that house, we needed to finance part of the project, but the banks didn't want to loan money on property so far from Seattle. We were out in the sticks. We finally arranged financing and were able to finish a really decent house.

We were able to pay the bills and still have some funds left over for investing in real estate. We were beginning to learn that real estate had possibilities. Over the next few years we bought a relatively new duplex and when we had the chance, we bought old houses that needed renovation and either rented them out or sold them. Things were going just fine.

Be careful not to judge people
By what the drive or by
What they wear.

Western Automation

After a few years working in the laundries, I got a little restless and decided to check out a job I heard about at Western Automation Corp.

They sold machinery and supplies to the local commercial laundry operators and installed and serviced what they sold.

I learned in the interview with Mr. Williamson, the owner of the company, that they were developing a new machine they intended to manufacture and market to department stores and laundries throughout the US. It was called a Vibra Steamer. The department stores used the system to remove wrinkles from clothing with a polyester blend before they were put on display. The laundries also used the machines to remove wrinkles after washing and drying shirts, coveralls and uniforms before they were delivered to customers. The steamer consisted of a conveyor that moved the garments on hangers through a large cabinet. The garment was blasted by live steam followed by hot air delivered by a powerful blower that finished the process.

The interview went OK and they decided to hire me which turned out to be a pretty good job. The shop on Western Avenue in Seattle was probably the most challenging part of the job. The assembly was done on the second floor of an old building. Supplies were delivered up a steep truck ramp to the level where the work was done. The machines were moved to the lower level for painting then trucked back up the ramp where they were crated and prepared for shipping.

Wes Seibold, another young guy from ND, and I worked together at Western for several years. We kept the assembly line moving, sometimes under almost impossible conditions. After a few years at Western, Wes started his own mechanical business that turned out to be quite successful.

I was involved with manufacturing and some installations. I went out of state often to service or install some of the systems. As sales for the units picked up, I worked with the assembly crew which consisted of six to eight people.

Elmer Williamson was one of the best people I ever worked for. He delivered parts and supplies for assembly of the machines in his Ford station wagon. He backed it up the ramp and scraped the rear end of his car on the concrete. He swept the shop every chance he had. He did whatever needed to be done to make production run smoothly. He made a big impression on me. He was a guy worth millions who associated with the people in his own socioeconomic circle but wasn't too good to get his hands dirty.

One day I opened my paycheck and found that the amount was considerably more than I had been getting. Suspecting a mistake, I went to the office to let them know and learned that Elmer had decided to give me a raise in pay. It was the first and only pay raise I ever got that I didn't need to ask for or was negotiated by a labor union.

My immediate supervisor was John De Koek Koek, who was head of manufacturing. He looked a lot like Don Knotts and at times was mistaken for him when he was traveling. Many of his actions were typical Don Knotts. John was a good boss and, although we had many challenges, I enjoyed working with him.

No story about Western would be complete without mentioning Art Berend. Art and I had been friends for years and we were happy to make him part of our crew. He always had a smile and a good word even when things weren't going all that well. We depended on his sense of humor to lift our spirits. Art worked in the machine shop where we depended on his ingenuity to help solve many of the challenges we had in developing and building our machines. Art was a joy to work with and a positive influence on me and our crew in the years I worked at Western.

The Vibra Steamer Systems were becoming a hot item. It was getting to the point that to keep up with demand, we needed a more modern facility. Eventually they built a new office and manufacturing building in Redmond with its own sheet metal shop. It had a sub-assembly line, two final assembly lines, a welding shop, an R & D department, and everything else needed to make things happen.

I ended up with an office in the manufacturing area where I worked on inventory and watched over our assembly lines. I never adjusted well to an air conditioned office. I preferred to be actively involved with the guys on the assembly line where I spent most of my time. It was actually a good job. I was treated well by the people in the front office. I was really proud of our work crew. We got the job done sometimes under adverse conditions. I enjoyed the respect and cooperation of our devoted crew.

When I was on vacation, Fred Laws, my right hand man, filled in. I hate to admit it, but things probably went better when I wasn't on the job. That could make a person feel a little insecure, but the job wasn't the only thing I had going. Our real estate ventures were beginning to work quite well. After I quit Western, Fred purchased the manufacturing division of the company from Elmer and operated it successfully for many years.

The crew at Western Automation. I'm the one second from the right.

Brothers

In 1966 my brother, Dwight, decided to come out to Seattle. He stayed with us for awhile. He got a job at Western and went to work in the shop helping with installation of equipment, running the lathe, doing sheet metal work, and anything else that needed to be done.

He bought an old trailer and moved it to a trailer park in North Seattle, but one day the roof started to leak. The rainy season in Seattle is not a good time to reroof anything, so we put black plastic over the whole roof and fastened it down with sticks and nails. That kept him dry all winter until he was able to do a permanent repair the next summer. It's a good thing he didn't live in a snobby trailer court or that type of maintenance might have been frowned upon, but it wasn't the worst looking trailer in the park.

After working at Western, Dwight proved his skills in the sheet metal and fabrication trades working for other companies. For the last couple of decades he has worked for the Port of Seattle as an operating engineer, and applied his sheet metal skills at Sea Tac Airport. I am very proud of my brother, Dwight, who now goes by Don. He and Linda have two great kids, Jon and Cristina. He worked steadily and has a nice home. I'm happy to have him as a brother and a friend. I can't believe he's sixty-one years old and looking forward to retirement. He and his wife, Barb, have a son, Shane, and four grand children. Jon and Erica now have a baby daughter, Noel.

I am also proud of my brother, Duane. He and his first wife, Christa, have a son named Donny who has spent most of his life in the Seattle area. Donny has one daughter, Kristina, who also lives in the area. He is now struggling with MS.

Duane and his wife, Ann, live in Minot, ND. He has three step children, James, John and Paula, and one granddaughter, Amanda.

Duane helped Dad on the farm for several years. We thought he would be the farmer of the family, but this was not to be. He went to work in road construction and didn't return to the farm. He started a landscaping business in Minot with a couple of smoking Lawn Boy mowers. He and Ann are very successful in this venture and it has moved far beyond mowing lawns. He now has a year around business excavating, landscaping, hauling soil and gravel, and doing snow removal in the winter. He has an impressive line of heavy equipment.

The Jussero boys: Don, Duane with the coffee cup, and myself on the right.

Becoming Unemployed

We had several rental units filled with good people, and the rental business was going fine. Caroleen had a successful career selling real estate and in her spare time she was working with me remodeling investment houses. Things were looking OK financially. In 1977 after more than a decade of working for Western, I decided to become unemployed. Some people called it retirement, but I called it unemployment. I preferred unemployment rather than retirement because I read about a study that said unemployed people live several years longer than retired people. It found that people on Social Security were much older than most people who were unemployed. They probably did another study to verify the first study. Either way I liked the idea of living longer.

I found there were definite disadvantages to quitting a full time job. I no longer had the company paying for gas for my truck and for my health insurance or my uniforms. It was a bit of a shock—sort of like falling out of the nest. I really enjoyed the people I worked with and I missed seeing them every day, but the advantages of being on my own schedule and having so much more free time seemed to work for me

We have been blessed with good tenants and our real estate investments are doing fine. There is no reason to change anything.

Health

There were several years when I worked at the laundries and at Western that my health wasn't very good. I developed asthma that often turned into bronchitis and pneumonia. As I look back, it was my own fault. I didn't maintain my health. I was destroying myself with a heavy smoking habit, too much alcohol, and no exercise. There were times when I landed in the hospital unable to breathe and on oxygen. I didn't think someone in their 20's or 30's could die from this problem, but I learned that people do, and I was close to checking out a few times.

I discussed what I could do to improve my health with my doctor. He suggested that I join a health club, stop smoking and drinking, and quit living the destructive life I was living. That wasn't the answer I wanted, so I changed doctors. I was having fun. Life was good except for my health. I did understand that my behavior wasn't sustainable and one day I would have to reform, but at the moment I was having a heck of a good time.

My compromise was to start going to church with Caroleen. Although I was raised as a Protestant, I figured it couldn't hurt to go to a Catholic church. They seemed like good people and I had married one. In the Catholic church Lent starts forty days before Easter. Lent is a time when Catholics give up something such as sweets or broccoli. Many times it's something they wouldn't miss too much anyway. It's meant to be penance for all the bad things you've done during the past year. At that time in my life, forty days probably wouldn't have been long enough to cover my mistakes. It dawned on me that if it worked, I could give up drinking for Lent. That was 1972 and I haven't had a drink in the last thirty-seven years. I wasn't totally dependent on booze, but I could see that I was a problem drinker. I feel that I had help with this from a force more powerful than myself. I sincerely hope God has a sense of humor because the remarks I've made about the church and religion were not meant to be offensive. I do know that he has blessed me with good health, a great family, and more material goods than I can ever use or need.

After reforming somewhat, I bought a bicycle. I hadn't ridden a bike since I was about fourteen years old and always considered them a toy just for kids. I got my first bike for Christmas when I was about ten years old and learned to ride it on snow, ice, and frozen ground. By the time the weather warmed up, I was able to ride pretty well. I rode to the neighbors and gave rides to two of my schoolmates, Irma and Martha Peterson. Martha sat on the back fender and Irma sat on the handle bars. Dad even rode the bike. He rode it to the mailbox and I wondered why a man of his advanced age (he was about forty) would ride a bike. It was a toy. After I got my bike as an adult, I realized that bike riding isn't just for kids. It's a great means of transportation and a good way to stay in shape. I have done a lot of bike riding since I started riding again, but I didn't really take bike riding very seriously until a few years after I quit my job at Western.

I started to consider longer bicycle trips. The crazy notion of a possible trip across the US entered my mind, but I was still quite nervous about riding in traffic. I even hauled my bike to jogging and bike trails in our area. If I were to do any cross country ventures, I had to get over the fear of riding in traffic. As time went on, my fear of traffic became more of a respect for the vehicles that I was sharing the road with. I found that if I were courteous, and rode as far to the right as possible, most people would give me plenty of room. I really learned to love riding bikes.

Charleen Growing Up

I am very proud of Charleen. She was a good kid and grew up to be a responsible adult. We had very little trouble with her. Her mother took care of most of the details of child rearing. I considered it a woman's job. That attitude doesn't work any more, but it was pretty much accepted years ago.

Charleen at about six or seven.

When Charleen was about four or five years old, she decided that she would leave home. She was upset about something. I explained to her that times were tough out there and it probably wasn't a great idea. If she had been about fifteen years old, I might not have tried as hard to discourage her. I told her that if she insisted on leaving, she would need certain things to live on such as food, clothes, etc. I told her go find a couple of paper bags. We made a sandwich and put it in one sack with a banana. Her cloths went in the other along with her cat. She stood there with both of her sacks and I opened the door for her, but she was having second thoughts about leaving a nice warm home. She said, "Dad, I don't think I'll leave. I think I want to stay." Besides her cat was getting pretty restless in that sack so she didn't run away from home.

During my employment years, we always took a vacation at least once a year whether we could afford it or not. Many years we went back to ND to visit our families. The first time we went back, Charleen was only a few month old so we made her a bed in the back seat of the Pontiac. The cars didn't have seat belts and there weren't any laws about restraining kids. Most babies grew to be functional adults with a few exceptions that weren't related to seat belts and car seats.

As Charleen grew older, we did a lot of camping. Camping seemed to bring the family together and I think it was because I was easier to get along with when I got away from the pressures of the job. At least, that's my excuse. We had port-a-potties in the trailer and Charleen and I played cards for the job of emptying them. The loser got the job of emptying those nasty buckets. Those camping trips and vacations were some of the best family times together.

After going to grade school in the Martha Lake area and a Catholic school in South Everett, Charleen went to Blanchet High School, a Catholic school in north Seattle. In the mornings before she drove to school, she took a shower. I tried to discourage her from the morning shower because it woke me up every morning. The plumbing was very noisy. I wasn't getting my point across that she should take her shower at night when it didn't bother anyone so one morning when she was in the forbidden morning shower, I turned the hot water off. She never mentioned anything, but she started taking a shower at night.

Charleen's first communion.

Before she was old enough to drive, I bought a small motorcycle. It was a Honda 50. It was just a little better than peddling a bike with a top speed of about 45 mph. She learned to ride it by cruising up and down our street. She learned to ride her first bicycle with hand brakes on the same street which had a downhill grade. I showed her how to pedal her bike, but I forgot to show her how to use the brakes. She managed to stop at the end of the street by dragging her feet on the pavement. I wasn't a great instructor. She learned to drive her first stick shift car on the same street. She had only driven automatic transmission cars when she bought a little Volkswagen with a straight shift. It was good she had that quiet street for safe practice.

From the Honda 50 motorcycle, we graduated to a couple of 90's. On a good day with a tail wind top speed was about 60 mph on the 90's. One day Charleen suggested that we take the cycles on a ride to Lake Cavanaugh where we had property. It was about a fifty mile ride, but she was only twelve or thirteen and didn't have a driver's license. I told her it wasn't such a good idea because that would be taking a chance of getting stopped by the police. We took a chance on getting busted and had a nice ride to the lake with no cops in sight.

On the way home I thought she should ride ahead of me for a short distance and, if for some reason, I got stopped, she could just keep going as if she didn't know what was going on behind her. I could distract the police until she was out of sight. It seemed like a great idea at the time, but the detail I failed to consider was just how far ahead of me she should stay. I overlooked the fact that all Honda 90's were not created equal. Her bike was the quicker of the two and with a lighter load, it went even faster. I watched as she rode out of sight. All I could see was a little white spot ahead which was her helmet, but I couldn't catch up to her. She arrived home long before I did. I asked her why she left me so far behind and she said, "Dad, I wasn't supposed to be aware of what was going on behind me." What could I say?

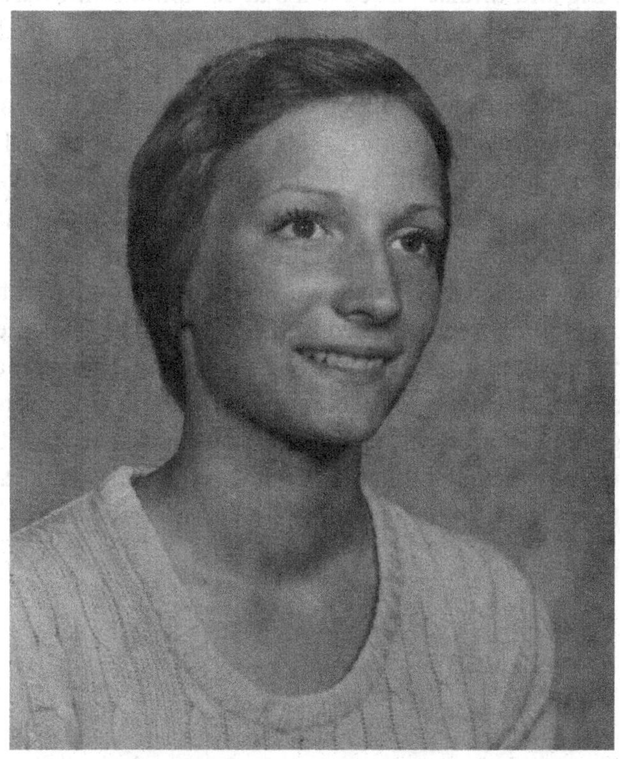

Charleen's graduation picture. Our girl grew up.

Family Pets

Charleen always had pets when she was growing up. Her first one was a kitten that I brought home in a paper sack. As soon as we let it out of the bag, it scampered up the draperies totally out of control. We almost always had at least one cat and dogs were also common in our family. At one time we had a St. Bernard and a Mexican Chihuahua. When we walked them, people laughed at the mismatched pair. We said the little one was the runt of the litter.

We got Queenie, the St. Bernard, when she was a pup and she turned out to be a good dog. When she grew up, we thought it might be fun to raise pups. We went looking for a mate for Queenie and found an ad in the paper for a St. Bernard named Thor. We went to check him out and he ended up coming home with us. We put him in the back of the pickup and every time he moved the truck would sway. He was huge. Not only was he huge, he was undisciplined so he did pretty much whatever he wanted to. Big and undisciplined is a bad combination. Charleen tried to take him for a walk but he dragged her down the driveway. He didn't understand the concept of leash.

Queenie fell in love with him and became pregnant. We only hoped that the offspring would be more like Queenie than Thor. I couldn't imagine having a litter of little Thors. All ten puppies arrived in the coldest part of the winter. We made a maternity ward in the garage with heat lamps and bedding to keep the little family comfortable.

Thor went to live with people who were better prepared to handle that big guy. Nobody really missed him except maybe Queenie, but she was busy raising her family. He isn't the first male to disappear and leave the female to raise the family. The pups turned out fine even without a father figure in their lives. We sold the pups and were back to one St. Bernard and a Mexican Chihuahua. That was the end of our St. Bernard raising enterprise, but it turned out to be a great experience.

Charleen with the Mama and her babies.

Charleen and Queen ready for a walk.

Charleen and Harley's Wedding

Charleen informed us in 1977 that she was planning to be married the following May. That got my attention. A wedding can get really expensive for the father of the bride. I approached Harley, my future son-in-law and suggested that he and Charleen should elope. I even offered him my credit card to cover the expenses up to a couple of hundred dollars. He thought I was kidding. It didn't work and they planned a conventional wedding with tuxedos, flowers, and all the other traditional stuff. The wedding went well and they were off to start their lives as a couple.

As it turned out we got a bargain. We got a good son-in-law and two neat grandkids out of the deal and they've been married for well over thirty years.

We'd known Harley's parents, Harold and Delores Spaeth for years. They had also migrated to Seattle from ND in the 1950's.

Justin was born in 1979. Charleen and Harley were excited about being mom and dad and Caroleen and I were anxious to become grandparents. One advantage of being married young, there's a good chance that you will be young parents and grandparents. It's more fun to interact with kids when you're forty than when you're seventy.

From left to right: Dave and Caroleen, Charleen and Harley, Delores and Harold.

Uncle Omer

In the mid to late 70's we did a lot of traveling with RV's. We bought our first camp trailer about 1970 which we towed with the 1965 Pontiac. We had the travel bug and tried several RV's looking for the perfect rig. We had years of experimenting with trailers, campers, and motor homes. We finally decided there was no perfect outfit.

In 1979 we had a new 1979 Chevy pickup and a small eight foot camper. We decided to go to Alberta to visit relatives on Mom's side of the family. We had been there a few years earlier and met many relatives for the first time. By the time we went in 1979, many of the older generation had passed on including Aunt Lillian, Uncle Emil, Aunt Marie Anne, and Uncle Edward.

On an earlier trip we stayed with Aunt Lillian and Uncle Joe. We met their daughter, Doreen and her husband, Emile, and Cousin Paul and his wife, Eloise. Over the years we had several opportunities to spend time with these fine folks and became close friends. We also had the privilege of meeting Uncle Omer who was one of a kind.

The road to his house was just two tire tracks through a field. He didn't know we were coming because he had no phone. He was a bachelor in his late 60's or early 70's living in a 16 x 16 foot cabin that he had built.

The road to Omer's cabin was more like a trail.

When we drove up, he was mowing hay with a team of horses. He loved his horses and did his work with them mainly because he'd always done it that way. He saw no good reason to change. His nephews had given him a tractor, but he didn't trust it. He seemed a little afraid of it. He walked to town on the railroad track and carried his groceries several miles home the same way.

Uncle Omer invited us into his cabin for a cup of tea. The only stove he had was an ancient wood burner that he used for heating and cooking. It was July, but he fired up his stove anyway. He went to a shallow well with a wooden cover on it to get some water in a quart canning jar for tea. Several flies flew out of the well when he opened the lid. We were having second thoughts about drinking his brew, but we didn't want to offend this good man.

I asked him why he used a jar to heat water. He told me that he once had a tea kettle, but the spout plugged up and he had to throw it away. The glass jar didn't have that problem. He put the jug on the stove and dumped in a generous amount of tea. By this time the stove was going good and the temperature in the cabin was about 100 degrees. The tea concoction was boiling vigorously. He said in order to make good tea, you needed to boil it well. It seemed like a good idea to me.

He said, "So, you guys are from the United States." I said we were from Washington State.

"I got a letter once from the US," he said. He dug through his paper work and retrieved a letter he received from Chicago a year earlier.

Uncle Omer lived on several acres of land that had been a homestead. He had a radio covered with a piece of tarp which was his only link to the outside world. He said the roof leaked when it rained and that wasn't very good for the radio, but the batteries were dead anyway. His bed was also covered with a tarp to keep it dry. The floor was bare boards with huge cracks between them. There was a big space under the door where wind could sweep in and there was no plumbing or electricity. To say that it was basic housing is a gross exaggeration.

The barn on the property wasn't a bad building. His horses had much better conditions than he did. His horses were his top priority. He loved them and nothing was too good for them. He also had a few chickens for eggs and meat. Omer lived much the same way people lived at the turn of the century and he had no plans to change anything.

We invited him to eat with us in the camper. "By Gosh this is a pretty nice caboose," he said as he checked things out.

The next morning Omer and I went for a walk. He wanted to show me his property. I had a hard time keeping up with him. He walked fast and told me the history of the land. He was proud of his acreage.

I learned a lot in those few days with this unique individual. I could see that he was content and happy with very little in creature comforts.

Omer's nephew helped him from time to time and made sure that he was OK. Eventually he built Omer a new house next to his cabin. He said he wanted a farm house—nothing fancy. It had a single room with a few conveniences such as a linoleum floor that he could sweep out.

Omer, Caroleen and I in front of his log cabin.

Aunt Virginia in Omer's cabin.

This is the stove Omer used to heat his cabin and brew his tea.

We learned a few years later that Omer died. His nephew found his body near the barn where he apparently died of a heart attack. I'm sure this is the way he wanted to go. I was grateful that I got to meet him. Spending time with Uncle Omer was like going back in time—almost a century. Life was much simpler then although it was physically much harder. It took all of his time just to make a meager living.

It's not the amount of stuff that surrounds you that creates happiness.

Dad's Last Days

In 1980 Caroleen and I were vacationing in Las Vegas in our pickup and camper that we parked behind a casino on the strip. We called Dad and Mom in ND and learned that Dad wasn't feeling well. He was having stomach problems and was afraid it might be something serious. We thought maybe it was an ulcer and were worried because it wasn't Dad's nature to complain. He had gone to the hospital for tests but they didn't have the results yet. We headed for home and kept in touch with the folks by phone. While we were on our way home, we stopped in Brooks, OR to see Caroleen's Aunt Hilda and Uncle Gerald. When we called home, we got the bad news. Dad had cancer of the esophagus and it had probably spread to other organs. He had been out to visit us a year earlier when Justin was born so he got to meet his great grandchild. It had been a special time for all of us. He enjoyed coming out to visit and came several times in his later years. He loved to ride the train. It gave him a chance to socialize with other passengers and make new friends. Dad loved to visit. He loved talking politics and occasionally discussing religion. The last time he came out in 1979, he wasn't feeling well and we suggested that he get some medical attention at the time, but he declined. I wish we had insisted on it. I think he suspected problems at the time, but didn't want to bother us.

Caroleen and I arrived home from Las Vegas and prepared to go to ND to spend some time with Dad and Mom. His wish was to stay around long enough to see his kids, grandkids, and friends one more time. Caroleen, Charleen, Justin and I drove to Minot, ND, where he was in the hospital. Duane and Ann lived in Minot and were able to spend time with Dad while he was hospitalized. He was happy to see us and said he knew we would come. When we walked into the room and saw how thin and pale he looked, we suspected that he didn't have all that long to be with us. He was well aware of how serious his condition was. He discussed different options with his doctor, but there was no cure and he accepted that he would be checking out soon. Knowing that he would soon not be able to eat and swallow, he decided to have feeding tube surgically installed in his stomach. That gave him more time. It was either live with the tube for a while or slowly starve to death which he said he seriously considered. He told me he wasn't afraid of death, but he was afraid of the dying process. He had watched his dad die a very painful death with a similar cancer. When Grandpa died in 1938, there weren't as many pain medications available for managing this horrible disease and Dad had seen his dad go through a very painful death.

There wasn't any more they could do for Dad at the hospital in Minot and he really wanted to go home for his last days. Mom and Dad had moved off the farm and into a nice home in Rolla, and he wanted to be there. They had sold the home place and a few acres to a young neighbor and moved to town. Moving from the farm was a big adjustment for them and I'm sure that Dad was never comfortable living in town. He was a farmer at heart and had been one all his life.

Caroleen, Charleen, and Justin returned to Seattle knowing they would never see him again. I'm sure that wasn't easy. I decided to stay to help with Dad. I thought the folks could use some assistance, and my schedule allowed me the time to spend with them.

We moved Dad home from the hospital in Minot in Duane and Ann's station wagon. Dad wasn't strong enough to ride sitting up for 120 miles so we made a bed in the back of the station wagon. I'm sure it wasn't very comfortable but he didn't complain.

He as able to get around the house without help for most of his last days, and when he could no longer eat, we fed him with the tube they inserted. It kept him alive but he continued to get weaker. He couldn't drink coffee and, being a Finn, that was tough.

Dad and I went for rides in the country from time to time and he enjoyed that. One day we were driving along and he told me he was seeing double—another sign the cancer was spreading. He looked at me and said, "I see Dickie and Dave." He never lost his sense of humor. I told him I was glad I was driving. We headed for Rolla and he asked me where we were going. I told him we were going home. He said, "You're going the wrong way. Oh, hell, I forgot. I thought we were still living on the farm."

His health continued to deteriorate. His eye sight was giving him trouble, and his speech began to fail. All this time he was losing weight and becoming weaker.

Dwight and Linda came back to Rolla with Jon and Christie. Jon was about three years old and Christie was a baby. It pleased Dad to see his kids and grandkids one last time. They had limited time to spend and needed to get back to Seattle for work, but their visit meant the world to Mom and Dad.

Our Uncle Herb was one of Dad's regular visitors. Herb had been married to Dad's sister, Elma, who died a few years earlier and he was taking Dad's illness very hard. Cousin Anne and her husband, Don, also lived in Rolla and were great support through this very difficult time. She helped so much and I don't know what we'd have done without her. Thank God for family and friends.

As time went on, Dad got weaker. One day he woke up with a bad cough and was having trouble breathing. He agreed to go to the hospital in Rolla. As we drove to the hospital he looked back and knew it would be the last time he would see his home. They told us at the hospital he had pneumonia. Dad was a very courageous man in life and in death. He said as he was getting weaker, "Don't worry, Son, life will go on."

Mom and I took turns staying with him at the hospital. There was a cot in the room where we could rest. After a few days, he went into a coma. After spending most of the night with him, I went home to get some sleep and slept longer than I intended. The hospital called and said he was gone. His passing was peaceful and painless in the end which is what he wanted.

Mom took his death hard and I think in those last days, they resolved any differences they had in the earlier days.

Dwight and Caroleen flew out for the funeral which was a large gathering of friends and family. Dad had lived in the community all his life and had lots of friends. After the funeral, we flew back to Seattle leaving Mom as a widow. She was also a strong person and I knew she would be OK. She was seventy years old, very capable, and had the support of many friends. Cousin Anne was there for anything she needed. Mom was a very religious person and relied heavily on faith to carry her through the difficult times.

Mom owned an old apartment building in Rolla. The tenants were mostly her friends, so Mom took an apartment for herself in the building. She seemed to prefer living there rather than in her house a few blocks away. It was probably lonely for her living in a house by herself. We called her periodically to see how she was doing. We also tried to go see her at least once a year.

Mount St. Helen's Eruption

On Sunday morning, May 18, 1980, we were in church in Everett when we heard a loud noise like a truck hitting the building. We later learned that the noise was the Mount St. Helen's eruption over one hundred miles south of us.

Fifty seven people were killed, 250 homes, 47 bridges, 15 miles of railway, and 185 miles of highway were destroyed. The eruption reduced the elevation of the summit from 9677 feet to 8365 feet and created a one mile wide crater in the mountain. The blast wiped out the forest for miles, laying the trees flat like giant toothpicks. It took several decades for the area to recover. Much of the area was prime logging territory, but it takes a long time for trees to grow back big enough to harvest. The death toll would have been much higher if the eruption had happened on a work day when the loggers were working.

The ash from the eruption covered the city of Yakima to the east, and the area surrounding the mountain was covered with a thick layer of ash. The ash from the eruption reached several states including North Dakota twelve hundred miles away. Duane said there was ash covering his vehicles in Minot a couple of days after the eruption.

Later that Sunday in May, we celebrated Justin's first birthday. He shares his birthday with a very destructive and unforgettable event.

Grandkids and Great-grandkids

Our grandkids, Justin and Cassie, spent a lot of time with us which we loved. Justin is our first and only grandson. In his younger years we spent a lot of time together. We skied together, but our most memorable venture was the bicycle trip to ND.

One day I decided to go skiing and asked Justin if he would like to come along and take a skiing lesson. He was about nine or ten years old and hadn't spent much time in the snow. As we were driving up to Stevens Pass, he looked out at the snow capped mountains and the deep snow along the road. He was so quiet it seemed as if he was concerned about something, so I asked what the problem was. He wanted to know how deep the snow was up in the ski area. I told him it was about eight or ten feet. He said, "Grandpa, how tall am I?" I assured him that it wouldn't be a problem and he had nothing to worry about. He took lessons and became quite enthused about the sport. We took Cassie for lessons a year or two later and she also caught on quickly, but didn't seem to enjoy it as much as Justin did.

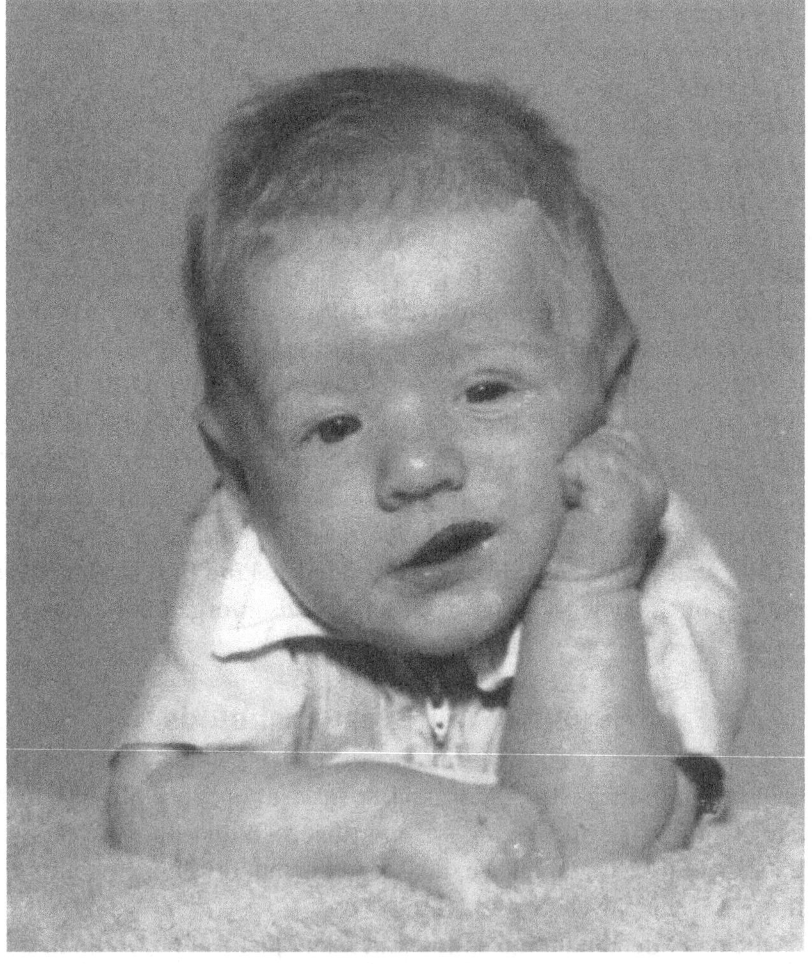

Justin at six months.

Justin has spent many of his working years in the hardwood flooring business. As the residential construction business melted down, there was a very high rate of unemployment in the flooring trade. He is now working in the salvage business and this seems to be working for him. He's a hard worker with a good work ethic and, although he's seen some hard times, things are coming together for him.

Justin has two kids, Ryleigh, born Aug. 26, 1999, and Caitlyn, born July 2, 2001. I am very proud of Justin and his family. Ryleigh enjoys some of the same kinds of recreation that I do. When he was about four years old he became interested in skiing so I took him with me to Stevens Pass where he took skiing lessons. Now I have trouble keeping up with him on the slopes. He turned out to be a great skier and has added snowboarding to his winter sports fun. He's also a strong bicycle rider and we've been riding together on the Centennial trail for several years. I look forward to more bike miles with my great-grandson.

Four generations of Jusseros from left to right: Me, Charleen and Justin, and Dad on the right.

Caitlyn is a couple of years younger than Ryleigh. She and I will probably always remember picking blackberries. We've had fun doing this for the last few years. When she was about six years old, I realized I wasn't doing as many things with her as I did with Ryleigh because she wasn't involved in biking and skiing. She was more interested in playing with dolls and making cookies and other projects with Grandma.

Caitlyn

I decided one day that it might be fun to build a playhouse for her. It turned out to be quite a project, but I had the time and most of the materials. We planned to celebrate her sixth birthday at our house and I intended to have the playhouse finished and set up in time for her birthday. With Caroleen's help as the painter and decorator, we had it finished and temporarily set in time for her birthday celebration. We presented her with a birthday card and a house key. She looked a bit disappointed with just a card and a lone house key. Other cards she had gotten had a few dollars cash but this one didn't. She looked at the key and said, "What am I supposed to do with this?" We took her to the playhouse and her eyes got as big as saucers. I told her to try the key and it fit! She spent the rest of the day in and out of her little house and each time she left, she locked the door.

The playhouse looked cute in our yard, but Caitlyn lived in Cashmere, WA, with her mother, Charity, stepdad, Guy, and her step sisters, Brenda and Carolyn. I anticipated moving it so I built it in seven sections for easy dismantling and assembly. We stacked it on a trailer, moved it, and set it up at their home east of the mountains where the kids could enjoy it. It was a fun project. I probably had more fun building the little house than the kids have playing in it.

The playhouse I built and Caroleen decorated for Caitlyn.

Our granddaughter, Cassie, was born on Feb. 8, 1981. We looked forward to babysitting for her when she was growing up and she did spend a lot of time with us. She served us imaginary tea in a huge dog house converted to a play house when we lived on 161st. She and I often sneaked off to McDonalds for an ice cream sundae with caramel topping. We both have a serious sweet tooth.

Cassie is my favorite and only granddaughter. She was a good kid and a good student. The years went by quickly and soon she was a young adult. I never had any doubts that she would be a success because it seemed as if she always had a plan for her life.

Cassie is now married and she and Vichhean have two delightful sons, Max and Alex. I get to see the little guys fairly often because they only live a few minutes away from us. I told Cassie that a third child, a girl, might be nice and asked when it might be arriving. She said, "Probably ain't going to happen." As I said, she seems to have a plan.

Vichhean has a great job with Siemens Industries. They have a nice home and Cassie has quit her job as a medical assistant to stay home to raise the kids.I have every reason to be proud of this young family. They are doing a lot of things right.

Cassie

By Grandpa

You've come a long way, kid
With eight years of school gone by,
But your whole life's before you
And I know you will try

To pick your friends wisely,
As you've always done,
The school years ahead
Will be rewarding and fun.

There will be temptations
That could lead you astray,
But just go by your conscience
And you'll get through them OK.

Keep up the good work
And I truly believe,
There will be no limit
As to what you will achieve.

You're a delightful young lady
Who stands out from the crowd.
And to be your grandfather
Makes me real proud.

A poem I wrote for Cassie when she graduated from the 8th grade.

Cassie at age fourteen.

Cassie and Vichhean

Max and Alex

Justin and Ryleigh

Mother's Health

In the winter of 1981 Mom's older sister, Bertha, died. When we went back for the funeral and felt the cold wind, I remembered those severe winters was one of the reasons we left ND. We spent many holidays with Aunt Bertha and Uncle Carl and the cousins when we were young and still on the farm. We were very close to Bertha's family.

Mom walked the few blocks between her apartment and Aunt Bertha's house regularly, but she told me she couldn't do it without stopping to rest. I suspected that something was wrong and we wanted her to get a physical exam. Mom was always a very active person who seldom sat down. Doctors and hospitals weren't part of her plan. I don't remember that she ever went to see a doctor, not even for childbirth.

I noticed at Aunt Bertha's funeral that Mom seemed to have aged a lot in the short time since we'd last seen her. Dad's death had taken a toll on her. We were concerned because heart disease ran in her family. Many of her relatives had died from heart problems—some at a very early age.

In late summer of 1983 Anne called to say that Mother had a heart attack, and the situation was critical. We left in the motor home with Dwight and drove straight through to ND. Mom was glad to see us and seemed to be alert, but we could tell her condition was serious. The doctors in Rolla suggested that more could be done for her in Minot so we transported her there by ambulance where she was treated until she was well enough to go home. The heart attack caused substantial heart damage, but she wanted to go home to recuperate.

We stayed with Mother in Rolla for a few days until we thought she was stable enough to make it on her own. As I look back, it wasn't a good decision on my part. I should have figured out a way to stay with her longer because she was weaker than we realized at the time. It became obvious that Mom would need help. We wanted her to go to the assisted care facility in Rolla until she was stronger, but she wanted no part of that program. I don't blame her. That's the last place I would want to go even on a temporary basis.

Dwight, Duane, and I talked the situation over and decided she could get more help in a Seattle hospital. Duane arranged for Mom to fly to Seattle in an ambulance plane using the Minot Air Service. Even though she had medical assistance on the plane and Duane accompanied her on the trip, the experience was quite stressful for her.

She checked into Virginia Mason hospital in Seattle where she stayed for a few days. The doctors determined that she was too weak for surgery and that she could stand a better chance of survival on medication, rest, and exercise.

She came home with Caroleen and me. This was a real downer for her because she was always a very independent person. The last thing she wanted was to be dependent on her kids although I'm sure she appreciated our efforts. Caroleen did a great job caring for Mom. I was gone a lot of the time taking care of the rentals. Mom seemed to be doing OK, but she wasn't very strong and didn't seem to be improving a whole lot because of the heart damage.

One day in November 1983 I was working at a duplex in Everett, when Caroleen's sister, Linda and her husband, Vic, drove over to tell me Mother had another heart attack and was in Steven's Hospital in Lynnwood. The situation was critical and she was in a coma. She never regained consciousness.

When I saw her on a breathing machine, I knew it was the end. I can still hear the mechanical device pumping air into the lifeless body of our dear Mother. The doctors indicated that she had no brain activity because of the extended period of time without oxygen. We had a decision to make. Would she want us to keep her breathing with virtually no chance of improvement? I think not.

As she always did in life, she came to our rescue. We didn't have to make the decision to pull the plug. She overpowered the mechanical monster that was breathing for her and went peaceful on to her next life. She died on November 17, 1983.

We knew it was her wish to be buried in ND with Dad at the Rolla cemetery. Caroleen, Dwight, and I went back to ND by train. Mother was in a different car going back to the area that she loved so much and where she spent most of her life.

She and Dad are buried side by side in the North Dakota soil where they made their living and raised their family. May they rest in peace.

Mother's Diary

For as long as I remember Mother kept a daily diary. She wrote about the weather and little things that occurred to her. Many times there wasn't much to write about because there wasn't much happening around the farm. A trip to town to do shopping, a neighbor stopping by to visit, or a call from one of us kids was always documented. There were no secrets or personal entries. She simply made notes on what happened that day.

After Mother was gone, I was looking at old photos and other memorable things from the past when I discovered her entry from Tues. Sept. 6, 1983—just two and half months before she died. The last few years, she made her notes on a calendar which was a gift from a local business and it would be the last entry she ever made. She indicated that she was sick that day and Cousin Anne's daughter, Linda, had been over to see her. They discovered that she was very sick and she'd had a serious heart attack which would ultimately result in her death a few months later.

There is little doubt that her heart problem was a condition that she had suffered with for some time, but Mother didn't have physical checkups or consult a doctor even when she wasn't feeling well. She had been sick many times and she always recovered. I'm sure she thought this episode was no exception. The fact that she wrote in her daily notes that she was sick that day tells me that she must have been in great pain. She wasn't someone to mention it otherwise.

It's possible that much of the heart damage that occurred might have been prevented if it had been dealt with even a few hours sooner.

AUG.						1983
S	M	T	W	T	F	S
	1	2	3	4	5	6
7	8	9	10	11	12	13
14	15	16	17	18	19	20
21	22	23	24	25	26	27
28	29	30	31			

OCT.						1983
S	M	T	W	T	F	S
						1
2	3	4	5	6	7	8
9	10	11	12	13	14	15
16	17	18	19	20	21	22
23/30	24/31	25	26	27	28	29

Sept. 1983

Sun	Mon	Tue	Wed	Thu	Fri	Sat
				1	2	3
4	5	6	7	8	9	10
11	12	13	14	15	16	17
18	19	20	21	22	23	24
25	26	27	28	29	30	

SUNDAY 4 247 — 78
going to crossroads this afternoon with Lois. went to the service here this m

MONDAY 5 248 — 72
Labor Day Mrs Hudson got a rug from [illegible] $[illegible].00, labor day. Clayton and Debbie got apt. No 1.

TUESDAY 6 New M. 249
Lois was over this Mor. I ordered some stuff from her. rain a little this Mor. [illegible] was over. I am sick today. Linda was over

WEDNESDAY 7 250

THURSDAY 8 251
Jewish New Year

FRIDAY 9 252

SATURDAY 10 253

36TH WEEK

SEPT. 4 to 10

Speak no ill of a friend, nor even of an enemy.

SEP OCT NOV DEC

Sept. 6, 1983, the last entry of Mother's journal. This was near the end of her very active, productive life.

Health Issues

IT WAS THE GOOD LIFE. We were traveling and had relatively good health except for some of my earlier self-inflicted problems, but I had resolved them. In the fall of 1990 Caroleen began having some problems and had to have surgery. They found she had a very rare type of cervical cancer. The doctor said that she was lucky because normally that type of cancer isn't found until it is no longer treatable. It was in the early stages and turned out to be treatable. But the word *cancer* was terrifying for us. We knew it was serious when the phone rang and the doctor wanted to see us immediately.

They started her on radiation therapy immediately which cured the cancer, but the side effects have been difficult to deal with ever since the treatment. She will probably always have some problems from the massive doses of radiation, but cervical cancer is fatal if not treated early. We were very fortunate they discovered it early and the treatment was successful. It served to remind us of how fragile life is. We need to live each day as if it's our last because one day it will be.

We both have a few aches and pains as we get older, but that's normal. At least we wake up every morning with a heart that's beating and a mind that still works even if not as well as they once did. Things could be worse.

Caroleen's cancer was over twenty years ago and there's been no return of that dreaded disease. We are now both seventy-four years old and have had a few health issues over the years but basically we're both able to function and manage to take care of business.

There have been many medical advances in our lifetime and many of these procedures give us a few extra years. We consider ourselves fortunate to have lived much of our lives in this period of history.

Motorcycles, Motorhomes, and Bicycles

And the New House we left behind.

IN THE EARLY 1980'S WE were still traveling and camping whenever we had the chance. Louie and Lucille Hoveland, friends we knew from ND, moved to the Seattle area about the same time we did. They also had an RV and we often traveled together. They were about the same age as our parents. One day I told Lucille that I was now an orphan because both of my parents were gone. I asked her if she would consider adopting me. We kidded around all the time. She said she would love to adopt me, but she had already adopted Gloria, another mutual friend, and wasn't sure if Louie wanted any more kids. But we had a mock adoption and I had a sister and another brother-in-law, Stan. Lucille and Louis both passed away years ago, but we miss them and Louie's accordion music a lot. We went to many old fiddlers' campouts with them and Gloria and Stan.

Over the years Gloria and I have convinced many people that we are actually brother and sister and I think we tend to believe it ourselves sometimes. I'd be proud to have Gloria as a real sister. She's a great person.

In 1985 I had some kind of a midlife crisis. I felt the most urgent need to buy myself a new motorcycle. I'd had many different cycles over the years beginning with the Honda 50 and worked my way up to a Honda 400. Now I had my eye on a Gold Wing 1200 cc. It could do some serious traveling as I later learned. I bought one.

The year was 1986 when I rode to ND on the Goldwing. This picture was taken in Rolla, ND, in front of my Cousin Anne's house. I celebrated my 50th birthday on this trip. The trip wasn't very popular with Caroleen and the rest of the family, but it was my birthday!

A New House

The first year I had my motorcycle, I just rode around the Seattle and Everett area. One day I decided to take a trip to Snohomish. As I rode between Clearview and Snohomish on Broadway, I noticed a piece of land overlooking the Snohomish Valley that really looked good. We had been looking for a building site farther north because the Martha Lake area was getting quite congested.

We decided to find out who owned the acreage and see if it was for sale. We knew, almost anything is for sale for the right price. The owner quoted us a number which wasn't negotiable because he didn't really care if he sold it or not. We decided to buy it.

Now we had a piece of land that needed a house. Caroleen did a great job coming up with a floor plan which would be her dream home. We decided to contract the work and not use a builder. This was a decision that I regretted several times during the next few months. Remodeling was fairly easy for me, but I had a lot to learn about new construction. Many times I wondered about the wisdom of building a house that big. It kept growing in size as we went along. When I thought of it as an investment, it made a little more sense.

We sold the home on 161st Place and also a small cabin we owned on Lake Cavanaugh. We also sold a rental house in the Martha Lake area to be able to afford this new home. I was happy to be rid of the cabin. It turned out to be just another piece of real estate to maintain on weekends when we could have been relaxing. There was absolutely no reason to own a piece of recreation property when tax money pays for public parks. We sold the cabin and the houses for several times what we paid for them, so as investments, they penciled out.

Caroleen continued to sell real estate as we were building. This, along with rentals, paid the bills and kept us in groceries. Things were fine financially.

During the building process, I'd sneak away to Stevens Pass to do some skiing. We had taken skiing lessons a couple of years earlier and it was a good way to unwind.

This is the house in Snohomish, WA, where we still live. We overlook a beautiful farming valley and can see Mount Baker in the distance.

Motorcycle Travel

When construction was finished and we were all moved and settled in the new house in the summer of 1986, I decided to get on the motorcycle and head for ND. That was how I celebrated my 50th birthday. There was no speed limit in Montana and that shortened the travel time considerably across a very wide state. I arrived in Minot and tracked Duane down at a landscape site across town. His wife, Ann, kidded me about riding my cycle back there. She said she wouldn't be surprised if I'd show up the next time on a bicycle. I told her not to rule it out.

Occasionally the weather can change your plans when you're traveling on a motorcycle. I got rained in while staying a few days with my Uncle Herb near Rolla. Aunt Elma had passed on and he was living alone. Their kids, Lillian, Dale, and Curtis were all living in Oregon, so he welcomed the company. Herb was one of my favorites. When I was young, he would cut my hair and give me a silver dollar when he finished. This was serious money in those days. After he cooked breakfast one morning, I offered to pick up the dishes. He told me not to stack the plates because then he'd only need to wash one side. He was always trying to figure out a more efficient way to do things. It made sense to me and to this day, I don't stack the dishes. It saves half the work. I thoroughly enjoyed my few days with Herb. It was the highlight of my trip. Thank God for the rain.

In those days it wasn't all work. Caroleen quit selling real estate after we moved into the new house. That gave us a chance to so some serious traveling for a few years. It's strange how things work out. We had everything—a big house and enough stuff to fill it,—yet we couldn't wait to hit the road.

We took a couple of extended trips across the country in the motor home. We spent some time in every state in the lower 48 over the next few years as well as several Canadian provinces.

Traveling by RV has always been one of my favorite ways to travel. It's nice to be able to stop when you want and not worry about meals or lodging.

When we first got the travel bug, we had a really nice twenty one foot Lindy motor home. We bought it in the early 80's during a period of a dollar plus gas prices. People couldn't wait to get rid of gas guzzlers so the price was right on the motor home. As soon as the price of gas went down, we all forgot about trying to conserve and went back to our wasteful ways. Caroleen and I were no exception.

Motor Home Travel in 1986

After my birthday trip with the Gold Wing, we were ready for some serious traveling. One reason for early retirement was to be able to see the US.

We decided that if we were to spend a lot of time in a motor home, we would need something bigger than the twenty one foot Lindy. We bought a twenty nine foot Pace Arrow in 1986. It was a 1985 model that hadn't been sold. After we bought it, I figured out why it hadn't moved from the lot. It was a total lemon. We drove that monster about 80,000 miles but I was never impressed with it. It seemed as if each time we used it, something went wrong and it needed to be repaired. That wasn't so bad when it was under warranty, but eventually we had to start paying the price for keeping it maintained.

Caroleen loved it. She could spend days—even weeks—riding and sleeping in our oversized, self propelled bed. My problem was getting rid of it. It looked like a choice between keeping the motor home and a divorce. I did the math and it was cheaper to keep fixing the motor home.

The Pace Arrow had all the modern conveniences that we had at home incorporated in that grossly overloaded truck chassis called a motor home. The appliances and fixtures worked fine most of the time. It was the times they gave us trouble that were frustrating. Being a plant maintenance engineer in my working life, proved to be quite useful, but the experience that I gained over those years proved to be inadequate to deal with some of the problematic gadgets that we were hauling around. Much of the frustration was due to my total lack of patience with unfamiliar situations. I could see no good reason to spend my retirement trying to keep that rig and all its systems working.

Another part of the problem was my choice in vehicles and it was obvious that other owners of Pace Arrows also had problems. We saw a motor home like ours parked in a campground that had large lemons painted across the front of it. They were trying to send a message, but unfortunately the message was too late for me. But Caroleen continued to love it.

There were a few things I learned on those trips. One was that as big as that motor home was, it wasn't as big as a house, and it's not a good thing to have too many disagreements when you're in such close quarters with your wife. At the house I could escape to my cave if things got too heated. Escaping out of the motor home could only mean a very long walk.

With the new house completed and rentals occupied, we had very little to do and a lot of time to do it. We didn't spend much time planning a route when we decided to head east. Going west was out of the question since we had a motor home that wasn't equipped with pontoons to handle that large body of salt water called the Pacific Ocean.

We left Snohomish with Caroleen reading the map. I was driving what was to become my least favorite vehicle of all times, but I didn't know it yet. Everything was still working.

We headed up the North Cascades highway. It is probably the most scenic road in the entire US. We found no other route in our travels more beautiful.

Caroleen's cousin, Leslie Deschamps and his wife, Loraine, live in Salmon Arm, BC, so we headed towards Canada. They invited us to park our rig on the spacious piece of property near their beautiful new home.

Once in the Rockies, we made it a practice to check out the numerous hot spring pools that are available to the public. After a long day of driving, the luxury of a dip in one of those natural pools was very inviting and the sulphur content in the water is thought to be quite therapeutic. Camping is available at many of those hot pool locations.

We headed out of the Rockies in Alberta on into Saskatchewan with its endless wheat fields, and then cut down into ND to visit Duane and Ann. Over the years we have claimed a parking spot at Duane's place complete with electrical hook ups and access to a hot shower. This is as good as it gets. It also gave me a chance to ride with Duane in his truck as he visits the numerous businesses in Minot that serve free coffee. Many of them are his customers and friends.

A couple of times I helped him with some projects. I ran one of his John Deere loaders for several hours one time and it was definitely the biggest machine I had ever operated. It is amazing that anything that big can be so maneuverable. It was a great experience and I didn't do any serious damage to the machine or anything in the general area.

When we arrived in Rolla, we parked at Don and Anne Hoesl's place where we once again took full advantage of relatives. It was always enjoyable spending time with Uncle Herb. We parked in his yard and spent the evening with him playing pool and blackjack. He had just bought a big, new tractor that let him get the farm work done quickly. That freed up some time for playing pool and enjoying the company of his buddies.

Uncle Herb with his new tractor. With this machine he was able to ride in comfort as he quickly got his work done.

After a few days in the Rolla and Hansboro area, we headed east again. We stopped briefly in Langdon to have breakfast with Gerald, my old school buddy, and Aime, who was a former neighbor. A few more days in the US and we headed north into Canada to see Caroleen's aunt and uncle, Mary and Bernard Deschamp. Then we were back across the border again into Minnesota and heading toward Minneapolis to see Bill and Betty Wygant. After that we were back on the road again like Gypsies bumming from one friend and relative to another.

We had a sixty gallon gas tank that managed to get us from one service station to another. It was terrible mileage for a car, but not bad for a house. And there were even bigger rigs on the road that must have had even bigger tanks and worse mileage. Many of them towed a car or an SUV behind, but we didn't. Towing a car behind an RV would be a challenge when it comes to backing up or turning around.

As we traveled, we always tried to find a Catholic church along the way on Sunday. Sometimes during the week I'd loose my patience and used up many chances to go to heaven. I hoped going to a house of worship would make up for those incidents. Caroleen always insisted on going to a Catholic church, but most any church works equally well for me.

We headed out of Minnesota then into Illinois and it got hot and humid. When the humidity reached 100%, it was a sure sign of a thunderstorm. We decided to visit my friend, Elmer, and his sister, Verna, and her family on the outskirts of Chicago. Verna and Elmer Raasakka were our neighbors and school mates in ND. It was there we experienced one of the hardest rain storms we had seen in a long time. Staying there was a chance to go through the Museum of Science and Industry in Chicago.

The next stop was Niagara Falls where we took a ride on the *Maid of Mist*, a tour boat that takes tourists clad in rain-suits out to experience the moisture from the water as it flows over the falls and splashes down on the river below. It felt like a winter day in Seattle and we spent money on that adventure!

So far the cost of the trip was mostly for gasoline and an occasional campsite. We found that the gas mileage varied with that rig. The mileage varied between nine miles a gallon and as low as six or seven mpg depending on whom I was talking to. RV drivers aren't noted for being honest about mileage.

We still had a few friends and relatives to visit so we headed toward Baltimore where we looked forward to seeing Cousin Carl and his wife, Eileen, and their girls, Cheryl and Ellen. Carl and I go way back to our ND roots where we had close contact from the time we were kids.

Cousin Carl, his wife, Eileen and their girls Cheryl and Ellen.

We left the motor home at Carl's house and rode the train to Washington, DC where we took in the usual sites. Of course, the White House was the main attraction. We were able to tour part of this impressive structure with minimal security checks back then. The White House is the ultimate example of a tax subsidized housing unit. Just one advantage of being President, is the short commute to the office just down the hall. Sort of like working at home.

The White House had one hundred and thirty-two rooms, which I would think is quite adequate. We were among the one million tourists who visit Washington, DC annually. That's one heck of a lot of company. We weren't even offered a cup of coffee. I hoped that, as tax payers financing the operation, we would have been extended more consideration.

Actually seeing memorials to Lincoln and Washington, Arlington Cemetery, the Ford Theater, the museums, and the war memorials were sobering experiences. We had a chance to see the changing of the Guard, the Capitol, and the Kennedy graves. Washington, DC is a fine place to visit but I still prefer our Washington state because it has better scenery and fewer politicians.

The capitol building in Washington, DC.

The White House.

We found our way out of Baltimore and headed toward Virginia and the Blue Ridge Mountains. Shenandoah National Park lies in the heart of the Blue Ridge Mountains of Virginia. We drove through that beautiful area of wilderness and wooded mountain peaks so rich in history. George Washington passed through the area during the French and Indian wars. There are battlefields of the Civil War on both sides of those mountains.

We stopped at Thomas Jefferson's Monticello while still in Virginia. He was the third President of the US from 1801 to 1809 and is known for drafting the Declaration of Independence in 1776. His greatest achievement, as President, was the Louisiana Purchase from France for fifteen million dollars and sponsoring the Lewis and Clark Voyage of Discovery. The US government gained control of the Mississippi River and doubled the size of the United States. That has to be one of the best real estate deals in history.

Prior to becoming President, Jefferson was a serious politician holding many offices including Governor of Virginia, Congressman, Minister to France, Secretary of State, and Vice President.

Jefferson loved architecture and started building his dream home in 1768 while he was still a young man. The building site of Monticello was a 5,000 acre view estate that he inherited from his father when he was only fourteen years old. He added many more acres during his lifetime in order to make it a self-sustaining operation. He employed as many as seventy-five slaves to help run his farms and gardens.

As I review some of the history of this time period, I wonder about some of the events that took place. It's a well accepted fact that Jefferson, as a young congressman in 1776, drafted the Declaration off Independence that stated all men are created equal and have certain inalienable rights. Decades later it's also true that this man's labor force consisted mostly of slaves. Do I sense some degree of inconsistency in the situation? Could it be that the whites considered themselves a little more equal than blacks? It was 1865 before slaves were finally allowed citizenship and civil rights.

Construction of Monticello went quite slow. Jefferson was in charge of every detail and he couldn't spend full time on the project. It seems he kept changing his mind about what he actually wanted. The plans started with eight rooms. Construction continued for twenty-one years until 1789 when he decided to remodel it and expand it to twenty-one rooms. Much of the original building needed to be demolished to incorporate his new ideas. Work on the new plan went on for another twenty years. It took about forty years to build his house or about half his lifetime. I think I would have spent less time building and more time living in my house, but who am I to say what Jefferson should have done?

Monticello turned out to be much more than a mere home. It became a monument to Jefferson and has impressed visitors for a couple of hundred years. He was able to spend several years in his completed mansion before he died. He is buried in the family burial grounds at Monticello.

Thomas Jefferson's home at Monticello.

While we were in the Charlottesville area, we decided to tour Ash Lawn, the home of James Monroe, the fifth President of the US from 1817 to 1825. It was only a couple of miles from Monticello. Those two

Presidents were close friends and it seems as if Jefferson had a great deal of influence on the location of Monroe's home.

Monroe was Minister to France under Jefferson's presidency and negotiated the Louisiana Purchase. He returned home and built his home, but it was obvious that Monroe didn't have the finances available that his neighbor did. He built a much more conventional home on a mere 550 acre site. He planned to retire to Ash Lawn, but lack of finances forced him to sell his beloved home in 1826. All his years in politics took a toll financially because those jobs paid small salaries and took away time from his farming operations and law practice. James Monroe died July 4, 1831.

In the mid 1970's Ash Lawn was bequeathed to the college that Monroe, Jefferson, and Tyler attended. After a major restoration, the college reopened Ash Lawn to the public. It is now an event center and houses many of Monroe's possessions.

Interstate 81 ties in with Interstate 40 at Knoxville, Tennessee. We were heading toward Nashville. Being a big fan of country music, the Nashville scene was something I could identify with. It represents much of my culture, or the lack of it, and I suspect there are only two types of people: the people who love country music and the ones who love it but won't admit it.

One of the big attractions in the Nashville area is a multi-million dollar family park with a dozen stage productions running daily. There are rides, restaurants and shops in a 120 acre setting. We saw a few good shows and spent much of a full day touring the park. We checked out the numerous souvenir and t-shirt shops even though I have never made it a practice to shop in them. I did find myself looking at the merchandise—also known as junk. I didn't find anything with any practical use. Where do these people find this stuff? There must be a catalog that shows all that stuff with anything of value purposely left out. The sad part is tourists buy this crap. I've seen little kids too young to read with t-shirts that say, "Grandpa and Grandma just got back from a long vacation spending my inheritance and all they brought me was this cheap Chinese made shirt." In a few thousand years archaeologists will excavate a landfill and find a lot of this useless refuse, dirty but still intact, and wonder why previous generations acquired that stuff.

We went to the Ryman Auditorium which was the home of the Grand Ole Opry from 1943 to 1974. The show was broadcast from there on the radio when I was growing up. We sat by our big battery operated radio and listened to the Grand Ole Opry. It was a really big deal on Saturday nights. The Opry show now takes place in Opry Land. The Ryman Auditorium is now part of Country Music history and is major tourist attraction.

The Ryman Auditorium is the original home of the Grand Ole Opry.

We enjoyed a bus tour of the homes of many famous country western stars. All the names brought back memories. Among them were the homes of Hank Williams Sr., Eddie Arnold, Webb Pierce, and many others. Roy Acuff's home is located in the Opry Land Park where he spent many of his last years.

Roy Acuff, Hank Snow, Lorrie Morgan, and many other familiar old time country western performers were part of the Grand Ole Opry show that we attended. Many of these famous people have passed on, but their music lives on. Although modern country music is popular with many people, the old stuff will continue to touch the lives of many people for years to come.

After several days in Nashville, we headed toward Memphis and the home of Elvis Presley. Graceland is impressive. His hangout where he did most of his entertaining was the lower level of this large home. There are few windows in that part of the mansion which I thought could be depressing, but it did have unique décor and furnishings.

Graceland, the home of Elvis Presley.

His private jet planes are also part of the tour. He had a Jet Star named Hound Dog II and a four engine Boeing 707 called the Lisa Marie. The Lisa Marie was more like a deluxe apartment than an airplane. It would take the proceeds from the sale of several albums to fill that thing up with fuel. Money was no problem for that famous entertainer, but, unfortunately, he had other hang-ups that affected his health. His fans were devastated by his very premature death. Thanks to technology of recording, his music will be enjoyed forever.

One of Elvis's private planes. This one was the Lisa Marie named for his daughter.

We left Nashville and crossed the Tennessee border into Arkansas heading for the Ozark Mountains. We were on our way to see our friends, Hank and Eulaine in Mountain View. There is no shortage of lively music and entertainment in Mountain View. Hank and Eulaine with their musical talent and their natural ability to entertain delighted their neighbors, fans, and tourists. We attended a couple of stage shows and jam sessions where Hank and Eulaine's talent was obvious. It was an enjoyable time in Mountain View visiting, listening to music and touring the area. Hank and Eulaine took us to the Blanchard Springs Caverns which are a spectacular attraction.

Hank and Eulane Bloominthal in Mountain View, Arkansas.

After several weeks on the road, we started making serious miles in a westerly direction. We drove a lot at night which didn't make much difference in the scenery. The route through Oklahoma, Texas, and New Mexico is not the most scenic path through the US. Every area has its own beauty, but in some states the beauty is much harder to zero in on.

Caroleen kept my coffee cup full and the country music playing on the cassette player as we headed toward Las Vegas. We ended up in Las Vegas only because it happened to be on the route home not just because it is one of the main tourist destinations in the world. Las Vegas is a city where you can come in a $50,000 Mercedes and go home in a $200,000 Greyhound Bus!

We stopped at the Hoover Dam about twenty-five miles out of Las Vegas. It was named in honor President Herbert Hoover even though it was finished during the Franklin Roosevelt administration. This mammoth project is 726.4 feet high and 1244 feet long across the Colorado River in Black Canyon. It took 4,400,000 cubic yards of concrete to build which is enough to pave a highway sixteen feet wide from New York to San Francisco. It took 3500 people to build it. Lake Mead, the reservoir behind the dam, is 115 miles long and 589 feet deep, one of the longest man-made bodies of water in the world. Hoover Dam supplies a good part of the electricity for Southern California, Arizona, and Nevada. Water from Lake Mead can irrigate 1,000,000 acres of farm land in three states. It also supplies water for many cities in Southern California through an aqueduct 240 miles long. Las Vegas may not have been possible without the power and water from the Hoover Dan.

After a day or two looking at the sights, and a great deal of time trying to find a $2.00 blackjack table, I was ready to escape the city of bright lights and noisy slot machines. Going there in an RV eliminates the cost of expensive hotels. It's possible to eat in the casinos fairly cheaply. We could get breakfast for $2.00 and a dinner buffet for only $10.00 so eating was quite inexpensive. I did find a $2.00 blackjack table and ended up breaking even which in Las Vegas, can be described as beating the system. If everyone broke even, the city would go back to blowing desert sand and cactus.

We called my cousin, Oscar Leino, and his wife Betty who lived in Pahrump, NV. It was a fairly new town in 1981 developed in an area near Las Vegas that had access to water. Water is at a premium in Nevada because the country is basically a desert.

Oscar and Betty left Portland where they lived for many years to move to Pahrump. He hoped it would be an improvement over living in Oregon, but I suspect it turned out to be a disappointment. The area was slow to develop and the opportunities were not what he expected. He and Betty later decided to relocate in Washington state where they lived their last days. We had a nice visit before we moved on toward home.

Reno, NV, was our next stop. The drive between Las Vegas and Reno is not the most exciting stretch of road, but we only had a few more hours of driving before we got into familiar territory in Northern California, Oregon, and finally into Washington and home.

After several weeks on the road and almost 8,000 miles, we arrived at our new house and settled down for the winter. The trip was a great experience, but when we got home we wondered about why we would leave a new house with thousands of square feet of living area for an overloaded truck with a couple of hundred square feet of cramped space.

But this is what Americans do. We build much bigger homes than we need, fill them full of stuff, and can't wait to get away from the stress of dealing with all of our treasurers. We hit the road and leave it all behind.

Over the next few years we took other long motor home trips and saw more of the country, but always returned to Washington where we have all of our stuff. It's good to see our friends and family after bumming for several weeks. It wouldn't have been possible for us to take those excursions if it had not been for Charleen and Harley keeping things going at home collecting rents, paying bills, and making deposits so we could keep gas in the motor home.

1987 Motor Home Trip

The fall of 1987 we packed up and headed out once again for a long trip across the US. This time we went our usual route through Spokane, across Montana, and into ND. We traveled this route many, many times because it's the shortest way home to ND.

In Chester, MT, we noticed the alternator wasn't charging. It was a broken belt, but we were able to get the necessary repairs done in that small town. We were soon on our way again.

We stopped in Minot and Rolla before we continued east. Just before the Minnesota border we noticed that a misalignment problem was destroying our front tire. That required front end work. After that problem was taken care of, we travelled toward Duluth, MN, and Lake Superior, the largest of the Great Lakes with 31,800 square miles of area. Lakes Superior, Michigan, Huron, Erie, and Ontario comprise the Great Lakes and are the largest group of fresh water lakes in the world.

We entered Canada in Ontario at Sault Ste. Marie, headed toward Ottawa, then on to Montreal, Quebec. This part of Canada was interesting for us but we had a little communication problem. Many of the people spoke French and we didn't.

We stopped at a service station and noticed anti-freeze leaking from the motor home. One of the radiator hoses was installed too close to a belt pulley and, after miles of driving, it had worn through the hose. We were lucky to get the problem repaired at the service station. The people were very helpful and friendly but up to that point, we hadn't felt real welcome in that part of Canada.

We dropped back into the US and drove through a corner of Vermont and New Hampshire then into Maine toward Acadia National Park. The weather wasn't great. The wind and rain gave us a good reason to move on south where we visited Martha's Vineyard.

In Gloucester, MA, we took a whale watching excursion. We really didn't have to drive thousands of miles to watch whales because we could do that in the Puget Sound back home. Sometime tourists do things that don't make sense. People from Massachusetts probably come to Washington to see whales.

We drove south along the east coast and the traffic was heavy. In Boston we checked out the USS Constitution also known as Old Ironsides. It earned its nickname by refusing to sink when enemy cannon balls bounced off its sturdy sides. After many fierce battles, the ship was considered unseaworthy. It was condemned and ordered to be destroyed. That aroused public sentiment and the vessel was rebuilt and returned to service. A hundred years after launching that famous ship, it was once again rebuilt and preserved as a memorial. In addition to Old Ironsides, we saw the Tea Party ship, The Old North Church, Longfellow's home, and many other historic sites.

We continued south along the coast and passed through part of Rhode Island and Connecticut then New York City which has no end of places to see and things to do. We saw the Statue of Liberty, Staten Island, Central Park, and the view from the top of the Empire State Building. Caroleen was a little nervous about our ride on their famous subway system. She looked across from where we were sitting and saw a rough looking, badly dressed, hoodlum-type guy watching her. He apparently sensed her concern as he smiled and said, "Don't worry lady. I'm an undercover police officer." We have no way of knowing whether it was true, but she felt a bit safer. He was just one of many different looking characters riding that train. We went to a Broadway show and saw *42nd Street* which we enjoyed.

The two World Trade Center skyscrapers dominated the skyline. As we stood on the top floor of one of those majestic buildings looking at the view, little did we know that a couple of decades later, those awesome structures would be reduced to rubble and thousands of people would die in a senseless act of terrorism that would affect much of the world. The great New York City and the US will never be the same.

A lot of New York City was showing serious wear. The bridges were rough and many of the streets were not the cleanest. New York was a great place to visit, but after a day or two, we were ready to move on to Atlantic City which was our next stop. That city has been a major resort destination for many years, but things started to happen when the casinos came on the scene. It allowed people on the east coast to do their "gaming' without having to travel across the country to Las Vegas or Reno. The casino community likes to call their activity "gaming" rather than gambling, but which it is depends on which side of the craps table you're on. It may be a game to casino operators, but it's definitely a gamble to the poor sucker putting his hard earned money on the table. Some of Webster's definitions of gambling include: *to risk anything of value on something involving chance, anything involving risk, and to squander by betting.* Although there's a slight chance that the player will win, the house always ends up the big winner.

When in one of these lively cities, there are other options besides gambling. There are always great shows to attend, as well as cheap food and many other attractions meant to entice people to come to these resort cities.

Atlantic City is famous for its boardwalk which is sixty feet wide and extends for miles along the ocean. It is a suspended wooden structure as compared to something built of concrete. There is probably activity under the Boardwalk as well as on top of it as the song implied. Something to check out on the next trip to Atlantic City.

After a couple of live shows, checking out a smoky casino or two, a free night in a casino parking lot, and we were ready to move on. We didn't improve Atlantic City's cash flow much except when we filled our motor monster with gas.

Philadelphia was our next stop. We found a parking spot on a busy street near many of the historic sites. The Liberty Bell, originally cast in England, was the main attraction. The Province of Pennsylvania paid about $300 for it in 1752, and it must have seemed like a good deal for a bell that weighed more than a ton until it cracked when they rang it. It was recast in Philadelphia using the same metal in 1753 and they rang it in 1776 to announce the adoption of the Declaration of Independence. The inscription reads, "Proclaim Liberty through all the land onto all the inhabitants thereof." The quote is from the *Bible* (Leviticus 25:10.) This historic bell was rung early on the anniversary of the Declaration of Independence until 1835 when once again it cracked. It hasn't been rung since although it's been struck several times to announce special occasions.

After taking in the sights we got back to the motor home to discover that it had been broken into. It happened in broad daylight in a busy part of the city. The thief broke the window on the driver's side, unlocked the door and stole the video camera and some change we used for parking meters. We learned that breaking and entering was common in that area. It left us with a rather poor impression of Philadelphia. After the broken Liberty Bell and our broken window, we were ready to say goodbye to Philadelphia with no future plans to return. It's amazing how one rubber headed thug can ruin a perfectly good day.

We temporarily repaired the window with a plastic bag and a roll of duct tape. It's pretty incredible the degree of ingenuity that can be accessed with a roll of gray duct tape. I was proud of my repair job until we started driving and the wind vibrated the plastic bag right next to my ear.

We headed for home after a short stop in Baltimore to see Cousin Carl and his family. There are a lot of historical Civil War sites in Virginia such as the courthouse at Appomattox where Lee surrendered to Grant to end the Civil War in 1865, but we didn't stop at many. We were just trying to route our trip through as many states as possible. When we got home we took satisfaction in boring people about how many states we had visited. Just for the record, we've been in every one of the lower 48 states which is quite impressive, wouldn't you say?

I was getting anxious to get home because I was really tired of that plastic bag drumming in my left ear. It seemed as if we were experiencing a lot of wind which can be a challenge when you're driving a small house that's poorly suspended on air springs and rolling down the road on six overloaded tires. A side wind is actually dangerous because it tends to push the rig all over the road. I kept hoping for a tail wind but that doesn't happen very often because the prevailing winds are west to east.

We passed through parts of West Virginia, Ohio, and into Kentucky. If there weren't a white line down the center of the road, there wouldn't be much to see in some of those states. Sorry about that, Ohio.

There were a lot of horse ranch operations in Kentucky which is famous for its horses and distilleries. We toured one of the booze operations. As we watched the bottles go down the conveyor belt it made me a bit thirsty as I remembered some of my experiences of years ago before I gave up that forbidden beverage.

In Independence, Missouri, we checked out President Truman's museum. He was the *Buck Stops Here* guy. He was vice President for less than three months when Franklin D. Roosevelt died. Truman served two terms and made one of the most awesome decisions ever made by one man. He approved the use of the new and powerful atomic bomb against Japan to end World War II. He was blunt and outspoken. His opponents said he was undignified, but his friends loved him for his straight forward approach. He told it the way he saw it—sometimes with very colorful language.

Kansas and Nebraska are agricultural states with miles of rich farm land. There is something beautiful about the expansive fields of grain that a farm boy like me can appreciate. We know how much work it took to make it happen.

On to Colorado and the beautiful Rocky Mountains. We stopped in Denver, the Mile High City, to see friends, Don and June Tate. They are Vic's parents. Denver was founded during the Pikes Peak gold rush in the mid 1800's and has since evolved into a leading commercial and financial center.

We left Colorado and headed for Utah and the Dinosaur National Monument which covers 206,000 acres in Colorado and Utah. The area is famous for its fossil remains of prehistoric reptiles. We toured an excavation site where they uncovered the remains of some of those huge animals. It has a semi-permanent shelter that protects the fossil hunters who have spent years of tedious labor uncovering the specimens. Paleontologists spend their lives studying those creatures.

The word "dinosaur" comes from the Greek word *dinos* meaning terrible and "*sauros* meaning lizard. They weren't really lizards but they were terrible. Imagine an ugly animal twenty feet high with huge dagger-like teeth. Some were eighty feet long and weighed eighty five tons. You can bet they were at the top of the food chain.

Next we visited Salt Lake City, Utah, the state capitol and also the headquarters of the Church of Jesus Christ of Latter Day Saints. Mormons make up the majority of the population in Utah. Brigham Young University in Provo is a Mormon institution, but students of other faiths are accepted.

We were getting closer to home when we crossed into Nevada. Jackpot is a usual spot to stop when we're in the area. It's just another gambling town with cheap or free RV parking and reasonably priced food. We commonly stopped in Nevada to pick up some liquor for our bar. It's much cheaper than it is in Washington because of tax differences. Even though I don't drink any more, we keep our bar well stocked for friends and neighbors who enjoy an occasional social drink.

While I was shopping for booze, the store owner asked us where we were from. We told him we lived in Washington, but were originally from ND. I said he probably wouldn't recognize the town we were from, a small town by the Canadian border called Rolla. He said, "That's where I'm from!" His name was Roger Juntunen and he grew up in Rolla. I didn't know him, but we did know many of his relatives. We found out we had a lot in common and had great time reminiscing about our days in ND and our many mutual friends and acquaintances.

Posing with Roger Juntunen and a Native American Statue in front of his store in Nevada.

We arrived home after more than six weeks on the road and about ten thousand miles of driving. I once considered full time RVing, but it was a welcome change to walk around a house that was anchored to concrete after bumming around in a bouncing motor home for such a long period of time.

It was a great trip and we saw a lot of the country, but there were still many states yet to see. We planned to go on another excursion in 1988. That gave us plenty of time to replace the duct tape and plastic window that was broken by that thug in Philadelphia. We found no good reason to go anywhere near Philadelphia after that.

The Liberty Bell in Philadelphia

The USS Constitution also known as Old Ironsides.

The Mayflower at Plymouth, MA.

The Twin Towers in NYC

The Brooklyn bridge between Manhattan and Brooklyn

A view from the Empire State Building in NYC

The Statue of Liberty

New York City skyline from Staten Island

Cousin Carl on the left, and me in Baltimore

1988 RV Trip

September 1988 rolled around and we packed up the motor home again and headed out for the third year. It was getting to be a habit, but we hadn't visited the southern states. Most of that part of the country was new to us, but some of it we'd seen before.

We took off and drove only as far as Idaho when the motor home decided to give us trouble. It would run fine for a while, then stall, then restart and run fine again. A mechanic in Grangeville, Idaho, diagnosed the problem. It was a partially plugged fuel filter. We had taken it to the service department at the company where we purchased it, but they couldn't find the problem. One of the many complaints we had with that motor home was the company and their service department.

A few days later we were at a camp ground near the Grand Canyon which is one of the seven natural wonders of the world. That giant gorge is 217 miles long and a mile or more deep, cutting through the rock of northwestern Arizona. Millions of visitors view the spectacular natural formations yearly. We decided to take an airplane ride over the canyon. The view from the air gave us an idea of the magnitude of the beautiful rock cliffs with the Colorado River running thousands of feet below. It was a nice, sunny day and the scenery was impressive, but the ride was rough due to air currents over the canyon. If I'd known how uncomfortable the flight was going to be, I might have settled for the view from the canyon rim standing on firm ground.

As we were flying low over the canyon, I couldn't help but wonder what would happen if the single engine on the plane suddenly stopped. It would be impossible to glide to an airport. It left two choices, either crash into the side of a cliff or let the airplane drop to the bottom of the canyon. Either of those options would make it unnecessary to spend any of our later years in a nursing home. Our days are numbered, but I couldn't help hoping that the pilot's days wouldn't run out while we were on that scenic ride. We landed safely and after that bumpy experience we headed east on Interstate 40 which, after a few day's driving, took us into the Carolinas. There is a town in North Carolina named Caroleen. Of course, we had to stop and take a few pictures there.

The owners of the plantations became rich mainly due to the availability of slave labor. They could build large mansions.

They weren't as generous when they built cabins for the slaves.

We drove down along the Atlantic through South Carolina, Georgia, and Florida. St Augustine, FL, was the nation's first city founded in 1565. The great cross marks the beginning of Christianity in the states that same year. Thousands of tourists enjoy the historic sites in the area along with miles of white, sandy beaches. Orlando is where the action is with the Cypress Gardens, Disney World, Epcot Center, and Sea World. It was a short drive from Orlando to Cape Kennedy, originally named Cape Canaveral, which became The Kennedy Space Center after President Kennedy's death. The NASA facility is the assembly building and one of the world's largest buildings. It's so big it creates its own weather.

Russia launched Sputnik, the very first artificial satellite which circled the earth in 1957. The US followed with our first satellite launched from there in 1958. Space exploration on a large scale began and the space race between Russia and the US was on.

The Russian, Yuri Gagarin, was the first man in space in 1961. In 1962 John Glenn was launched into space from the Cape and was the first American to orbit the earth. The 1969 launch of Apollo 11 put

Neil Armstrong and Buzz Aldrin on the surface of the moon when they landed the Eagle. They were the first men to walk on the moon. There have been hundreds of launches both manned and unmanned from the Cape since then, but the space program came to a close this summer in 2011. It spanned more than fifty years and resulted in thousands of discoveries that we use everyday.

A space vehicle assembly building at Cape Kennedy.

We left the Cape and drove to the southern tip of Florida which is at Key West. It is an overseas highway 128 miles in length built on a group of small islands or reefs linked together by numerous bridges. It was a beautiful drive with no lack of great scenery, sandy beaches, and water front RV parks. Key West is the southernmost city in the continental US. It's a resort city built on a small coral island that attracts a serious number of tourists each year. In the 1960's Key West became the first US city to get a city financed facility that converts salt water to fresh water.

Our motor home in a park on the Florida Keys.

We started north from the Keys and drove west through the Everglades which are full of tourist traps. We spent good, hard-earned money to take a boat trip expecting to get a close up view of an alligator. We did see some birds and learned from a tour guide about the wildlife that inhabits the area, but we didn't see any alligators. As we left Everglade City heading north, we saw several alligators sunning themselves in the swampy water along a road called Alligator Alley. They are possibly the ugliest things that were ever created. Only another alligator could love something that looks like that. They might not like how we look either except as a snack. They probably think we taste like chicken. Even without spotting an alligator in the Everglades, we thought it was a great habitat for a variety of species and well worth seeing.

An alligator in a swamp near Everglade City, FL.

We left there and continued on our journey toward Georgia where we drove through the countryside with crops that were not familiar to us. The peanut and cotton fields are much different than the wheat fields of ND.

We were anxious to reach Plains, GA, a small town with a population of only a few hundred and the birthplace of the 39th President of the US. Jimmy and Roslyn Carter grew up in Plains and moved back after their time in Washington, DC. Jimmy grew up on a farm three miles outside of Plains with his sisters, Ruth and Gloria, and his brother, Billy.

Many people marvel at how a man of such humble beginnings could aspire to become President. After graduating from Plains High School, he went to college in GA and continued his education at the US Naval Academy in Annapolis, Maryland. Following his father's death in 1953, he returned to Plains to run the family farm business. He and Roslyn and their sons Jack, Chip, and Jeff raised peanuts and ran the Feed and Supply store his father had established until Jimmy got started in politics. In 1963 he was elected to the Georgia state senate and served two years. He also served four terms as governor before deciding to run for President in 1975.

He was inaugurated as President in January 1977, the first President of the US from GA. He and Rosalyn and their family spent four years in the White House. He was a one term President.

Plains, GA, is a typical small farm town in spite of its famous family. The Carters are active in their local church and regularly teach Sunday school classes.

His brother, Billy's, service station was still operating. It was a Phillip's 66 gas station with a couple of gas pumps and a service shop. Billy proved to be somewhat of an embarrassment to his famous brother because he made the news with his behavior after frequenting the local pubs. He was quite the partying type.

I discovered an unpretentious cemetery while checking out the countryside by bicycle early one morning. I found a freshly covered grave with Billy Carter's name on the headstone. He had died a few weeks previously.

Billy Carter's gas station in Plains, Georgia.

As of now, Jimmy Carter is 80 years old and still very active. He has written many books, gives speeches frequently, and is active with Habitat for Humanity. He has no problem strapping on a tool belt and working with the organization that he has done much to promote. Although his years as President could have gone better, he is a great humanitarian and people have a lot of respect for this distinguished man.

Jimmy Carter's campaign headquarters in Plains, Georgia.

We left Plains and went through Alabama and Mississippi on our way to Louisiana and New Orleans which the locals pronounce *na leens*, with their catchy southern accent. We took a couple of tours of the area and learned about the Battle of New Orleans. We found the cemeteries really interesting. They entomb their loved ones in vaults which can hold several bodies above the ground because of the high water table. They couldn't keep a casket in the ground during really wet, rainy conditions. Vaults solved the problem. Even though the Bible tells us that the dead shall rise, it wouldn't be a blessed event to see a friend or relative float by in a casket.

We took a tour bus through the historic areas of New Orleans, past the French Quarter and many of the great mansions on St. Charles Ave. After the tours, we spent the evening in the French Quarter on Bourbon St. where we found one continuous party. We found numerous jazz clubs where we enjoyed Dixieland music and endless New Orleans entertainment. It was an unforgettable experience.

It's a short drive from New Orleans to Texas which is the second largest state in the US. It's a state full of very friendly people. We spent our first night in Galveston camped on the beach. The city is built on Galveston Island about two miles off the Texas mainland in the Gulf of Mexico. It is linked to the mainland by three causeways and a ferry system. It is one of the busiest dry cargo ports in the US.

A disastrous hurricane struck Galveston in 1900 killing about 6,000 people. It was one of the worst disasters in the history of North American. A massive sea wall of concrete, steel, and granite was built following the storm to guard against future hurricane damage.

We drove on down to Brownsville on the very lower tip of the state. We crossed into Mexico and had a glimpse of the poverty affecting our neighbors to the south. Even though there are many countries that are much poorer than Mexico, it's an amazing contrast in living conditions when you cross the border between the US and Mexico.

We took a short drive to Port Isabel and over the bridge to South Padre Island which is a long, narrow island that sweeps north in an arc for more than 100 miles. We discovered that in that part of Texas the weather can be quite changeable. We saw the results of a hurricane that had done considerable damage to the area just before we arrived. Going over the bridge from Port Isabel, a camper had blown off a pickup and landed against the guardrail. It was reduced to a pile of wood splinters and tin. The morning of the storm that did so much damage with wind and rain, we had enjoyed breakfast on a beautiful, sandy beach parked near the waters of the Gulf of Mexico.

Not far from where we were parked, there were a couple of older rather weather beaten trailers, a few old cars, and some questionable looking characters that looked as if they might be semi-permanent residents of that little piece of sand. They called it "Bum Buck City." The name seemed to fit the place, but if they'd had all the money in the world, they couldn't have bought a more beautiful ocean view. I wondered at the time if we couldn't learn something from them.

Breakfast on the beach at South Padre Island, Texas.

I suggested to Caroleen that we spend the winter there and get to know our neighbors. A couple of weeks without a bath, a few months without shaving or getting our hair cut and we'd fit right in. She always wanted a place with an ocean view and the price was right with this one. My idea didn't get much traction so we filled up with gas and pointed the beast in the general direction of home.

We crossed the rest of Texas and the south west corner of New Mexico before we finally arrived in Arizona. We anticipated staying in some of the best RV resorts in the US. Phoenix is well known for its heat, sand, and cactus, but they really have a feel for building RV parks to attract snowbirds from the northern states.

The AZ summers are unbearably hot, but the winters are usually sunny with reasonable temperatures that give many people a chance to escape the snow banks and nasty winters in their home state. Many live in RV communities where they have pot luck dinners, play cards, swim, golf, or any one of the countless other activities that fail to be even remotely productive. We enjoyed a few days in one of those resorts, but several months of that lifestyle wouldn't work for me. I do a pretty good job at being non-productive in Washington on the rainy days of winter.

On the last leg of the trip we stopped in Nevada towns for reasonably priced food and RV parking. We usually took in a couple of live shows and played a game or two of black jack. Gambling, blowing sand, and prostitution is about all Nevada has going for it, but Las Vegas draws tourists from all over the world. Many of those people spend money freely and that keeps the lights burning brightly. But if that money wasn't spent in Las Vegas, there's a good chance it might actually be squandered!

For all the negative things I say about Nevada, we travel through there to avoid the freeways of California. The freeway route in CA is quicker if a person is lucky enough to live through the experience. If an accident doesn't kill you, the stress of driving those multi-lane race tracks with a clunky motor home might.

We got home to the gray days of winter in western Washington, but we'd had enough sun to get our vitamin D level up to where it should be. It was time for the motor monster to become a lawn ornament until our next adventure. It was a good trip, but it felt good to be living in a structure without wheels.

It was time to get the mail and the next credit card bill so we could assess the financial damage we did on that venture. It wasn't pretty.

We'd used enough gas to keep the oil companies in Saudi Arabia in business. The only gas I used on the next trips I took, was in a camp stove that I carried on my bicycle which was a kind of penance for wasting so many of our precious natural resources on those motor home trips. They were my act of repentance of my previous traveling sins.

Graduating to a Bike

When spring came, we were back in the motor home with two bicycles strapped on for exercise. In the early morning hours, I'd ride the bike around the area where we were camped. I discovered that I was seeing as much in a few minutes on the bike as several hundred miles of driving the motor home.

We were getting settled in a campground one evening when a couple of young fellows rode in on bicycles. They were loaded down with all the necessities including camping gear, cooking utensils, clothing, etc. They were traveling under their own power. No gas stations involved. We learned they were crossing the US on their bikes and it made me wonder if I could do that. I was in my 50's, but they were in their 20's. It was food for thought. It seemed a little crazy, but the more I thought about it, the more obsessed I became with the idea. By this time my body was beginning to recover from my early years of abuse and neglect. I could ride several miles on the bike and not be totally wasted.

I still had the motorcycle, but after another trip to ND and one to Alberta, it was just sitting in the garage. I was riding the bike more and more and the motorcycle less and less. After walking around it for a couple of years, I decided to sell it. It was an expensive toy I no longer played with. It was probably a good idea because when you put a normally reasonable person on two wheels with too much power under his butt, he sometimes goes a little nuts and I was no exception. I was beginning to get speeding tickets from driving the freeway speed limit on country roads. Several times I hadn't even shifted into a higher gear before the spinning blue light appeared out of nowhere. If I'd stayed with the Goldwing, I don't think I'd have had to worry about high cholesterol or heart disease killing me.

I advertised the bike and the first guy that looked at it bought it for cash and rode off a happy man. I shed a couple of tears as I watched my Goldwing quietly roll down the driveway with its excited new owner. I won't totally rule out another motorcycle when I'm too old to ride a bicycle, but for now, I've graduated from a motorcycle to a bicycle and it's working quite well. I've already ridden more miles on the bicycle than I ever did on the motorcycle. The Goldwing only had 30,000 miles on it when I sold it.

Before I even considered getting serious about cross country bicycle rides, I needed to know if I was physically able to pedal a bike up a mountain pass. I'd never attempted a mountain and had only negotiated a few hundred feet in elevation at best on local hills. If I couldn't climb a mountain pass, I might just as well forget cross country riding because no route across the country is level.

One day I decided to ride up Stevens Pass which has an elevation of over 4,000 feet. It hadn't seemed especially steep when I'd driven it. I left on a summer afternoon with a jug of water and a bag of peanuts. Skykomish was about a sixty mile ride and I planned to stay in at a hotel on my way back. Skykomish is about seventeen miles from the summit. I stopped there on the way up to inquire about accommodations. By that time I had ridden about forty miles and only had less than twenty miles to go. What I hadn't considered was the fact that in that last twenty miles I needed to climb over 2,000 feet in elevation. I thought I'd be back in Skykomish before dark and before dinner, but it was almost dark when I reached the top. I had eaten lunch in Index many hours earlier, but had worked that off and had eaten all of the peanuts on the way up. The last few miles were really rough. I pedaled about twenty revolutions then rested for a few minutes before doing it all over again. I finally reached the top and the sign said "Stevens Pass, 4300 feet." I felt a sense of accomplishment and serious pangs of hunger. I'd never worked that hard in my life, but it was downhill from there back to the hotel and some real dinner.

After I'd coasted downhill for a few miles, I turned on my headlight, but the light was very dim and I still had an hour's ride to Skykomish. In no time the light went out completely. The batteries were dead. I was coasting down the pass in the dark with only the light from the moon. Each time I saw car lights in my mirror, I pulled off on the shoulder, stop, and let them go by. I didn't want to be road kill. When I finally reached Skykomish, I was ready for a good meal, a shower, and a warm bed. What I didn't know was that the railroad track was about thirty feet from the hotel and every time a train went by, the old building quivered and shook. It was a long night.

That trip up the mountain was a prime example of doing something on the spur of the moment, totally unprepared. But I did learn a valuable lesson which I should already have known. It's stupid to do something like that without proper planning and preparation. Since then I have climbed many mountain passes, but I always have extra batteries for my headlight and a couple extra bags of peanuts.

A Bike Ride with Justin

Our grandson, Justin, shared my enthusiasm for bike riding. We went on many rides during the next several years. They were mostly local rides, but I could tell that he was becoming a strong rider and I was getting much stronger. We actually made a good pair in spite of our age difference. I could usually out ride him, but that changed as time went on

One day when we were riding, Justin said, "Grandpa, let's take a long ride sometime." I asked him what he considered a long ride and he said, "To Spokane." That was all I needed to urge me on to some long distance riding. We started making plans. I knew we needed to do more training before taking on that kind of a challenge. We rode several hundred miles over the next couple of months and I started to lay out all the things we would need for our trip.

Justin and I finally got our bikes loaded with all the gear we thought we would need. We quickly found out that what we needed and what we actually took along weren't the same thing. We took many things we didn't need that weighed down our bikes and took up the space of things we should have taken. I knew nothing about how to load a bike correctly. We had all of the weight on the back of the bike which is not the way it should be. Justin looked at my bike and said he thought it looked like I had a big bag of potatoes on the back. Even at his age, he recognized a poorly loaded bike. We had panniers that Charleen made for us and they worked well, but I threw most of the stuff in a big bag and tied it on the back with bungee cords.

My bike was a Schwinn mountain bike that I had the bike shop re-gear for loads, touring, and hill climbing. I had them put on a good set of street tires. Justin's bike got the same treatment. His bike was a $100 garage sale special that the owner of the bike shop said was a better bike than mine.

Everything was loaded and we were ready to leave on our trip to Spokane where Justin thought we would turn around and ride back. Caroleen and Charleen knew when we left that I had an even longer trip in mind. I figured that if we could ride 300 miles, we could ride 1300 miles and that would take us to Rolla, ND.

It took us five or six days to reach Spokane. By that time we both felt considerably stronger than when we left. In spite of all of our training, after riding 300 with fully loaded bikes, we were in even better condition and had more confidence in our abilities.

When we got to Spokane, I asked Justin what he thought about riding to Rolla. He said, "Where's that?" I told him it was about another 1,000 miles and he said, "Let's go!" His fourteen year old confidence was contagious.

We continued east on Highway 2 toward the Rocky Mountains. We had already gone over Stevens Pass, which is over 4,000 feet and we did it under adverse conditions. It rained most of the way across Stevens. I commented to Justin that this was a really rough climb. He looked down at the rear gear cluster and told me it might help if I used first gear. That made me wonder who was taking care of whom. I shifted down and the climb was much more tolerable.

Our clothes were soaked from sweat and rain when we reached the summit. I suggested that we change our wet clothes before we started down the other side. Coasting doesn't generate any heat and being wet, we could really get a chill. I changed, but Justin decided not to take my advice. By the time we reached a motel about half way down the mountain, he had learned a lesson. He said he had never been so cold.

Going through Idaho, we had more rain. When bicycling, you may wish for good conditions, but you take what you get. There were times while pedaling in the rain and wind that I wondered why I was doing this and Justin must have wondered from time to time what his old fool grandpa had gotten him into, He seemed to lose his enthusiasm when the conditions were the worst, but he kept plugging along.

One day we were rained in near a supermarket somewhere in Idaho with nothing to do but wait out the rainstorm. I decided to make a sign to put on the back of Justin's bike that would encourage truckers to give us more room when passing. I found a piece of cardboard in a dumpster and with a felt pen; we made a sign that read:

Truckers, please give
us plenty of room.
This could be your son.

After we attached the sign to the bike, they passed at a safe distance and often gave us a friendly honk with their air horn. Justin thought that was great.

One of the days we had a rain delay. It gave us time to print a cardboard sign to amuse truck drivers. It worked. We received a friendly honk on their air horns as they passed us.

As we approached the Rocky Mountains, we faced our biggest challenge of the trip. Logan pass was 5,600 feet and our highest climb ever. I wondered how Justin would hold up and hoped I had the strength to make it to the top.

We stayed in a motel just below the mountain so we could get an early start. We had limited time to ride to the top because after 11:00 AM all bikes were ordered off the road. They considered it too dangerous to have bikes on the road with the high volume of tour busses and the tourist traffic after that time of day. If we didn't make it to the top in our allotted time, we would have to wait until the following morning somewhere along the road. That would make it a long night as there were no accommodations on the way to the top.

We got up in the middle of the night, had breakfast and started up the pass using our headlights the first couple of hours. I hadn't slept well anticipating the grueling climb, but Justin seemed to be in fine shape.

We ground our way to the top only to be approached by some goofy redneck wanting to pick an argument. He said bikes had no business on that road and we were breaking the law. I asked him if he read the sign at the beginning of the climb that said bikes were legal to ride during designated hours and we were well within the time frame. I suggested that he go check it out but have his wife read it because it was obvious that he didn't know how to read. That didn't make us friends, but I wasn't in any mood to take his crap. I though afterwards that I was glad it didn't end up in a physical altercation because he was much younger and considerably bigger than I was, but my legs were strong so I probably could have out run him.

We were relieved to reach the top of Logan Pass in Glacier Park and we were about to enjoy some serious downhill riding. There are two kinds of riding that all bicyclists love. One is downhill and the other is with a tail wind. We were about to experience both of those conditions on our ride down the east side of Logan Pass.

The highway is built with a very short rock wall as a barrier. It's possible to ride close to this wall and view the scenery thousands of feet straight down. I was enjoying the view and looked over at Justin who was riding down the center of the highway. I told him to get over and look at the view. He said, "No way, Grandpa."

We had some effortless riding, cashing in on the energy we burned going up the pass. This is the reward of biking. If you climb a hill, there's a downhill slope on the other side, although there are times when you reach the top, see a short down hill and an even steeper hill in the distance.

We reached a level roadway and had a really nice tail wind. I could see Justin coming up behind me quickly, but he didn't seem to be pedaling much. As he passed, I saw that he had found a large garbage can lid that he hooked to the back of his bike and was using it as a sail. I was proud of him.

A couple of guys happy to be at the top of the pass. We were looking forward to miles of coasting down the other side with a tail wind. I'm on the left and Justin is on the right.

Montana is a wide state with lots of small towns on the northern route. We had no trouble finding motels. We had tents along, but used them only in case of emergency which only happened once. Motels were cheap and the restaurants had plenty of greasy food. It was very different crossing the state at ten or twelve miles per hour as compared with eighty to eighty-five with the Goldwing. We were able to see a lot more. With a full face helmet on a motorcycle, you look straight ahead, hang on to the handlebars and go like hell, but you don't see a lot.

It was a good feeling to see the Rocky Mountains in my rear view mirror and a reasonably flat road ahead. We worked our way through Montana in nine or ten days and arrived at the ND border in good shape. The bikes held up well except for a couple of flat tires which were to be expected, but we were prepared for flats.

We arrived in Williston, ND, in drenching rain. We were longer getting there than we planned and ran out of daylight. We were traveling with our bike lights looking for a Motel when we finally spotted a Motel 8 in the distance. A motel with beds, heat, and shower sounded really good. We rented their last room and settled in for the night.

The next day we woke up to sunshine. ND weather can change quickly. Riding out of Williston the road looked flat and in a motorized vehicle you would swear it was flat. We soon learned that we had some elevation to contend with. It was a steady climb heading east. It wasn't like climbing a mountain. It was mile after mile of gradual grade with no end in sight. We were happy to stop in Stanley that night where we found a motel. Justin had relatives who lived nearby so we called them and they came to town and had dinner with us at the motel café.

We arrived in Berthold about noon the next day where we stopped at the Tumbleweed Café for lunch. It is a popular café in the area and I looked for my friend, Ray Hennessy, who farmed nearby. I asked the waitress if he ever came in and she said that he came often about this time. Just then he walked in. He saw the bikes outside and quickly figured out who they belonged to. He laughed and asked if we had ridden them all the way from Washington then said, "Boy, you guys are nuts." People from that part of the country don't do crazy things like ride a bike for hundreds of miles. They use their energy in much more productive ways. I asked about his wife, Pat, who I went to Picton Grade School with many years earlier.

Minot was only a couple of hours farther east and that would be our next stop at my brother, Duane's, house where we stayed with him and his wife, Ann, for a few days. We wouldn't be paying for motels in Minot.

After a few days, we packed up the bikes and headed for Rolla, about 120 miles farther east. As we headed out of town, we saw what looked like a survey party on the shoulder of the road. They had a tripod set up. We got a little closer and saw that it wasn't a survey party but the local TV crew waiting for us. Duane had alerted them, but he would never admit that he did. We were interviewed and had a spot on the evening news. It was our fifteen minutes of fame.

That night we made it to Rugby, the geographic center of North America, where rented a motel. We couldn't wait to watch ourselves on the evening news.

We reached Rolla, our final destination, the next day. My old home town hadn't changed a great deal over the years. The population is still about 2,000. We rode to my cousin, Anne's, house where she and Don shared their home with us while we were in town. Don was the local optometrist and both he and Ann were very active in the community. They were greatly missed when they retired a few years later and moved to Wenatchee, WA. Their kids, John, Pam, Carla, and Linda weren't at home so they had plenty of room for a couple of tired bicycle riders.

Don offered to let us use his pickup and I didn't hesitate to accept his offer. It felt pretty good to be off the bicycle seats after 1400 miles. We were able to tour the country and surrounding towns in style thanks to Don loaning us his new wheels.

The local newspaper took a few pictures and interviewed us for an article they wanted to publish. We were enjoying our brush with notoriety.

After our time visiting around in Rolla, we loaded our bikes in Don's pickup, packed our gear, and he drove us to Rugby where we boarded the train back to Everett, WA. We were on our way home. The trips was great for both of us, but for me it wouldn't be my last long bike ride.

Southern Route Bike Trip

In 1996 I started to get the urge to go on another long bike ride. The winters in Seattle are long and wet so it made sense to ride my bike through some of the southern states where I could find some sunshine. I started to plan.

I borrowed some Adventure Cycle maps from a guy we met on our bike trip to ND. The route I chose went from San Diego, CA, to St. Augustine, FL. My plan was a solo trip because it's not easy to find people willing to ride 3,000 miles on a bicycle, but Charleen had reservations about me riding by myself. She considered this type of venture too risky for a sixty year old guy. She thought I would need someone to keep me out of trouble. She thought her husband, Harley, should get a bike and ride along.

Harley liked the idea so he bought a new bike, and we did several hundred miles of training. I decided to ride my old Schwinn. It needed a new chain, a couple of new tires, and it was ready to go. It wasn't the kind of bike that people would steal because it looked pretty rough—kind of like the old geezer riding it.

We flew to San Diego, rented a motel and got an early start toward Campo, CA. We climbed most of the day and it was a rather rough way to start a trip. We pitched our tents in a campground about sixty miles east of San Diego and it was the coldest night anyone would ever want to spend in a tent. The water froze in our water bottles and the toothpaste was too thick to come out of the tube. We ate breakfast in the laundry room to warm up a bit. The conditions weren't good so it could only get better. A bike rider never knows what the next day will offer.

A couple of days down the road we pulled into Palo Verde after a pretty good day's ride. We found a combination store, bar, and motel. Harley asked the owner if he had any rooms. He said he did but they weren't cleaned. Harley told him we didn't care about clean. At that point all we needed was a spot to spread out our sleeping bags. He offered the guy $20.00 for the room and the owner accepted it. It was a low budget trip even though we had credit cards with us.

We rode through the Imperial Valley where the farms were impressive and the irrigated land very productive. A large part of the produce we enjoy is grown in that part of the US. It's hot, dry country, and we carried a few extra gallons of water because water was hard to find. We didn't need the extra weight, but the water was necessary.

Quartzsite, AZ, is a desert town that is overtaken by snowbirds in the winter. Many of the campers park out on the sand near a good sized cactus and spend the winter in the sun. It looked like a good place to pass through, not a place we wanted to spend a long period of time.

We stopped at a campground and checked it out. There was space available, but it was covered with rocks. We asked the manager if he had anything with grass and he said he had never heard of grass in that area, but the campground down the street had smaller rocks. Sleeping on rocks in a tent in ninety degree weather didn't sound very inviting so we rented an old trailer house. It had air conditioning and a shower. Pure luxury The park we stayed in that night was called the Quartzsite Yacht Club. By this time we'd seen all the sand and cactus we cared to enjoy but we still had a lot of desert ahead of us.

Eventually, we pedaled into Phoenix, AZ, where the Seattle Mariners were for spring training. We thought it would be a shame not to see our local team play. We watched the Mariners beat the Milwaukee Brewers

9 to 3 then went looking for a motel in the area. We found a room for $125 per night. That was outrageous. We wanted to rent a place to spread out a couple of sleeping bags, not buy it.

We settle for a spot in a pretty rough park where we camped next to the dumpsters. We could see homeless people across the street watching TV in their tents. Even under those circumstances, sleep came easily and quickly. It was a thirty mile ride from Peoria, where we spent the night, to Apache Junction on the east side of the Phoenix area. Apache Junction is one of the most beautiful parts of the city and it is where former ND neighbors, Duane and Eileen Herrala, now live. We called them on our way through and Duane offered to come to where we were with his truck and take us to their place to spend the night. The offer was too good to pass up, so I quickly agreed before he changed his mind. We had a great evening talking over old times. We were up at 5 AM and he had the coffee ready. What hospitality.

We rode on to Bylas, AZ, a town that normally would never be mentioned because it has no motels and no campgrounds. When we got there, the sand was blowing like crazy, and it was obvious why the population didn't increase. Harley wasn't feeling well. We thought he may have had some kind of food poisoning. He was running a fever, had no appetite, and was freezing in ninety degree weather. He decided to have a nap behind a little store. I went looking for a spot where we could set up our tents. The local police said it would be OK to camp in a small area behind the police station but we would have to share the area with several horses.

I went back to Harley where he was sleeping on a pallet wrapped in two jackets with a hood over his head and told him about the options. He said, "Hell, we need to get outta here." We looked at an American flag on a nearby pole and it was pointing due east. We had a tail wind so we decided to head toward the next town, Pima. With the tail wind we got there in about an hour. We found a motel and settled in. Harley still wasn't able to eat so he went to bed. I had a hamburger and a milkshake and joined him. Mileage-wise we had a good day under some very adverse conditions. It was pretty good for a guy who was so sick he could hardly stand up. He's one tough dude.

The next day we rode through an Indian reservation. It was obvious that they didn't get the best land. It wasn't a part of the country a person would want to live. The locals were friendly and it seemed as if alcohol flowed freely. Alcoholism is a big problem on reservations and beer cans flying out of car windows tell the story. Most of the cars that passed us were a party on four wheels. The entire area was covered with litter. Plastic bags were hanging from the fences and on the cactus. It seemed as if nobody cared.

We stopped at a store to buy some refreshments and the beer business was thriving. A rather large, inebriated woman came stumbling out of the store as we rode up. She seemed to like Harley. I told him he may have missed his chance and that she might look better after a few beers. He said he didn't think there was enough beer in the store to make that happen.

Harley's 39th birthday was our last day in AZ. We were looking at New Mexico sand and I thought it looked just like Arizona sand. I was ready to see some grass—the kind you mow that is. After so many days crossing AZ, the sand and wind were getting tiresome. Our last night in AZ was a cold one in a primitive campground in the mountains.

We rolled into NM and stopped to buy some gas for our stove which used regular gas. It took thirteen cents worth. When we went in to pay for it, the attendant thanked us for stopping. I told him we really liked to spread the money around and were glad to share it with him.

New Mexico isn't the most exciting part of the country, but it is sparsely populated so the traffic wasn't so bad. There were a number windmills around there because the wind was always blowing.

We were in and out of the mountains in NM, and it was time to deal with the continental divide. One day we climbed 6,000 feet and the next one was over 8,000 feet. The scenery was great and we found a lot of interesting places. Silver City was one of the attractions. It is a town that was thriving in the 1880's after gold and silver were discovered, and now seemed to enjoy a healthy economy. It was a fine place to rent a motel and spend the night.

After a few more days of pedaling, we stopped in Las Cruses, NM. It had been a tough day. I developed a blister on a part of my body that I don't normally discuss. I stood up to pedal most of the day. Standing up is like adding another gear to the bike and at my age I needed all the advantage I could get. According to my notes, we traveled seventy-eight miles that day. I did almost all of it standing up.

As we headed toward the Texas border, we passed a guy dressed like a monk walking along the road. I stopped and asked him where he was going. He told me it didn't matter because he was walking for Jesus. He had been walking for four years. He walked and prayed all day and said he expected to do it for the rest of his life. It might have been some kind of penance for something he had done. In any event, it seemed like a tough way to spend your life.

Texas was a challenge. We hit more than our share of head winds and dust. The people in Texas were a friendly bunch who were courteous to bike riders and accommodating in every way.

We were only stopped once by the police on the whole trip and that was in Texas. We were riding through San Antonio early on Easter morning on Interstate 80. The traffic was light, the shoulders on the road were wide, and we were really making time when we saw a blue light coming up behind us. Bicycling on interstates is not legal in many areas especially through cities. We knew that but thought we'd take a chance. We had only one choice. Plead ignorance. That proved to be easy for a couple of nuts from Washington riding loaded down bicycles for thousands of mile. The patrolman headed us off the freeway down a ramp that led us right to a McDonalds. We didn't get a ticket, but he could have arrested us. That might not have been the worst thing that could happen. A night in jail would have been more comfortable than sleeping on Texas rocks in a campground.

The main roads in most states have restrooms in the rest areas. Not so in many Texas rest areas. Often the only bathroom facilities we found were trees where you had to watch where you stepped. We rode through a variety of terrain—mountains, ranches, farmland, and desert. Texas has it all and it's a big state, especially traveling by bike. Some of the most beautiful farms and ranches had oil wells for added income. Nice way to live. We found many of the ranches with the big homes were owned by business people in Houston and other cities in the area.

A couple of days into Texas, we met a couple of young guys on bikes heading east on much the same route we were heading. We rode together for several days. The four of us arrived in Del Rio, a great little Texas city. While traveling together, we rented motels with two beds. Harley and I used the beds and our guests slept on the floor in their sleeping bags. It wasn't very neighborly, but we paid for the rooms while the two young guys stayed for free. Harley and I had a little more slack in our budget than they did and the arrangement worked just fine.

The man at the bike shop in Del Rio recommended a Mexican restaurant as a good place to eat. We arrived there to find the place closed. The owner saw us at the door and asked if he could help us. We told him we had hoped to have Mexican food at this restaurant but were sorry to bother him since it was after his regular hours. He said not to worry about that and come on in. He turned on the music, brought us complimentary chips, and salsa, then proceeded to cook the best Mexican dinner I have ever eaten. We had the place to ourselves except for the owner who sat and visited with us throughout the meal. True Texas hospitality. The next morning we stopped to say goodbye to our new friend at the El Zarape restaurant and found him all smiles.

We were beginning to see more trees and grass in that part of Texas and it looked good. A few miles out of Del Rio we came to Bracketville. They filmed a lot of movies in that town including *The Alamo* with John Wayne. The town claimed to be the movie capitol of Texas.

We had been riding in mostly dry weather to that point, but the rain was about to catch up with us. We decided to take a different route than our two new friends and hoped to catch up with them later. We rode in heavy rain and lightning for about forty miles to Uvalde where we rented a cheap motel. We decided to take the afternoon off, dry out our gear and wait out the storm. It's not a good idea to ride in lightening. The weather had turned cold and it was no fun. We needed the rest anyway.

A few days later we were camped for the night near the Louisiana border. We heard some activity in our campsite, but neither of us got up to investigate. Whatever it was helped itself to the breakfast that Harley had packed on ice for the next morning. We suspect it was either a raccoon or a bear. A bear would make a better story, but we will never know for sure.

Just into Louisiana, we rented a motel for $18 and it was an absolute pit. We went to the local restaurant and found our old riding buddies, Mark and Chris. They had taken a longer route, but we slacked off and we ended up at the same place. They rode on to a campground out of town. The four of us rode together again for awhile.

In Bogalusa, LA, one of the locals told us about the Box Car Sandwich shop where we went for breakfast. It was a small café in a converted box car run by an older woman and her two middle aged sons. They were very interested in our bike trip and we visited all through breakfast. People in the south seem always to have time to socialize. They are warm, friendly folks.

After pedaling into Mississippi, we rode south and east along the Gulf of Mexico. The scenery was beautiful although the traffic was heavy. It's a major tourist area with a lot of casinos. Hurricane Katrina destroyed much of the area as well as much of New Orleans since we rode through. After a couple of days in Mississippi, we were in Alabama headed toward Dolphin Island. It wasn't a good day in Alabama. We rode in rain most of the day. When the pavement is wet, it's hard to see broken glass and other hazards. We had three flat tires, two for me and one for Harley. After thousands of miles, we were starting to have more flat tires. The glass and debris we'd been running over was taking a toll on the equipment. With all of my bike riding I hadn't had many flats, but bad luck finally caught up.

Our bad luck was about to change. We saw a white car stopped ahead of us with a man standing there waiting for us. He was a Baptist minister from the area. He offered to let us stay at his youth facility in town and told us how to find it. The place was a huge dormitory with accommodations for at least one hundred people. It had a large kitchen, several bathrooms, a laundry room, and guest bunks for sleeping. He opened the place up and told us to make ourselves at home. He said he was living by himself now because his wife ran off with a bicycle rider. We hoped he was kidding. We figured there were a couple of possibilities. One was that he was happy his wife was gone and that was why he was being so nice to bike riders, and the other was he planned to kill the four of us in revenge. I don't know about the other guys, but I slept with one eye open that night. We actually had a good night on Dolphin Island. Harley, Chris and Mark took advantage of the kitchen and prepared a great meal while I did the laundry. We were all still alive the next morning so, after another good meal, we took the ferry to Fort Morgan, then followed the shoreline to Gulf Shores and on to Florida.

On Sundays we tried to find a church along the way and weren't particular as to denomination. They were all pretty similar. In the south we found mostly Baptist churches. The people were friendly and the sermons were fine.

In Bonifay, FL, we once again parted company with Chris and Mark who took a different route. The four of us had many enjoyable miles of riding together. They were good company.

We rode on to Green Cove Springs and pulled into the parking lot of a motel where we met two bicyclists that we'd been hearing about since we were in AZ. These two women left San Diego on March 2nd just a few days ahead of us and had traveled the same basic route that we did. It was interesting to swap stories about the trip. It's always nice to talk to and compare experiences with fellow bicycle riders.

We hardly ever saw a live armadillo in FL, but we saw lots of those slow, dumb animals dead along the way. There was armadillo road kill everywhere. It was a reminder that bike riders could end up just as dead if we weren't paying attention. The closer we came to the Atlantic coast, the heavier the traffic became. We were careful not to meet the fate of the armadillo. We were only about thirty miles from our destination—the Atlantic Ocean, and St. Augustine, FL.

I began to think back on our trip which had been great. The journey on the bike was many times more interesting than the final destination. St. Augustine was a beautiful, historic city, but we didn't take much time to check it out.

We got a motel room and checked on our return tickets from Jacksonville to Seattle. That was when we found out we had a problem. We were two weeks ahead of our scheduled return date, but we were ready to go home. After more than an hour on the phone with various agents at American Airlines, they were able to accommodate us on a flight out of Orlando. We stayed over night in St. Augustine, then rented a car and hauled our bikes and baggage to Orlando where we caught a flight home.

Since we left San Diego in early March, we had ridden our bikes for forty-two days averaging about seventy miles per day for a total of 2940 miles. We saw incredible country, made many new friends, and had a trip neither of us will ever forget.

Leaving San Diego

Rest stop

Entering New Mexico

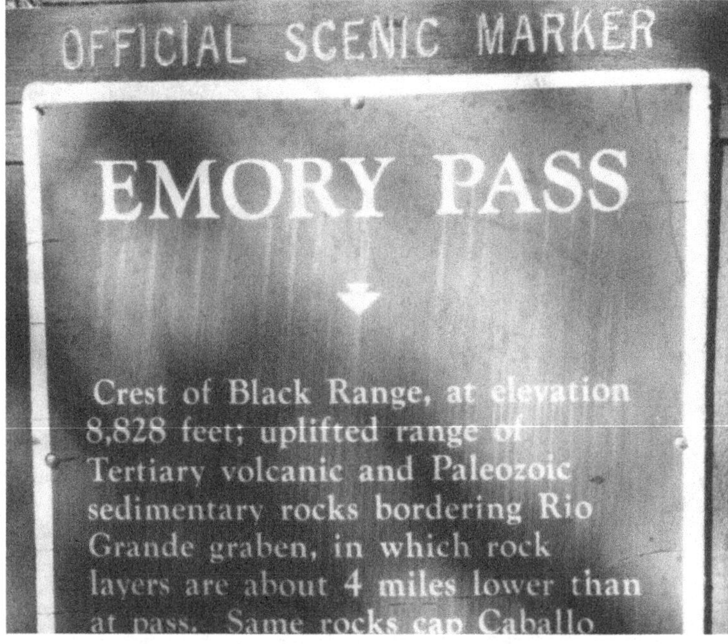

Emory Pass was a pretty good climb.

The Arizona desert . . . . miles of it.

Duane and Eileen's home in Mesa, AZ.

Owners of the El Zarape restaurant in Del Rio, Texas

A wet day in Alabama.

Plenty of sun in Florida

Just a few miles to go to reach our destination.

St Augustine, Florida. We made it.

Year 2000

THE TWENTIETH CENTURY CAME TO an end. In spite of the hype that computers would fail and without computers the world, as we knew it, would end. The change from the 20th century to the 21st century was quite uneventful. The sun still came up on January 1, 2000, and very little had changed except the calendars. It was a slow news day. There were no great disasters to report.

The year 2000 was also when I had planned to take another bicycle trip. I hoped to finish a trip across the US that started in 1993 when Justin and I rode from Snohomish, WA to Rolla, ND. The ride from Minot, ND to Bar Harbor, Maine, was another 2800 miles so I started to ride more in the spring trying to get in shape for a long, long ride.

As I was training, I was hoping to find someone to ride along and keep me company. I started by trying to convince Dave Schmid to ride along. Dave and I volunteered at Habitat for Humanity and we got along quite well. He thought it sounded like fun, but he was having a problem with one of his knees and he would need to tend to this before he could consider a trip of that length. Taking that much time from his job at Boeing also posed a problem. It looked as if I might have to make the trip alone if I were going to do it the summer of 2000. It's not easy to find someone who would agree to pedal a loaded bicycle for that distance.

I continued to take long rides still planning to do the trip, but I didn't feel that I was getting stronger in spite of the training. I felt extremely tired after what I considered a fairly easy ride of fifteen or twenty miles. It wasn't normal.

I decided to have a physical check up which was a good idea since I hadn't seen a doctor in some time. I went in and explained to him what I had in mind and he suggested a treadmill test. He hooked me up to monitors and I started walking. The faster I walked, the more he turned up the speed. I thought I might die on the spot. He finally told me the test was over. I was dripping with sweat and barely able to stand up. I was totally exhausted.

I went home, and he said he'd call if there were any problems. The next day he called. I wasn't home, so Caroleen talked to him and told him I was out. He wanted to know where I was and she told him I was on a bike ride. He told her it was important that I call him as soon as I got home. That sounded urgent so when I got home I made the call immediately. He said he needed to see me as soon as possible. Something showed up on the stress test that we needed to discuss. He thought we'd need to do more tests. He said that one thing was for sure I could forget about the long bike ride. That was definitely disappointing, but I think I expected that it was possible that something serious could be happening. Further tests showed that I had a severely plugged artery in my heart and it would require immediate attention if I had any intention of growing older.

Growing old is not ideal, but the alternative isn't very exciting either. I still had a lot of things I wanted to do before I checked out. I was only sixty-four years old and, in spite of partly plugged tube in my ticker, I was in pretty good shape physically. According to the doctor, I needed by-pass surgery which is a pretty serious procedure. It isn't anything that anyone would look forward to, but I didn't have much choice in the matter. I didn't even have a lot of time to think about it. The surgery was scheduled immediately and I was in and out of surgery in the next day or two. Although this is a complicated operation, the success rate is very good. Over the years, the odds of surviving are definitely in your favor.

I had a three way bypass which meant there was more than one artery with problems. In a few months I felt better than I'd felt in years. Immediately after surgery there was some discomfort and I had to be careful not to do much physically. It was several weeks before I could ride my bicycle again.

A few months later on one of my lasts visits with the doctor, I asked him if I should limit my physical activity. He told me not to change anything I'd been doing before the operation. I assumed this meant that a long bicycle ride would not be ruled out, so I started to plan again for the trip that didn't happen in 2000, maybe in 2001.

That gave me another year to work on my friend, Dave. I think I was beginning to wear him down because he was starting to talk more favorable about the bike ride. He bought a new bike. That was a positive move. The surgery on Dave's knee was successful and his doctor felt that bike riding would be good low impact exercise. This was starting to fit with the plan. We began to do some serious rides as training to get our legs and butts in shape for the ride.

In July 2001 Dave and I started sorting through our camping gear and attempted to assemble the necessities for living off our bicycles for several weeks. We would actually become homeless, except for the supplies we could carry. That was a sobering thought. We might be homeless, but we wouldn't be broke as long as Caroleen and Kim kept paying the credit card bills that would be arriving in the mail. If we maxed out the credit cards, we might have to work our way back home but who would hire us? We were one old man who looked like he escaped from a nursing home on a rusty bike and his riding partner who had two years growth of whiskers and a funny hat. Who would hire a pair like that?

Year 2001 Bike Trip

It was Monday, August 6th. The packing was done and the long anticipated trip was about to begin. I put my bike in a cardboard container for transit, and Caroleen took me to the train station in Everett to catch Amtrak to Minot. I went ahead to take care of some business, and Dave followed a few days later. We planned to leave Duane's house in Minot and head east on the bikes.

Things were going as planned. The train got into Minot on Tuesday evening two hours late, but after an uneventful trip, Duane was there to meet me in his new pickup. I stayed with him and Ann for a couple of days before I used his pickup to run up to Rolla. After visiting friends and tending to a few details, I headed back to Duane's place in Minot.

On Saturday, August 11th, Dave called and said he was on the way but would be four hours late. Amtrak doesn't have a great record for being on time. The passenger train shares tracks with freight trains and the freight always gets preference. If someone has to wait for another train, it's always Amtrak that waits for the freight trains.

I met him at the depot a few blocks from Duane's house. The train was about to leave for Minneapolis and Dave's bike hadn't been unloaded. That was serious. We asked them to double check their baggage cars because the bike had been loaded in Everett so it must be somewhere on the train. After a slight delay they finally located the large cardboard box containing the bike and much of Dave's luggage. How could they misplace something that large? Obviously, airlines aren't the only ones that lose luggage.

The weather looked promising on the morning of August 12th. Duane and two of his buddies decided to ride along on their bikes for our first day on the road. Ann came along with the pickup hauling our luggage and a picnic lunch. We welcomed the company and this was a great way to begin the trip to Maine.

We arrived in Rugby, ND, where we spent the night camping in a noisy campground near the highway. Duane, Ann, and their friends returned to Minot, and Dave and I were on our own with about 2800 miles ahead of us.

Duane, Ann, and the old guy . . . me.

The next day wasn't a good day. We were bucking a headwind which takes a toll on the body as well as the mind. The prevailing winds are the reason most people ride west to east. The head wind only lasted for about twenty miles so it turned out to be a fair day's ride after all except for the fact that my Themorest mattress fell off the bike somewhere during the day. I had it tied on with bungee cords and I haven't trusted bungee cords since then. I still use them and like them, but I don't trust them. This unfortunate bungee failure cost about one hundred dollars and a few nights in the tent sleeping with no padding between me and the ground.

We arrived in Pekin, ND, that night. It's a very small town in the eastern part of the state. It looked like a great place to spend the night. We found a city park and hurriedly set up our tents, because it looked like rain. We settled comfortably in our tents and were ready for a well earned night's sleep when the wind came up. Thunder and lightening followed and we were about to find out if our tents were water tight. It was a typical ND summer storm. With the crashing thunder and the spectacular lightening show, we didn't sleep a lot, but we did stay dry.

We woke up to a beautiful morning. The sun was shining as we broke camp and loaded our gear on the bicycles. As we rode out of town, a lady living near the park approached us and asked us where we were headed. She said she was watching the storm the night before and was prepared to rescue us if the weather situation had become critical. Small town people are definitely aware of unusual people in the area and we, no doubt, fit that category.

Leaving Pekin, ND after surviving a thunder storm in the city park. We learned that this lady had been watching over us and was ready rescue us if necessary.

By August 16th, we were in Fargo about to leave ND. We were ready to check out Minnesota. The last day in ND was a good day for riding. We had a tail wind all day and rode 94 miles. It was one of the best days of the whole trip. The next day we were in Hawley, MN, where we went to the post office and picked up the new Thermorest mattress that Caroleen had sent from home.

Riding out of Fargo was tough because we had a head wind and an uphill ride for much of the day. That part of MN has more trees and lakes than ND and it seemed to have more rural population than ND. Maybe they had smaller farms.

After a few days of enjoying the MN country side, we decided to treat ourselves to a motel room. We found a Budget Motel in Long Prairie where we negotiated a great rate for a room. I handed the clerk my credit card and she said, "Heck, I know you." She recognized my name on the card. She was from Rolla, had gone to the same school as Caroleen, and was a good friend of my cousin, Lillian. I knew her from decades earlier when she was living in Portland and roomed with Lillian. She was MaryAnn Nolting.

I called Lillian from the motel and told her about meeting her friend, MaryAnn. We had planned to see Lillian and her husband, Dale, while we were in the area. They lived in Annondale, MN, where they retired after living in Portland, OR, for many years. We decided to meet them in Royalton, which is about fifty miles from their home in Annondale. They offered to load our bikes and luggage in their van and drive us to their house for the night then haul us back to Royalton the next day so we could continue the trip east. We couldn't pass up an offer like that. We had a fine ride in their van, a place to sleep in their new home, great food, and a good visit with Lillian and Dale. These two bicycle riders really appreciated their hospitality.

They dropped us off in Royalton the next day and we headed for the Wisconsin border which was only a short day's ride. The first night in Wisconsin we camped just out of Oscola where we met a young couple from Everett, WA. Reed and Jean were also traveling to Bar Harbor by bicycle.

The hills and the hot, humid weather were somewhat of a challenge the first few days in WI. That beautiful country is not the easiest riding, but we enjoyed the scenery. We were looking forward to getting to Hancock, WI for a visit with Dave's parents, but we were still a couple of day's ride away. The weather continued to be hot and humid which was normal for WI at that time of year.

August 25th was a long day. We rode about ninety miles and five of the twelve hours were in a steady rain. We decided to treat ourselves to a small rental cabin at the campground in Nelcoosa, WI. We were only a short day's ride from Hancock where Dave's parents spend their summers. His sister, Kris, and her family were also there. They were set up in a mobile home at the Woodlake Campground and they offered us their tent trailer to sleep in which we gladly accepted. It was a great place to sleep after so many nights in our tents along the way.

Before heading out the next morning, we loaded our bikes while Dave's mom prepared sandwiches and snacks for the road. She made sure we were well stocked with tasty provisions that would last for many miles. This saved us from needing to stop at roadside service station deli's that served questionable grub that wasn't quite lethal, and far from exciting.

When riding with loaded bicycles, food is really important. A bike rider uses several times more calories in a day than normal activity requires. Occasionally, we stopped at a supermarket and loaded up on groceries for the times we did our own cooking in campgrounds.

Our campground cooking had a routine. Young Dave heated water on the stove and tossed in anything that seemed remotely edible. Older but wiser Dave (that would be me) went through the food inventory to come up with something to contribute to the concoction. Old Dave would come up with a package wrapped in clear plastic. Young Dave would ask, "Where did you find that?" Answer, "In with the rest of the food." It wasn't moving so it went into the soup but was later identified as left over pizza we bought in Rugby, ND, two weeks earlier.

We often made hobo stew which consisted of as many food items as we had with us mixed together and boiled on a one burner stove then seasoned with Tabasco Sauce and salt and pepper. It wasn't great, but it worked until morning when we had pancakes or oatmeal, bran, coffee, and Gatorade before leaving camp.

About midmorning we typically looked for a restaurant for a second breakfast. Most greasy spoon cafes put together a pretty good breakfast. They seem to start out great in the morning, but they usually weren't a great place to eat dinner. Maybe the hot, greasy air in the kitchen takes a toll on the chef.

For bike riders it's hard to beat a buffet. It doesn't need to be a great spread, but the chances of finding something relatively fresh and desirable are fairly good. When you do find something you like, there's usually lots of it. Pizza was Dave's favorite meal. We could not pass a pizza parlor without stopping. He could smell pizza for miles. I liked pizza too, but the fat content was of some concern. I justified eating it by telling myself that I needed some grease for lubrication for my knees and joints while I was riding. I used the same reasoning with ice cream and milkshakes. I'm not sure the medical community would agree with my rationale, but it worked for me.

Our route took us through an Amish settlement where we were able to see how well the simple life worked for those friendly, hard working folks. Life was really good for them without all the modern conveniences available.

The bikes did fairly well, but we did have a few problems with tires and had a couple of axles replaced on Dave's bike. The original equipment rear axle and tires weren't quite up to the task and we found ourselves stopping for repairs more often than we liked.

For Dave we were in familiar territory. Most of his family lives in the Chicago area. We spent the night with his sister, Kathy, and her husband, Russ, in Rochester. After a great visit with them, we rode several miles on an old railroad bed that had been converted to biking and walking trails on our way to Crystal Springs, IL. Kathy had arranged for a room for us at the Super 8 motel and while in the area, we spent time with Dave's other sisters, Kim and Kary. I also had the chance to have dinner with Elmer Raasakka and Verna Urban who were old friends and neighbors from ND who lived near Chicago.

After a good rest and visit, it was time to hit the road and continue our trip to Maine. We loaded our bikes and luggage in Kary's van and she hauled us back to the bike route. After all that hospitality, great accommodations and food, we were once again on our way to cheap motels, camping, and greasy food courtesy of our low budget trip.

It was already Sept 2nd, and we had been on the road for four weeks. The time had gone fast and it had been a great trip. We got into Joliet, IL, just in time to attend services at a Lutheran Church. I felt it was important to get religious inspiration at least once a week because it seemed as if someone greater had been protecting us on the road, and we had a lot of miles to go.

We were in Indiana for a few days and saw more corn fields than we could possibly enjoy. If there hadn't been an occasional field of soybeans to look at, that route would have been very monotonous.

There were many good camping opportunities which beat a stuffy motel room any day especially when the weather was dry. We found that Monroeville, Indiana, was an especially memorable city. Several mapped bicycle routes go through the town and they take particularly good care of bicyclists. They welcomed riders with a beautiful city park which had showers, a kitchen, laundry facilities, and a good place to sleep. It couldn't get much better for two weary bicycle nuts.

Dave drying out laundry that he washed at the motel.

We crossed the state line into Ohio with a nice tail wind. It looked like Sept. 8th would be a fairly easy day even though it was still hot and humid. We stayed in a motel in Napoleon, OH, then headed towards Grand Rapids for breakfast. That was where we met a young fellow named Matt Pulka who was riding his bike from OH to CA. Matt was an interesting fellow who had written a screen play about his bike riding and was working on a book.

We rode on to Huron where we rented a motel room and got our first glimpse of Lake Erie. It was looking like rain. We stayed there before we rode on toward Vermillion, but we started having tire trouble. We rode into town with Dave's back tire held together with duct tape. I wouldn't recommend anyone should leave on a bike trip without duct tape and bungee cords. Dave bought two new tires and considered naming his bike *Firestone*. This was about the time the company was having serious problems with the quality of their tires.

On September 11, 2001, Dave and I were in Painesville, OH, only a few hundred miles from New York City when terrorists flew into the World Trade Towers killing thousands of people. It was a sunny morning and we were about to have breakfast when we heard the news. We stayed in Painesville to do our laundry at a local Laundromat where we could listen to the news about that tragic event on a small radio that we carried.

We learned that a plane crashed into the Pentagon and yet another plane, headed for the White House, crashed in Pennsylvania. We learned later the heroic efforts of some of the passengers had caused the plane to crash in Pennsylvania killing everyone on board rather than let it destroy the White House which was the intended target. The incidents shut down airports across the entire country for a time and changed air travel and our country forever.

We left Painsville and continued our trip along the lake to Geneva, OH, where we rented a motel and watched CNN's coverage of the carnage that took place earlier that fateful day.

Our route took us into Pennsylvania for several miles where we camped on the shore of Lake Erie and had a refreshing swim before returning to our tents for the night. From there it was on to New York where we decided to cross into Ontario to see Niagara Falls from the Canadian side. It was a good choice because the view from Canada is quite spectacular.

As we approached the border, the traffic was backed up for several miles because of the added security put into place following the World Trade Center incident. We went to the pedestrian crossing with our loaded bicycles fully expecting to be delayed by an inspection of our luggage by the border patrol. We were pleasantly surprised when we were asked a few simple questions and allowed to pass into Canada. Apparently they didn't consider us a serious threat. Most of the questions involved their curiosity about why people would decide to ride bicycles for such a distance. I didn't have a good answer other than a possible lack of brain cells or an excess of nervous, misplaced energy.

Back on the US side, we were by the Erie Canal which reaches from Buffalo to Troy, NY, on the Hudson River. It connects the Great Lakes to the Atlantic Ocean. We rode many miles along the canal on a trail that was once used by horses to tow freight and passenger vessels through the canal in the 1800's. The canal was finished in 1825 and is now combined with three shorter canals to form the New York State Barge Canal system that covered a total of five hundred twenty four miles.

Outside Altan, NY, we were riding along when a guy in an SUV stopped us as we approached his car. His name was Vince and he wanted to hear about our riding experiences. He also had a bike trip planned and wanted to discuss bike touring. He offered us a bag of cookies which we eagerly accepted. He later e-mailed Dave after he had taken his trip and told him it was less than enjoyable due to bad weather.

With New York behind us we rode into Middlebury, Vermont. Our intention was to coordinate our trip with the fall colors the northeast is famous for, but we were about two weeks early for the peak colors. It seemed like a good time to treat ourselves to a cheap motel because it was beginning to look like rain. It turned out to be a good decision. We stayed at that motel for two nights because of the rain. It was one of the few days of the trip that we didn't ride at least a few miles. We used that time to send some of our extra baggage home. We didn't need the extra weight going over some of the serious mountains coming up.

We wished we had lower gearing when we pedaled over Breadloaf Pass. We hadn't considered the mountains in that area to be a great threat, but if we were to ride that route again, we'd spend a few extra dollars for better gearing. A couple more mountain passes and we were through VT and NH which was the last state before we rode into Maine—our target state and the end of a great ride.

The roads in NH and Maine weren't the best. The traffic was heavier than it had been and there were many challenging hills before we arrived in Bar Harbor, Maine. We found a nice campground in Acadia National park. Camping season was over so we had our choice of great camping sites. After a few hours of riding around the park sightseeing and relaxing in Bar Harbor, we were ready to head home to Washington.

Anodale, MN, where we spent a night with Lillian and Dale Mitchell in their new home.

A choice camping spot on Lake Erie.

Cruise ship visable from Arcadia National Park.

Taking in the fall colors in Arcadia National Park. This couple drove us to the airport when we left Maine.

Oregon Coast Bike Trip

THE BAR HARBOR TRIP WOULDN'T be the last time Dave and I would load up our bikes and venture out. In 2003 we decided to ride the Oregon coast from Astoria to Crescent City, CA, a journey of about four hundred miles. That trip would be much shorter than the last and we kept an easy schedule of about fifty miles per day.

We loaded the bikes on the van and hauled them to Cousin Nestor's place in Astoria where we left the van for our return trip home. After an enjoyable evening with Nestor which included a fish dinner at one of his favorite restaurants, we settled down for a good night's sleep. We woke up to rain that lasted most of the day. We started the ride by going to church for a little inspiration. After a breakfast at the Pig and Pancake Cafe, we headed out and rode for a couple of days in intermittent rain. We decided to rent a motel room since the forecast was 100% chance of more rain. What could we expect? After all, we were on the Oregon Coast.

The Oregon coast is a popular route for bicycle touring. We met several bike tourists and among them were Alison and Keith, a young couple riding from Alberta, Canada, to the Mexican border.

The state campgrounds on the coastal route offer hiker/biker rates which are just a fraction of the regular rates. The hiker/biker camps share the same clean bathrooms and showers with the regular campsites and there are always accommodations available for hikers and bikers even if the main campground is full.

My brother Dwight and his wife, Barb, were touring the coast at the same time with their pickup and trailer. We had made no plans to meet them, but agreed to watch for each other on the road. As we were riding out of Newport, I looked over and saw their rig stopped at a stoplight so we waved like crazy to get their attention. They told us they were staying a short distance away at South Beach state campground and invited us to camp with them. We set up our tents on their site. Dwight made French toast in the morning which was a welcome change from pancakes.

The campground we shared with Dwight and Barb near Newport, OR.

The scenic Oregon coast.

The hiker/biker camps are an excellent place to meet other bike riders. Many times fast friendships develop and riders team up and ride together for a time. We met a young man from Holland named Martin (pronounced Marteen) who joined us for pancakes at breakfast. He was traveling from Alberta to San Diego, CA and wasn't in a great hurry. He expected to be on the road for three months.

As we were riding along enjoying the scenery, we met two young women, Karmen and Trish, riding from the Yukon Territory in northern Canada to Mexico and planned to continue down Baja. We told them about our new friend, Martin, and suggested they slow down a bit and let him catch up with them. They seemed to think that might be a good idea. That night we were setting up our tents at Bay State campground, when Martin rode in with Carl, a California guy who was riding from Bellingham to the CA border. In the morning we made pancakes for the four of us. By this time we were beginning to be known as the pancake boys and I was described as the old guy with a really big frying pan.

We told Martin about the Yukon girls. I told him that I didn't remember a whole lot about young girls, but these two were probably worth catching up to and suggested that he pick up his pace a little so he could catch up with them. He seemed quite excited about the possibility.

The weather was beginning to dry out and we had spectacular scenery plus a tail wind. At Harris Beach state park we had our breakfast of pancakes made with blackberries Dave picked on site. A biker from Germany named Holgar joined us.

The ride was coming to an end. We rode into Jedediah Smith Redwoods state park to camp near the giant redwoods for a couple of nights. On Monday, September 22, we rode into Crescent City, CA, to go to church and confirm our rental car reservation. We spent the afternoon on a relaxing ride back to our campsite and around the park. The next day we rode back into Crescent City, loaded our bikes and luggage in the rental car, and headed back to Astoria. We dropped off the car and headed home with the van.

We received a postcard from Martin and the Yukon girls. He finally caught up with them down the road in CA and a friendship developed. They met again in San Diego and Martin escorted his two new friends across the border into Mexico. The girls continued their adventure in Mexico. Dave received an e-mail from Karman and Trish after their trip ended. They indicated their Mexican experience was quite stressful. The encountered mad dogs, dead dogs, outlaw kids, wind storms, extreme heat, and a flasher who stalked them. They decided to end their trip in LaPaz. Although they had some positive experiences, they considered the trip too dangerous to continue. Apparently they arrived home with positive memories of their US ride, but were not so keen on riding in Mexico.

Dave and Holgar, a cyclist from Germany in a hiker/biker camp on the Oregon coast.

Giving Back

World Vision and Food for the Poor

I was born and baptized Catholic. Before Mom and Dad were married, she was Catholic and Dad was Lutheran. Later in their marriage, they reached some sort of compromise and we started going to Protestant churches. Before I was married and even afterward, I enjoyed attending churches of various denominations and found that although they may have a slightly different approach, they have many similarities. They are all basically trying to accomplish the same things. I also believe that it's not the name of an organization that makes a difference, but the devotion of the members and the leadership that makes it successful. For many years I have been attending the Catholic church with Caroleen. Charleen was baptized and confirmed Catholic.

Many years ago we had a priest named Father Lane. One Sunday there was a fund raiser for the Missions. I have always been a believer in supporting some religious organization and he really got my attention. He went on about the idea of giving part of your income to a good cause, mainly to the church. He said according to several passages in the Bible, the more you gave, the more you would receive, but it wasn't a good idea to give for that reason alone. That made sense to me. It's not to get a lot back that a person should give, but for the love of God. But still it sounded like a pretty good investment. We weren't getting any kind of a return on CD's.

After mass I told him he made a pretty good case for tithing and that he would be a good financial advisor. He probably thought I was taking his sermon much too lightly, and he said I should trust him and give it a try.

I'm not sure he appreciated my off-beat sense of humor, but we actually had almost always given part of our income to the church and

I know we've been blessed financially because of it. There is no other reason that a couple of North Dakota farm kids would be as fortunate as we have been. We did start to give even more and Father Lane was right. The more we gave, the more we received.

I've always believed that anything we have should be shared. We in America hold a disproportionate amount of the world's wealth and we use more than our share of the world's resources. I feel that it is our duty to share with the worlds' less fortunate. We have many poor people in the US, but the poor here would be considered wealthy in many of the third world communities. The richest 20% of the world's people consume 86% of all goods and services while the poorest 20% consume just 1.3%. Americans spend eight billion dollars per year on cosmetics. That's two billion more than the estimated annual amount needed to provide basic education for everyone in the world. Of the 6.7 billion people on earth, 40% live on less than $2 per day, and 15% of the world's population live on $1 per day. The US with 4.5 % of the world's population lives on $105 per day according to the book *The Hole in our Gospel* by Richard Stearns.

These few statistics aren't the kind of news that's very popular and it doesn't sell well, but they make the point well. Someone said that if one person is tragically killed, it is news. If one million people die of hunger each year, it is a statistic. Unfortunately, such statistics don't consume the news, but they are things people need to know.

Roughly one out of four children in developing countries is underweight. Some 350 to 400 million children are hungry. About one in seven people worldwide do not have enough food to sustain themselves. Approximately 25,000 people die each day of hunger or related causes. That's the equivalent of about nine million people each year.

We are more likely to hear about the rate of foreclosures on real estate that shouldn't have been bought in the first place because the buyers had no money. Financing should not have been available under those circumstances. We hear what the media reports, not what society needs to know.

Water is a continuing problem in many developing countries. Not only is water a scarce commodity, but many times the water that is available is contaminated with water borne bacteria and parasites. In many areas obtaining this tainted water involves women and children carrying it in buckets on their heads, sometimes for miles. As many as five million people die each year of water related illnesses. A water-well in those communities is considered a miracle and is a life changer for so many. The children are free to go to school rather than spend much of their time carrying water. It also makes growing food a reality in many instances. People are survivors and, if given a chance, they can do quite well with very little. Clean water, some food, and a roof over their head make all the difference.

I have seen some communities in Jamaica where people live next to the garage dump and their only income is from a few items salvaged from the rubble then sold to recyclers. Much of their food is salvaged from these same sources because there are no government programs to bail them out. Their shelters are built from plastic and pallets they salvaged. A good day is finding a bucket full of aluminum cans or bottles that might sell for a dollar or less. Now that is poverty

We saw small children working with their parents sorting through tons of rotting garbage because there are no child labor laws protecting them. If the whole family doesn't work, it would mean severe hunger. When a loaded garbage truck appears at the dump, the kids all run toward it competing to be first to pick through its smelly cargo.

Some of the families had livestock and they became scavengers too. I was amazed to see cows and hogs living on a diet of garbage. Even the animals had to adapt to poverty.

I'm very passionate about supporting organizations that help the world's poor. One of my favorite charities is Food for the Poor which concentrates on the most desperately poor segment of the population providing communities with improved housing, sanitation, and clean water. You can reach them at: 6401 Lyons road, Coconut Creek, FL 33073 phone # 954-427-2222.

Some other organizations I like a lot are:

1) Cross International—370 W. Camino Gardens Blvd.—Boca Raton, FL 33432 800-277-7575.
2) World Vision—34834 PO Box 9716 Mail Stop 325—Federal Way, WA 98036 800-974-7794.
3) Catholic Relief Services—PO Box 17090,—Baltimore, MD 21298 888-277-7575

All of these organizations have low administrative costs and are prominent in helping the poorest of the poor worldwide. I have been on tours with Food for the Poor in the very poorest parts of Jamaica and on a trip to Honduras with World Vision. They were life changing trips and I feel you can't go wrong supporting any of the organizations I have listed.

Sponsoring needy children in underdeveloped countries is something else very close to my heart. Although many organizations offer sponsorship programs, the main one that we support is World Vision. We have sponsored children through them for many years and find it very fulfilling. It is great to have such a close relationship with families in distant countries.

Sponsorship means donating a few dollars each month that the organization uses to help support a child in a selected community in a very poor country. The contribution not only helps the child but is pooled to improve the community as a whole with such things as clean water, improved housing, education, and instruction in more efficient farming techniques. A few dollars can buy so much and mean so much to a poor family.

When you become a sponsor through World Vision, you receive a picture of the child and information on the country and the general area where the family lives. The program is set up so you are able to send letters to the child and the letters are answered with the help of a World Vision interpreter working in that particular community. The kids love to get letters from their sponsors and it's one of the greatest joys of sponsorship to receive a letter and pictures from the family.

There is also a program set up to encourage sponsors to visit the kids and families they are working with. I had the opportunity to do that a few years ago in Honduras where we have two sponsored kids. After a flight from Houston, I arrived in Honduras. Giavanni, a World Vision representative, picked me up at the airport in Tegucigalpa. I checked into a hotel and they picked me up early the next morning for the trip to the country with two World Vision staff members. The roads were absolutely terrible, and this is from a guy raised in ND. We were in a 4-wheel drive Toyota pickup that had good clearance, but it was still scraping over large rocks. The roads were not even fit for goats. I hung on to the panic handles on each side of the cab and tried to keep my head from hitting the top of the cab. After a five hour drive, we arrived at the Yoro development project where we met Sandi and her family. Sandi was our first sponsored child. We had a short visit with the help of the interpreter. It felt as if I knew her after so many years of exchanging pictures and letters. I wasn't disappointed. She's a great kid and has a beautiful family.

Next we headed for another community where Philipe, another sponsored child, lives with his family. We spent the night in the town of Progresso in a hotel with no sheets on the bed, no shower head, and a plugged sink. They don't spend a lot of time on maintenance in Honduras. We headed out over more roads that consisted of broken pavement and large rocks. We stopped at a remote World Vision office and met the staff that worked in the area. It was a great group of people who were very devoted to improving the lives of the people. After leaving the World Vision headquarters, we drove to Philipe's home. They are subsistence farmers. They have a small plot of land and grow most of their produce. They did the work by hand. Philipe's mother prepared lunch for us and it was a great meal. We had chicken which was not common because most of their meals are served without meat. They had butchered one of the few chickens for us. Their home was a structure built of a poor grade of lumber. There were spaces in the walls where you could see outside. They had a rusty metal roof with a dirt floor. The kitchen wasn't in the main part of the house. It was located away from the main living area because of the smoke from cooking. They did most of the cooking on a wood fire that was not well vented.

Somehow they had electricity run to their home. There was one lone bulb hanging from a cord and a receptacle to plug their radio into. The radio was probably their only source of information from the outside. They were very proud of the fact they had a radio. We were treated royally. Anyone involved with World Vision was treated with great respect.

Because Philipe and his family had sponsors, their housing improved over time. His dad wrote me a letter inviting me to see his beautiful new home that had a roof that didn't leak and a solid wood or concrete floor. Our granddaughter, Cassie and her husband, Vichhean, now sponsor Philipe's sister, Christianne. Our daughter, Charleen and her husband, Harley, are the proud sponsor of two children in Honduras. It is a worthwhile venture and I know they will continue to help in this way.

I also had the opportunity to join a working tour of a World Vision project. People from around the US arrived to help construct housing for needy families. We arrived on the building site and were greeted by a group of children all dressed up in their good clothes. They sang a few songs and were all smiles as they watched their new homes materialize. Adobe construction is the typical building material used in that part of Central America, but it was completely different than any construction material we were familiar with. The adobe block is made from local clay soil that is readily available on most construction sites. The clay is mixed with water into mud that is dried in the sun for several days in wooden forms. They result in large blocks that weigh about thirty or forty pounds. The blocks are mortared together with adobe mud to form the walls. They do all the mud mixing by hand with a large hoe. I watched a small local woman mix adobe all day hardly ever stopping for a break. I would have been wiped out in a very short time. Those people were not afraid of hard work.

The inside walls were also made of adobe which makes the walls very thick and tends to cut down the square footage to about 400 square feet. The outside of the structures were covered with a type of stucco or plaster used for preserving the adobe. The roofs were made of clay tiles which were also produced locally. The floors were hard surfaced—usually concrete. The adobe homes were known to last up to 100 years.

I'm not sure how much help we were on the construction site, but the locals tolerated us for a couple of days. It did give us a chance to interact with the local people and see firsthand what World Vision and its contributors are doing in that part of the world. We also had the opportunity to view some finished adobe homes. The proud owners were happy to show us their new homes. The houses had upgraded kitchen stoves that were vented to the outside which was a much healthier situation than the open fire method that depended on venting through the walls and ceilings. The new stoves were quite efficient and only took a few sticks of wood to make a clean, hot fire. Wood is scarce. I saw people walking by on the road with large pieces of salvaged scrap wood on their shoulders.

We saw one home where a lady used one of the rooms of her house to start a store. The inventory of her little business consisted of fewer products than the average American has in their pantry. She started her venture with a micro-loan of a few dollars borrowed from the World Vision bank. Many of the businesses were started with as little as a $30 loan. The repayment rate is excellent. The welfare and government programs like we see in the US are scarce or nonexistent. It was absolutely amazing to me how resourceful our neighbors to the south have become in dealing with their extreme poverty.

We toured a sheet metal factory where the workers build small corn silos from galvanized sheeting. The soldering irons were wood heated. The seams were formed over a 4 x 4 beam with hammers and pliers. They cut the metal outdoors on the ground with shears that would have been abandoned long ago in the US. The end result was an impressive piece of work that any sheet metal person would be proud of.

We passed a road improvement project where several people with large white bags filled with rocks and soil were filling holes in the road. They filled the bags and dragged them to the part of the road that needed grading. They dumped them, spread out the material, and went back for a refill. A simple wheelbarrow would have made all the difference in the world, but it wasn't available due to budget limits. Their system in Honduras would have a financial advantage over our labor and cost intensive system, but I wouldn't trade our roads for the roads in any of the developing countries.

When I arrived in Honduras, I saw many school buses. They weren't used to haul school kids since most of the kids walked to school. They repainted the old school busses acquired from the US that we consider worn out, and used them for years for local and long distance public transportation.

Part of our tour was a trip to a school building where mothers brought their children hoping that someone in our group would give their kids the benefit of sponsorship. There were kids of all ages from infants to about ten years old. There was very little noise and the kids all seemed well behaved. They were all dressed in their best clothes to impress potential sponsors. That is where I met Maria. She was a sweet little one about three years old. When I got home, I told Charleen about her and she agreed to sponsor her. The relationship has been ongoing for years now and Maria is getting the benefits of sponsorship. She is growing up to be a great young lady with opportunities that she wouldn't have if it weren't for the World Vision Sponsorship Program.

We have another sponsored child named Gayane, who lives in Armenia. She has been one of our kids for years. She is about twelve or thirteen years old now and is an A student who wants to be in the medical field. It would be impossible if it weren't for World Vision. An education is not available for all kids world wide. The kids are eager to learn and consider it an opportunity to go to school. It is a joy to be able to help these kids reach their goals.

Years ago we started donating towards building small houses in developing countries. The basic Food for the Poor house was 12 x 12 feet with a small deck in the front. The little homes are built in communities where potable water and public restrooms are available. The structures are made with 2x4 stud walls exposed on the inside and roofed and sheeted with galvanized material. Some have electricity, but many don't have such a luxury. They usually do their cooking on a small portable stove. They aren't great homes by much of the world's standards, but they are an improvement over plastic and pallet shelters built with salvaged material from a garbage dump. It's a luxury to have a dry place to sleep and a way to lock up their meager belongings.

Some of the homes are as large as 12x24 feet if they have a large family. Harley and I had a chance to get involved in the building of a couple of those homes. Typically, the houses are built by local contractors sometimes with the help of a group of volunteers from the US.

Food for the Poor also has a program to provide motor boats and equipment for fishermen. Their daily catch can be multiplied many times over using a row boat. They can better provide for their families and communities.

I was very impressed with what we saw when we toured Jamaica. We stayed at the John Bosco Boy's Home managed by two Catholic nuns. Many of the boys are orphans or homeless kids. The home is partially supported by Food for the Poor and they had arranged the accommodations for our tour group. This is a self contained farming operation where much of the food for the home is produced on site. I was quite impressed with the farm. They accomplished many tasks the same way we did when I was a kid in ND. The kids are taught the importance of hard work. Each kid has the responsibility of a job. Some fed the chickens and others cut hay by hand for the live stock. There was even a butcher shop on the grounds where they processed their meat products. They taught the boys about real life.

Their main meat was pork. They have a very modern pork producing operation that is state of the art. They produce most of the meat consumed by the residents and they market the rest to help finance the organization.

The residents get a formal education so they are prepared to take advantage of whatever opportunities come their way in adulthood. The Boys Home is just one of many worthwhile project sponsored by Food for the Poor.

I strongly encourage everyone who can to get involved with this program. It is a great experience to visit the kids and families in the sponsored communities. It's a great way to take a vacation and learn about the people and cultures in those developing countries. It is my wish that my family continue to work with the poorest of the world's poor. I regret that I didn't get involved with these programs when I was younger. It has made me more aware of the problems of the world and makes me appreciate my life in the US much more. We are truly blessed—probably more than we really deserve.

A small home built and financed by Food For the Poor. Our group had the opportunity to work on this project in Jamaica.

A typical Food For the Poor community. These homes are built for families and are about 12' x 24'. That's not much bigger than a bedroom in a home in the US.

John Bosco Boy's Home is financed partly by Food For the Poor. Kids from the street learn to be self-sufficient by growing much of their own food and maintaining the operation. Everybody has a job.

A very happy family is presented with a new house. This house had no electricity and had exposed 2x4 walls. By our standards this wasn't even basic housing, but it was a great improvement for these people. It allowed them to lock up their meager belongings and be safe from predators.

A road crew filling pot holes with rocks and gravel on a country road in Honduras.

A one-man construction project—a sack of cement, a bucket of water, a wheel barrow and a shovel. Notice there are no flag people and no fancy concrete truck.

On a recent trip to Honduras with World Vision, we learned about house construction with adobe. The blocks are produced by putting mud in wooden forms and allowing it to dry in the sun. The finished blocks sell for a few cents each.

These men are mixing adobe mud that is used as mortar as they build adobe block houses. You don't find these people jogging for exercise.

We helped build an adobe house. It was a great experience, but I'm not sure we were a lot of help. I'm the guy bringing up the rear.

This is a kitchen in a house in Honduras. The walls are left open to vent the smoke from cooking. Notice the lack of custom cabinets and granite counter tops.

123 {{finished house half page A newly completed adobe home. The adobe blocks have a stucco finish on the outside and are expected to last as long as 100 years. The locals considered them mansions.

The stove in this photo is a great improvement over the non-vented open-fire method of cooking. The stoves are quite efficient. A few small sticks of wood make a nice, hot fire.

Having lunch with our sponsored boy, Phillip, and his family. Two employees from the World Vision office in Honduras, Waldina and Allison, made this visit possible. They provided transportation, and acted as interpreters which was great as I don't speak Spanish and the family didn't speak English.

The Mendez Family. My granddaughter, Cassie, sponsors Christianne, Phillip's little sister.

The Mendez family now has a new home thanks to the efforts of World Vision.

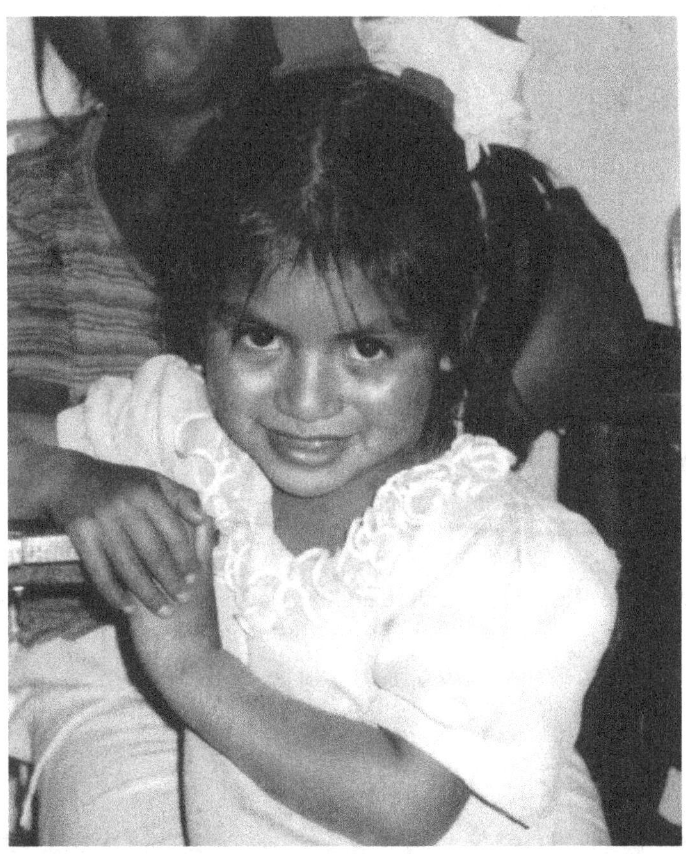

World Vision had an event to promote sponsorship. Mothers brought their children to this public center in hopes that their child would have the benefit of being part of the sponsorship program. This is where I met Maria. Who could resist this beautiful child? I told Charleen about her when I got home and she and Harley agreed to be her sponsors. Many kids found sponsors from people in our group. The sad part is that many did not and had to return home disappointed. This program changes the lives of these kids and their families and it provides many benefits to the community.

Habitat for Humanity

A FEW YEARS AGO WE decided to sell some of our rental houses and downsize to some of the smaller, more manageable units. This left me with more free time. I was a little bit bored and too young to vegetate in the recliner with a TV remote, but too old to get into any real trouble. With all that extra time I needed some way to direct my excess energy into something productive. I had the necessary tools and many years of experience in maintaining houses and I was looking for a project.

One Sunday a speaker from Habitat for Humanity came to our church and talked about starting an operation in Everett where I spent a lot of my time. Habitat for Humanity helps low income families get into new homes. The families agree to work a certain number of hours on the building project in return for a no interest loan and payments geared to their income. Much of the labor for construction is provided by volunteers and a lot of the material is donated by local businesses. All of this helps people move out of substandard housing and into their own affordable home. I decided to give volunteer work on these houses a try.

I checked into the building site where they were building a house for a family from Viet Nam and discovered that I knew the man. He was a maintenance worker at our church and I was happy to be able to help someone I knew.

Starting at Habitat for Humanity was a lot like starting a new job. The first days were somewhat stressful until I got into the groove. New construction wasn't my specialty. I spent many, many years remodeling and repairing, and found that I had a lot to learn about new construction, but learning wasn't all that bad. When you stop learning, you stop living.

I finally got to the point where if I screwed something up, I was able to fix it and nobody was the wiser. I found it very liberating not to be working for wages. I always felt a certain amount of stress when I was on a payroll. If

I had trouble and took longer than I felt I should have for a job, I felt guilty. My screw-ups were costing somebody something. With Habitat things don't always go as planned, but I go home at the end of the day thinking of the line from a country Western song, *It ain't worth nothing but it's free.*

Working with a crew was a change after working for more than two decades by myself. I began to realize how much I was missing and I started to feel comfortable working with people again. I had forgotten how much fun it was. We only work one or two days a week, but I work with the professionals every chance I get. Recently I was working with my friend, DeDe, who is an expert plumber and he said that I was the best seventy-three year old apprentice he ever had. I felt good about that until I found out I was the only seventy-three year old apprentice he'd ever had.

Many of our crew are fellow retirees who usually have plenty of time. There are also people who work full time, have family responsibilities, but still manage to put in considerable time on Habitat projects. I truly admire them. Jan, the construction foreman on the last couple of jobs, is one of those people.

For a few years we spent several weeks on Maui in Hawaii. That gave me the opportunity to check out the local Habitat for Humanity on the island. I found that I had a limited capacity for sandy beaches and salt water. After about a week of swim suits and sun screen, it felt good to strap on a tool belt and do something productive. I enjoyed working with the remarkable people at Habitat. I had a chance to work with Mike Gerry, who later became construction superintendent. I learned a lot from him on the construction sites.

Many of the homes that I worked on were for local Hawaiian families and I found them to be impressive people who really appreciated our help on the projects. Many of those people had waited years for their new home. Several of the Habitat homes are built on choice view property. The building lots are provided for native Hawaiians by the government. It is an especially good program in Hawaii where prices are so inflated that homes are totally out of reach of much of the population. The fact that building sites are more readily available on Maui makes the program work much better than in Everett where it's difficult to find affordable building sites.

Habitat for Humanity is a good outfit and I strongly recommend that anyone with extra time and a few skills should contact their local chapter and help some deserving family get into a home.

A Habitat House on Maui, Hawaii

A Habitat House in Everett, WA

Fifty Years and Counting

Caroleen, Charleen, and Harley decided to arrange a special vacation for our fiftieth wedding anniversary. I went along with the idea mainly because I was outnumbered. Actually it sounded like a good idea. After fifty years of wedded bliss, it was only fair that we spend our anniversary doing something other than watching CNN or reading a book.

Grandma Caroleen in the Alps. Still looking good after 50 years of marriage.

We decided to fly to Zürich, Switzerland. Charleen and Harley planned to meet us there, rent a car, and take a motor trip through parts of Europe. We would end the road trip in Rome then take a ten day cruise on the Holland America, Noordam. If I had to do the driving it wouldn't have happened, but Charleen drove and Harley navigated. Caroleen and I just sat in the back seat of a rented VW and enjoyed the scenery. Sitting in the back seat might have been more exciting fifty years earlier, but there's no doubt we would have missed some of the scenery.

We drove from Zurich into Germany to the Dachau Concentration Camp. Dachau was built by the Nazis as an extermination camp for Jews and other political prisoners. Many of the prisoners worked in arms factories that were also built there. The Nazis performed many medical experiments on the 3500 prisoners at Dachau and almost all of those prisoners died. Thousands more were executed or died of starvation or epidemics.

US forces liberated about 32,000 prisoners at Dachau on April 29th, 1945. Unlike other Nazi concentration camps, the Dachau furnaces were never used to exterminate Jews. From Dachau we drove to Salzburg, Austria, where we toured a massive salt mine.

Dachau concentration camp buildings.

It was a scenic drive through many quaint towns and villages then through the beautiful Austrian Alps on the way to Venice, Italy. Venice is the largest car-free city in the world due to the fact that it was built on 118 islands. We parked the car in one of the parking lots and took a ferry into the city which was founded in 452 AD. We did as all tourists do—we took a tour of Venice in a gondola. It is a city of historical buildings. The streets of the city consist of 177 canals which go under 455 bridges. Floods are a constant threat. The islands the city is built on consist of white clay and sand which has allowed the structures to settle over the years.

Venice is a beautiful city in very serious trouble. Pollution of the canals has been a problem throughout time. Industrial and human waste has definitely affected the water quality. Air pollution has taken its toll on the statues, buildings, and paintings that Venice is famous for.

Caroleen and Charleen in Venice.

We left Venice, picked up the car, and headed for Rome. The scenery was great but the traffic in Italy is pretty crazy. It seemed as if most of the drivers were younger people. Considering the way they drive, I think nobody lives long enough to be an old driver.

In the US on a multi-lane highway, the four or five foot clearance between cars is off limits to traffic. This is not so in Italy. This part of the road becomes the motorcycle and scooter lane. Those suicide riders go flying by up to 50 or 60 miles per hour dodging rear view mirrors and truck beds. The car drivers are not much better.

After implying that the life span of Italian people is probably adversely affected by their driving habits, I decided to check out the facts. The expected lifespan of Italians is two to three years longer than that of people in the US. That told me that more people than I suspected survive this bumper car mentality and live to enjoy old age. The moral of this story is if you want to live longer, live in Italy, but I still recommend that you stay out of traffic as much as possible.

We survived the trip from Venice to Rome and got settled in a condo within walking distance of Vatican City which is the administrative and spiritual center of the Roman Catholic Church. Vatican City included the Basicilla of St. Peter, the Vatican palaces, and a museum. It is the smallest independent state in the world with a population of about 1,000 people on a little over 100 acres.

We spent a restful first night in Rome in our rented apartment. The next morning we decided to walk to the Vatican for a self-guided tour and the possibility of seeing the Pope as he traveled his regular route around the grounds. The building where we stayed was in a fenced area with access to the street through a gate. Outside the gate there was a narrow sidewalk dividing the busy highway from the fence. Traffic was flying by only inches from us as we stepped out. We were very careful and got to the Vatican along with thousands of other tourists, cameras in hand hoping to get a picture of Pope Benedict as he slowly passed by standing in some kind of an open vehicle. By zooming in with the camera, we managed to get a few pictures of this very popular Pontiff.

The artwork and architecture of the church is breathtaking. The Basicilla, The Vatican Palace, and the museum cover thirteen acres. It's a massive historic work dating back hundreds of years to the times of St. Peter who is interred on the grounds.

Rome is known as the Eternal City and dates back more than 2,000 years as an important center of civilization. We saw the ruins of the Coliseum, one of the chief landmarks of Rome where Romans watched trained fighters called gladiators battle each other or fight wild animals. The audience also watched persecuted Christians killed by lions. It makes me wonder what sort of people would enjoy that type of activity.

We saw many of the sites of ancient Rome from the top of a double decker bus. The city was originally laid out for horses and carriages. Now the streets are filled with cars and buses to the point of constant gridlock. In spite of the high price of gas, people are still driving or rather sitting in traffic. It was a good decision to turn in the rental car when we got to Rome. We were ready to spend a few days on board the Noordam for a relaxing Mediterranean cruise.

The Vatican

Pope Benedict

Our first port was Dubrovnik, Croatia. The city is famous for its walls that were built centuries ago for security. The wall is 6,250 feet long, 80 feet high, and 20 feet thick in some places. They started building the walls in the 12th century and continued construction for 500 years.

On May 14th we were docked at the beautiful island of Corfu, Greece, just west of the Greek mainland. We saw some of the local sites by a horse drawn carriage which I thought was kind of a rip-off, but that's what tourists do. When a ship comes into port, the local vendors, merchants, and tour operators have a good day. This is a large part of the local economy.

The next historic port was Santorini, Greece. Santorini was once an active volcano known as Stongyle, but a massive volcanic explosion in 1628 blew it apart resulting in four separate islands. Santorini is the largest section. The ship was anchored near the cliff side town of Fira.

There are several ways to reach the town. Harley and I decided to walk the steep path which turned out to be a good workout. Caroleen and Charleen rode donkeys to the town. A cable car was also available for the less adventurous. The view from this elevation was great. There were cafes and shops available for some great shopping.

Kusadase, Turkey, was the next port. We took a full day tour of Ephesus, a 2,000 year old city that had been abandoned in the 15th century. Archeologists began to uncover it in the 18th century, but much of it is still buried under several layers of silt. History tells us that St. Paul and St. John helped establish a flourishing church in Ephesus. The Basilica of St. John honors the holy man's tomb. Nearby we attended mass in the House of Mary which is where the Blessed Virgin spent her last days.

Then we were on to Valletta, the capitol of the island country, Malta, located south of Sicily in the Mediterranean Sea. We took a walking tour of part of the town including St. John's Cathedral. It is one of the main historic sites with impressive architecture and art. It was May 19th, the day of our 50th anniversary, so we treated ourselves to a horse and buggy ride to see the sites. After the tour, we enjoyed a great buffet on board the ship and had an extra dessert for good measure then spent a relaxing evening on board the massive ship, Noordam. Harley and Charleen brought a cake and a bottle of champagne to our cabin to top off the evening. That was the finest way to celebrate that fifty year milestone.

On May 20th we stopped at the Port of Messina, Sicily, and arrived back in Rome on the morning of May 21st. We spent a couple of days relaxing in the same condo we had before we went on the cruise. The first night back in the condo we felt water dripping on our pillows. Water dripping on you when it's not raining, eliminates the possibility of a leaky roof. I was concerned about the quality of the water that was dripping on us knowing there was a bathroom directly overhead. Caroleen went to sleep in the living room since most of the water dripped on her side of the bed.

The next morning we told the very nice Italian lady managing the complex about our experience during the night. She hit her forehead with her hand and said, "Ma Ma Mia," which I think is the equivalent to someone in the US saying, "Oh, Sh..!"

We learned the source of the water was someone in the condo directly above us trying to take a bath with a hand-held shower arrangement called a bidet. A bidet is not a substitute for a shower and is not meant to wash the whole body. It is designed to cleanse only a very private part of the body. Apparently the tourist wasn't familiar with the fixture and was confused, but the fact that there wasn't a shower curtain and the flexible hose assembly was only two feet long should have been a clue that it wasn't intended for bathing. Our hostess admitted that it had happened before.

After surviving our 50th anniversary excursion, we boarded a plane in Rome, headed for Zurich, then on to Boston where we stayed overnight. The next day it was on to Seattle by way of Dallas where it was business as usual.

Fifty years goes by very quickly. Enjoy them all, but especially enjoy those years when your body doesn't hurt, your skin doesn't sag, and your hair is its original color because life is like a roll of toilet paper. As more time goes by, the faster it goes.

The great ship Noordam

2009 Ocean Cruise

THE FALL OF 2009 WE decided to take a trip to New Zealand to visit our friends, Geoff and Judie McNeil. It was a long overdue trip as we had promised our friends years ago that we would come down for a visit.

New Zealand is a long distance from the US with a large body of salt water you either have to fly over or float across to get there. There are two things that I dislike about traveling and both of them are flying. It's about a fifteen hour flight with few places to land that don't require pontoons. I hate being confined in an uncomfortable seat in an aluminum tube with recycled air for that long.

Flying is getting to be a hassle because of all the security measures. The pat-downs make Caroleen a bit uncomfortable. She thinks anyone who touches her like that should at least take her out to dinner and a movie first

As we got more serious about this adventure, I mentioned the possibility of taking a cruise ship to Australia then fly from Sydney to New Zealand. Before I could change my mind, Caroleen had reservations with Holland American on the Amsterdam. With deposits made there was no backing out. Why would anybody fly for seventeen hours when they could spend thirty days or more on a cruise ship? It makes no sense in terms of time and financially it's devastating, but the arrangements were made and that is what we would do.

Cruise ships are not a bad way to go. We had spent some time on those floating resorts and enjoyed it. The size and accommodations never fail to amaze me. The food is great, the service superior, and there is nothing lacking. After being raised on outhouses and Sears catalogs, to have the end of the roll of toilet paper folded just right was almost too much for this country boy.

There are several options on board ship for meals. The formal dining room works for most people and especially well for people who own suits and neckties. I eat because I'm hungry not to make a statement about what I'm wearing or about my finances. I'm not social enough to be comfortable eating with people I don't know, so we chose other options such as the buffet. It's sort of an assembly line arranged for blue collar people where you just go down the line, pick and choose anything that suits your fancy, and there's no lack of choices. I always like to see what I'm buying but on the ship it's something I've already bought. The meals are included in the price of the cruise.

Not everything, however, is included, such as the casino. I learned years ago that a casino would only work for someone who flunked math in school. The percentages just don't calculate. Alcoholic drinks are also extra, but that wasn't a problem for me. I had my share of alcoholic fun years ago and I do quite well with free coffee. Caroleen thinks I'm the most boring person ever to go on a cruise. I spend most of my time in the library or the gym where you never have to wait in line like you do at the buffets or dining rooms.

Cassie and Vichhean drove us to Seattle to board the Amsterdam on September 26, 2009. We got settled in our cabin, had lunch, and sailed to Vancouver, BC where we picked up more passengers. Our cabin was one of the lower priced accommodations down by the water line not far from the drive assembly. I could feel each revolution of the prop as it cut its way through the water. It was a little like a vibrating bed, but it wasn't coin operated and we quickly got used to our cabin. There is really no need to rent the expensive cabins because there are lounges and great places to relax all over the ship. There is little time to be bored on a cruise because there is always something to do. If you don't feel like doing anything, that is acceptable too. There are live stage shows daily, usually after dinner. If that doesn't suit you, there is a current movie available in the theater. When they stop at a port of call there are always tours available for the tourists. They often end up in a shopping area designed to separate the tourist from his money. We prefer taking a private tour or sometimes a taxi to see the non-commercial sites away from the sandy beaches and resorts.

After a couple of days of reading, writing, and vegetating, we docked in Long Beach. We'd been in that area of LA before and had seen the

Queen Mary docked there. Since it wasn't a new port for us, we spent the day getting familiar with the Amsterdam.

On the morning of October7th, we were near Nuku Hiva, one of the Marquesas Islands in French Polynesia. The ship anchored off shore and we were shuttled to the island on one of the life boats. We went on a tour of the island in the back of a well used four wheel drive pickup before we were shuttled back to the ship to sail on to Tahiti. We had time to take a relaxing walk in Papeete, Tahiti, before we went on to Moorea where *South Pacific* was filmed about fifty years ago. The islands in the South Pacific were beautiful but we spent such a short time at each location we didn't get a chance to know them very well. They all seemed similar in both scenery and culture.

Wesley, was one of the waiters in the buffet where we ate most of our meals on board ship. Many of the staff were young people from the Philippines who spent six months on board ship before returning home for the rest of the year. The buffet dining area is the training site for these kids before they advance to the main dining room.

After several more days of island hopping, we arrived at Pago Pago, American Samoa. It is the capitol and is on the island of Tutuila which is a territory of the US. Tourism is a big part of their economy, but tuna processing provides jobs for about a third of the population. Pago Pago was under the control of the US Navy until 1951, and has a harbor equipped to handle most types of vessels. We took a bus tour where we saw some of the damage caused by a tsunami that swept across the island a short time before we arrived.

The American influence was obvious as we toured that beautiful island. The bus we rode on was quite interesting. The company purchased bare truck chassis and they built the bus body by hand on the truck frames out of tin and plywood over a wooden framework. I was really impressed with ingenuity in the design and construction of the bus bodies. It was hard to tell that they weren't factory built.

On October 18th we crossed the International Dateline and totally missed Sunday. We jumped from Saturday to Monday. That really messes with a person's mind and screws up the calendar.

The tour bus and our guide. The picture of the baby on the bus is her niece.

The next port was Suva, the capitol of Fiji. It has an excellent harbor and is able to accommodate commercial shipping traffic and cruise ships. Tourism employs a great number of the population of Fiji. The scenery and resorts attract thousands of people from Asia, Australia and the US. We took a taxi tour of the country side and saw several villages. The people seem happy and friendly. Their homes are adequate and they make the most of what they have.

We docked at Port Vila, Vanuatu on Efate Island on October 22nd. Port Vila is the capitol of a rather small country with a population of only about 390,000 people. The island is about 1200 miles northeast of Brisbane, Australia. The average monthly income is about $300 but there is no welfare, no pensions, and no nursing homes. Families take care of their parents. Homelessness is not a big problem. It is an island with happy, friendly people who take care of one another.

We arrived in Cairnes, Australia, on October 25th after sailing the inner route between the Great Barrier Reef and the east coast of Australia. We took a cable car ride over the rain forest as part of a bus tour of the area. Cairnes is the stopping off place for tourists interested in snorkeling and diving on the Great Barrier Reef which is one of the world's greatest wonders. It is the largest coral reef system in the world and is composed of about 3,000 individual reefs, 900 islands and stretches for over 1600 miles over an area of almost 133,000 square miles. The reef contains billions of tiny organisms, and countless numbers of whales, dolphins, porpoises, sea turtles, sharks and fish. We spent several hours sailing in view of the great natural wonder, but the real action was below the surface of the water. To truly appreciate all the natural beauty of the reef, a person needs to be involved in underwater sports.

A couple of days later we arrive in Brisbane, Australia's third largest city and the capitol of Queensland. We sailed fifty-five miles up the Brisbane River escorted by the local pilot-boat to our port of call. I spent most of the morning on deck for that scenic trip up the river.

We went on a bus tour to the Quala Sanctuary where we saw many of the native animals including dingos which are wild dogs. We also saw Tasmanian Devils, a vicious animal about the size of a badger, wombats, kangaroos, and cute, cuddly Koalas.

A Tasmanian Devil.

A Koala

Making friends with a kangaroo.

On October 31st we docked at Sydney, a city of over four million people and the capitol of New South Wales. We docked with a great view of the world famous Opera House and the Sydney Harbor Bridge.

It was the end of our cruise. It had been over thirty days since leaving Seattle and I hate to admit it, but I could get used to living like that. A week or two on board a ship is a vacation, but a month or more becomes a life style. I would never have believed that a country boy could learn to enjoy living on a luxury liner, but I guess anything is possible.

Before leaving Sydney we took a four hour tour of the city and the Opera House. We learned that the Opera House was an architect's nightmare. There were numerous challenges designing the structure and more headaches building it. It is different and it is quite impressive, but a simpler design might have been more practical.

The famous Sydney Opera House

We flew from Sydney to Christchurch, New Zealand, on Sunday Nov. 1st. Our friends, Judie and Geoff, met us at the airport. We drove several miles between the airport and their home which overlooks the harbor in Lyttleton. We thoroughly enjoyed the view from their house. Most of the shipping traffic docks in Lyttleton including many of the cruise ships. It was late spring or early summer in New Zealand in November and the weather was nice but changeable. Their climate is similar to the climate in the northwestern part of the US. It was nice to see trees and gardens coming to life after we had just ended the gardening season in Washington.

Our friends set us up in their bedroom and insisted on turning over the whole main level of their home over to us. They slept in a small basement room that Geoff had recently finished. I really felt that we had taken over their home and I mentioned it to Geoff. He said, "Well, you have!" He tells it like it is. I like that.

The next couple of days we took some drives around Christchurch and found it to be a beautiful, clean city with very friendly people. I got to take a few bike rides. Geoff knew I liked bike riding and suggested that we rent bikes and do a couple of rides. The ride to Governor's Bay was a treat and, as a bonus, we had a ferry ride back across the bay. We took the train to Springfield and took our bikes along so we could ride to Sheffeld for lunch. We had a meat pie which was a tasty treat. People in New Zealand love meat pies and sausage rolls and I could really get to like them too.

We had a good ride of about forty miles. Caroleen and Judie picked us up at Loburn. We hauled the bikes back to the rental shop and went on home to rest our legs.

After several days in beautiful New Zealand, Judie and Geoff took us back to the airport and we flew to Sydney to catch a flight to Hawaii where we spent a few days in our condo before flying back home to Seattle.

Judie and Geoff

We arrived in Honolulu only twenty hours after leaving New Zealand and that included a several hour lay-over in Sydney. The lay over was so long that Security became suspicious of us hanging around the terminal and put us through an extra security check.

From Honolulu we took a short flight to Maui and took the opportunity to get caught up on the maintenance of our condo while the people who were renting units in the complex were relaxing by the pool. It was a good way to break up the long flight between Sydney and Seattle.

On November 15th we arrived back in Snohomish to the real world just in time for the holiday season. We were only nine days short of being gone two months, and it had been a wonderful way to spend the time.

The Amsterdam

As a post script to our trip to New Zealand: Christchurch and much of the surrounding area that we enjoyed so much was devastated in the fall of 2010 by a powerful earthquake that left the city in shambles. Almost two thirds of the 160,000 homes in and around Christchurch were damaged, but because of rigid building codes and good luck, there was no loss of human life. Geoff and Judie's home was damaged but was still habitable. Hundreds of aftershocks occurred in the months following the initial quake.

Unfortunately, there was more bad news from New Zealand in February 2011. There was another shaker that destroyed much of downtown Christchurch that took many lives and left countless people injured. Many of the homes damaged by the first earthquake were left uninhabitable.

Geoff and Judie are still living in their home, but they will haul drinking water in jugs for quite some time. The electricity was back on line, but they lived in their home like campers. Although their home was severely damaged, they are making it work.

The horrible destruction of that beautiful area will take years to rebuild, but I'm confident the people of New Zealand will do it.

The view of the harbor from Judie and Geoff's living room.

Pot-pour-ri

First Impressions

HERE'S A GUY WITH AN almost new car and a pretty impressive suit posing like he is a real important part of the universe. I happen to know that he was living in his aunt's basement in a room with a bed, a hotplate, and an old refrigerator. He has access to a toilet and shower in another part of the basement. He had very little money, owed on his car and, if it hadn't been for his aunt giving him a deal on his rent at $25 per month including utilities, he'd have been in even worse shape.

You guessed it. I am that guy. That time in my life was a real learning experience. I definitely needed to get my priorities straightened out. I feel quite comfortable now, not owning a suit and driving a car that is a decade or more old, but paid for. Maybe there's a message here:

Don't let anyone impress you by the way he looks.
It could be deceiving

This was me in my Dapper Dan days.

Worth

MANY PEOPLE SAY THAT MONEY doesn't matter. It's probably people with adequate wealth who feel that way. Money is definitely necessary in our system. It's a means of exchange and anyone who has at sometime in their life known a situation when there wasn't quite enough to go around, would agree that a few dollars makes life much more comfortable.

We do need money for the basic requirements of life. But money is still just a unit of measurement and it should not be a measurement of the worth of your life. We don't want to make the mistake of confusing net worth with true worth.

It's more important to be known as resourceful than known as wealthy. It has been proven that money beyond enough for the basics of food, housing, health care, etc, doesn't make people happier. There are many more things more valuable than money such as family, reputation, work ethics, kindness, and a sense of humor.

Don't be a slave to money. Let your money work for you. Don't be so busy trying to impress people and making a living that you don't have time to make a life. There are few of us, as we experience our final hours on earth, who would regret the fact that they didn't make lots of money. There are many things more important. It's what we get that makes a living. It's what we give that makes a life. This method of accounting considers true worth above net worth. Most bankers wouldn't agree with me as everything is geared to the bottom line.

The secret to happiness is not having much, but
In wanting little.

Things I'm not proud of

THERE ARE MANY THINGS THAT I have done in the past that have worked quite well and that I'm very proud of. Needless to say, there are a few things I've done that wouldn't set a great example for future generations.

I smoked for a great many years and although this was acceptable behavior years ago, it was a physically destructive, stupid activity. I would be in much better health now if I had never smoked. I have also been known to take a few drinks of alcohol. An occasional social drink is fine, but I tended to let it get out of control. Some people can handle it and some can't. I found that the best way for me was to abstain completely.

Drinking and smoking, as well as drugs, will definitely shorten your life. It's not a smart way to live. There is no positive side to this type of living. There are no winners.

Remember when

REMEMBER WHEN CASH WAS USED to buy things? What a concept you say, but that's the way it was. People would either carry cash or a check book to access the money in their bank account and there better be enough in the account to cover the checks. Some people still use checks. I carry at least one check blank to cover me in the event of an emergency, but I depend mostly on a credit card for convenience and I don't mind having the bank loan me money until the bill comes in thirty days later. We pay the account in full and there is no penalty and no interest. The credit card system also gives me the flexibility to pay the minimum payment each month with a small amount of the proceeds going toward the loan principal but most of it being applied to a ridiculously high rate of interest. With the latter option, I could go out and have a hundred dollar dinner with friends and pay for it over several years and it would probably cost three hundred dollars with interest. We do have a choice. I actually saw someone paying for a meal with cash one day, so I know that businesses who take credit cards also still take cash.

The credit card system
is a great way to buy things we don't need
with money we don't have
to impress people we don't know

Some changes we've seen over the years

WE WERE ALIVE BEFORE TELEVISION, penicillin, polio shots, frozen food, Xerox, plastic, contact lenses, Frisbees and the pill. We were alive before radar, credit cards, split atoms, laser beams, ballpoint pens, pantyhose, dishwashers, clothes dryers, electric blankets, air conditioners, drip-dry, no-iron cotton and before men walked on the moon.

We got married first then lived together. We thought fast food was what you ate during Lent. We came before house-husbands, gay-rights, computer-dating, dual-careers, and commuter-marriages. We were around before day-care centers, group-therapy, and nursing homes. We had never heard of FM radio, tape decks, electric typewriters, artificial hearts, word processors, yogurt, and guys who wore earrings. For us, time-sharing meant togetherness not a condominium. A chip meant a chunk of wood, hardware meant hardware and software wasn't even a word.

In 1940 "Made in Japan" meant junk and "making out" referred to how you did on an exam. We'd never heard of pizza, McDonalds or instant coffee.

When we hit the scene, there were 5 and 10 cent stores where you actually could buy things that only cost a nickel or a dime. Ice cream cones cost a nickel, but you could get a double scoop for a dime. For a nickel you could ride a street car, make a phone call, buy a Pepsi, or enough stamps to mail one letter or two post cards. You could buy a new Chevy Coupe for $600 but you couldn't afford the gas that only cost eleven cents a gallon.

In our day cigarette smoking was fashionable. Grass was mowed. Coke was a cold drink and pot was something you cooked in. Rock music was a Grandma's lullaby and Aids were helpers in the principal's office

We were certainly not before the differences between the sexes was discovered, but we were before sex changes. We made do with what we had. And we were the last generation that was so dumb as to think you needed a husband to have a baby.

Thanks to boom boxes
We are the last generation that can hear.

I would like to credit the author of this piece but I don't know who wrote it. I have had a copy of it in my files for many years but I don't know where it came from. Because I don't know who the author is, doesn't mean it isn't still true.

Education

MANY THINGS THAT I'VE ACCOMPLISHED in life have been very satisfying, but these endeavors have been the result of a great deal of help along the way from my wife and family, and many other wonderful people who have encouraged me. My teachers in grade school and a couple of years of high school deserve much of the credit for my success. Although the years I spent in school were few by today's standards, they provided a basic education that enabled me to function in the world as it was then and is now. I'm sure there were times that more education would have been an advantage.

There will be kids reading this that will think that dropping out of school is acceptable. After all, Grandpa didn't do too badly with limited education. But I want to make it clear that I don't feel this is an option in this day and age and won't be in the future either. I strongly urge all young people to pursue higher education. The income levels for college graduates are considerably higher than for high school graduates. The unemployment rate is much lower as well.

I have lived through some of the best times in history as well as some years that weren't so good. When I was young, there were blue collar jobs that paid a living wage, but these jobs are very quickly disappearing to be replaced by fast food and other service jobs that don't pay very well. This is where people with limited education could be headed in our present economy.

This is the way it is today as I see it.

Artificial intelligence usually
Beats real stupidity.

The Plant Engineer

My brother, Don, and my son-in-law, Harley, both work as engineers for the Port of Seattle. SeaTac airport is under the jurisdiction of the Port and that is where both of them work. Although their work is not all glamour, as they occasionally need to unplug a toilet or work on a sewer pump, these jobs are about as good as it gets for the blue collar worker. The pay is good, and the benefits are great with a good health plan and liberal vacation and sick leave.

Years ago I had a similar job working for some of the commercial laundries in Seattle. Another advantage of these jobs is every day is different, as opposed to an assembly line job or punching keys on a computer. Another positive aspect is they can't send these jobs offshore. Blue collar jobs require hands on action. You can't replace a valve on a boiler or repair a broken conveyor by calling an 800 number and talking to a computer geek. Although robots have replaced many people in industry and computers have moved into the workplace, the plant engineer still needs to think things out and make repairs using the advantage of years of experience.

I feel that a college education is helpful for success because many jobs require certain credentials to get that job or to run a business. But I feel it's also important to learn to repair and build things. The ability to work with your hands as well as your mind increases chances for success and tend to make people more self sufficient. Office and sales jobs are not for everyone and we are not all cut out to be professionals or to run a business, but there will always be a market for people to keep things running and to build things. Too many people are afraid to get dirt under their fingernails.

Throughout my life I have done jobs that required me to work with my hands and there's no doubt that I'd have been more effective in many instances if I'd had a few years of higher education. Usually I was able to bluff my way through with BS and determination, but this probably won't work in the future. Times have changed. I was fortunate to be raised on a farm where it was absolutely necessary to repair things and learn to do things. We didn't have the option to throw things away and replace them with new like we do today. I still tend to keep things running longer than conventional wisdom would suggest. We are living in a throw away economy. It's a shame, but our whole economy would collapse if we all refused to throw away perfectly good stuff that just needed a simple repair.

The Engineer

by
Dave Jussero

He goes to the job, this hardy soul.
He works underground as if he were a mole.

There is little doubt strange hours he keeps
For he goes to work when most everyone sleeps.

He's taken for granted almost by all,
But let something go wrong
And he's the first one they call

He fires the boilers and does pretty fair
At keeping most things in real good repair.

He does his job right and you better know,
If he did it wrong the boiler would blow.

And if this happens, I'll tell you, my friend,
He would never be taken for granted again.

Though he's seldom seen, you need have no fear,
For working below is the Plant Engineer.

I wrote this poem for my brother, Don, years ago for his birthday. It was printed in the Union newsletter.

Dad's Family

THE FOLLOWING IS A SHORT vignette about my dad's sisters and brothers. It is an incomplete survey of each of them. It's important to pass along what I know so future generations in my family will have some idea of their heritage.

Aunt Lempi ~1895-1979

Dad's sister, Aunt Lempi, is someone I remember well. She was the oldest of the family. My earliest memories of her are the years she was married to John Kangas and lived on a farm in ND. She had two daughters, Sylvia and Vivian. John died young so Lempi was a widow at a fairly young age. She moved to Astoria, OR, to be near relatives. Vivian also lived most of her life in Astoria where she married and had one son, Eddie. Sylvia settled elsewhere and didn't maintain contact with the family or relatives.

Lempi spent much of her time visiting relatives. She would come to our farm and make herself at home for a period of time and then move on. She seemed to have relatives and acquaintances in various places. She was a mixed blessing to Mother. She was a great cook, but she tended to take control of the kitchen which caused some tension between them. Dad and the older kids didn't mind having her around, but the smaller kids pretty much stayed out of her way. Her personality didn't impress the younger ones because she tended to be quite strict and tried to discipline them in a way they weren't accustomed to.

When she wasn't traveling, she spent much of her time with her nephew, Nestor Leino, and her daughter, Vivian. She considered Nestor's place home but was displaced when Sally and Nestor were married.

When we were living in Seattle, Charleen was a baby and Lempi came to live with us and baby sit while Caroleen was working. This seemed to work for me, but Lempi didn't have a great track record of getting along in situations like this and stress built up between her and Caroleen. It became obvious that this wasn't going to work so I asked her if she would like to visit in Oregon. I needed to make a trip to Portland and I asked her if she would like to ride along. She accepted the offer and she spend most of her remaining years in Oregon. She lived well into her 80's.

Aunt Lempi had a slightly harsh personality, but she meant no harm. She just had a different way of handling things. When she was in her 70's, she would walk to Astoria from Nestor's farm which was about a two mile walk to volunteer at "Loaves and Fishes", a charity helping the hungry. She had no driver's license and never owned a car.

Aunt Hilda ~ 1897-1956

Dad's sister, Hilda, and her husband, Gust Leino, had five children, Victor, Nestor, Oscar, George, and Julia. They lived in ND on a farm in the same community as I was raised. I have a vague memory of when they sold everything at an auction and moved to Oregon about 1939 or 1940.

These were tough times and the depression had taken its toll on everyone. The Leino family was no exception, and the fact that Gust had an alcohol problem must have added to their difficulties. The family settled in Astoria, OR, which had a healthy logging economy at that time. Gust was used to hard work so he and the boys went to work in the woods as loggers. Unfortunately, Gust died fairly young of a heart attack while logging.

Aunt Hilda passed away after years of being disabled by health issues that included diabetes which also affected her vision.

Cousin Nestor Leino

When the family was still living in ND and Nestor was old enough to work, he went to live on a farm with another couple. He told me once that his family was poor and they just had too many kids so they sent him to live with this couple that didn't have any kids. It seemed to work for him.

In the fall of 1955 when I arrived in Portland, it was close to Thanksgiving, and everyone was going to Nestor's place for a festive meal. It didn't take long to learn that Nestor's place was where the action was. That is where the family usually ended up when they went to Astoria. Aunt Lempi was living at Nestor's place then and she was a great cook. I remember Nestor and Oscar from a time they came back to ND to visit in the late 40's.

Nestor was the kind of guy who made friends, not enemies. He lived on his small farm near Astoria where he ran his business. Most of his work involved working with his trucks, tractors and other farm machinery. He hauled cattle to Portland, tilled gardens, cut and baled hay, and in his spare time he worked as a carpenter with his brother, George.

Nestor remained a bachelor until he was about forty years old when he married Sally. He got an instant family out of the deal. Sally came with four young children and that worked fine for Nestor who always liked kids. Their family grew to be very close. Sally preceded him in death, the kids left home, and Nestor was once again living alone. He never retired and worked into his eighties when he died of a heart attack. His family and many friends around Astoria still miss him, his ready smile, and good words for everyone.

Cousin Victor Leino

The last time I saw Victor in the late 50's or early 60's he was living in Coos Bay, OR with his wife, Eva. He was working in the harbor as a longshoreman. We didn't get to spend a lot of time together before he died as a young man from a heart attack.

Cousin George Leino

I knew George quite well and he and Nestor worked together a great deal. George went in the home remodeling business when the logging and lumber business went into a decline. George passed away from natural causes when he was in his seventies.

George and his wife, Glenna, had three daughters, Jane, Mary, and Connie, and one son, George Jr., who is also a carpenter. George Jr. lives with his wife and family in the Astoria area.

Cousin Oscar Leino

After spending time in the military during WWII, the Leino boys returned to Astoria except for Oscar who spent several years in Bolivia, South America.

The first time I saw Oscar was when he and Nestor came back to the farm about 1948. They drove up in their 1935 Ford. Duane and I were playing in the yard and we had no idea who they were. We didn't have a telephone so visitors were usually a surprise. It was a timely visit because we were moving from the Laughlin farm to the Miller place and they were a great help.

The next time I saw Oscar was when he visited ND with his wife, Rosa. He had married Rosa when he was living in Bolivia where he was very successful working in construction. He paid cash for a new 1955 Ford and a fully furnished home in Portland. That impressed me.

They lived in Portland while they raised their three boys, Robert, James, and Charlie. We were living in the Seattle area and for many years while our families were young, we visited frequently. We always saw them when we went to Portland and when they periodically drove to Seattle.

After many years, Oscar moved to Nevada with his second wife, Betty, They later retired to Bellingham, WA, where he died of natural causes in his early 80's. I'll always remember him for his offbeat sense of humor.

Cousin Julia Leino Coulter

When I went to Portland in 1955, the first place I stopped was Aunt Elsie's. Julia and Don Coulter also lived in the area. I had met Julia a few years earlier in ND when she came to visit with Elsie and Reader. Julia was a great cousin and we became very close over the years. Don helped me get a job at Portland Chain where he was working. It paid much better than washing cars at Harbor Ford. He was also the best man at our wedding. Don spent his last years in a wheelchair as a result of diabetes. Julia enjoyed good health for several years after Don's death. She died of cancer in her 80's.

Julia and Don had one adopted son, Mark, who still lives in Portland.

Aunt Hilja ~ 1899-1985

The last time I saw Hilja she had moved to Portland from Detroit to be with relatives. She and her husband, Ed Heagle, had a daughter named Grace.

Ed and Hilja spent most of their lives in Detroit where they owned a home. They also lived on a farm in ND not too far from our home for a few years. She was a widow for many of her last years. Aunt Hilja was a jolly person who enjoyed a good joke and had no problem with a slightly off color joke.

Aunt Elsie ~ 1902-1999

I owe a lot to Aunt Elsie and Uncle Reader Moore. If it weren't for their help, life would have been much more difficult when I arrived in Portland. Actually, I might never have gone to Portland if it hadn't been for those terrific people. I might have ended up in Detroit or some other part of the country where there would have been far fewer opportunities.

Elsie had one son who died as a very young man. I have no further history on him which is unfortunate as he was my first cousin.

Aunt Elsie lived to the ripe old age of ninty-seven. She lived independently through most of her advanced years, but her last years were difficult with many health issued including dementia.

Aunt Elsie and Uncle Reader

Uncle Oscar ~ 1904-1972

I first met Uncle Oscar in Astoria when he and his wife made a trip to the west coast from their home in Detroit to visit relatives. Oscar left ND as a young man and worked for General Motors in Detroit until his retirement. I had the opportunity to visit Oscar and his wife, Ellen, in the 60's. I was doing an installation job in Chicago for Western Automation. I had a weekend off so I drove to Detroit to see Oscar and Ellen. I had a great visit with them, but even in those years Detroit wasn't a place I would want to live.

A few years later I was doing another job in Chicago, and I again took a weekend trip to Detroit. Oscar and I were able to spend some of his last days together. He was dying of cancer at the time. I think this meant a lot to both Uncle Oscar and Aunt Ellen as they had no children.

Richard ~ Born 1907-1980

My dad was born June 18, 1907. As I was the oldest son who lived at home until I was sixteen years old, he is the one of the Jussero family I knew the best and have written the most about. He was an exceptional man and I'm proud to be his son.

Uncle John ~1909-1967

Dad's younger brother, John, and his wife, Dorothy, also lived in Detroit. John held a position at Ford Motor Company. He left the farm as a young man and worked for Ford until he died from cancer.

When I was growing up in ND, I remember John and Dorothy spending part of their vacation with us on the farm. They always drove a new Ford product. This may have been part of his company benefit package. It was obvious they were doing quite well financially, and I was impressed. Those weren't great times on the farm.

Aunt Ellen ~ 1912-1987

When I arrived in Oregon, Aunt Ellen and her husband, Jim Crabtree, were retired in Astoria. She and her first husband, Bob Sheaffer, had three girls, Arlene, Nona, and Ramona. We visited her and Jim when we were in Astoria. She had a great sense of humor and we had a lot of fun during our times together. She died of cancer.

Aunt Elma ~ 1915-1977

Elma was one of Dad's younger sisters. She was raised in ND. She married Herb Moilan and they had three children, Lillian, Dale, and Curtis. They raised their family in the same general area as our home. They were farmers except for the few years they spent in Portland where Uncle Herb worked in the shipyards during WWII.

Our farms were only a few miles apart so we had the opportunity to visit quite often. My brothers and I were near the same ages as our three Moilan cousins so we had a great time together while our parents visited.

Aunt Elma spent her last days with Lillian and her family in Portland. Elma had a difficult and painful death with cancer leaving Herb a widower. He continued to farm in ND until he was in his eighties. He retired in Portland and passed away after spending his last years near his family in Oregon.

We've been in close contact with Lillian and her husband, Dale Mitchell, over the years. They've now moved to Minnesota to be near their son, David, and his family. My cousin, Dale, passed away a few years ago after being disabled for a time. Curtis still lives in Oregon.

Mother's Family

MY MOTHER WAS NAMED DORA Cadieux and was born in Alberta, Canada. Many of my mother's family still live in Canada. A few migrated to the US and I had the chance to know them better than my Canadian relatives.

Uncle Edward Cadieux ~ 1900-1960

Edward was the oldest of the Cadieux family. He was born in Ontario and raised in the Lac LaBiche area of Alberta. Unfortunately, I never had the chance to meet Uncle Edward. He died of heart problems before I was able to make a trip to Alberta. Edward and his wife, Maud, had five sons, David, Paul, Gerry, Jay, and Earnest and two daughters, Louise, and Margaret. Ernest and Louise are deceased. Louise had Parkinson's and her daughter, Linda died of Lou Gehrig's disease.

When Edward was younger, he worked in the construction of the Lac LaBiche Inn, a facility built by the railroad to encourage tourism in the area. The building later became a hospital. He also worked with Grandpa Cadieux on some of his ventures including a taxi business. All of the Cadieux kids learned what it meant to work hard at a very early age because a living didn't come easy.

Because Edward was the oldest in the family, he took on a lot of the responsibility of helping raise his younger siblings. Uncle Edward and Aunt Maud spent many years raising their own kids as well as helping their extended family of brothers and sisters after Grandma Cadieux died. My cousin, David, remembers his mother making clothes from flour sacks. Those were tough times. My mother spoke highly of Uncle Edward and Aunt Maud.

Uncle Edward died of heart disease.

Cousin David Cadieux

David, his wife, Bernice, and their family, Joan, David, Silvia, Marilyn, Erlene, Louberta, and Amy, live in the Lac LaBiche area where David spent many years in the premixed concrete business. We had the pleasure of spending time with David and his family in 1987 at our family reunion in Snohomish. He and Bernice have helped me a lot with questions I've had about the Cadieux family while I've been writing this book. David is struggling with Parkinson's disease. He is eight-one years old.

Cousin Paul Cadieux

Paul and Eloise live in Edmonton, Alberta, where they are now retired. Paul had a construction company where he built and remodeled houses—many times under very adverse conditions. The North Country winters can be quite severe. It's not a great climate for home construction. They have two daughters, Melody and Heather.

We've been in close contact with Paul and Eloise over the last several years. They make it a point stop when they come to the US and we've had the pleasure of spending time with them when we go to Canada.

I was semi-retired the first time we visited Paul and Eloise in Edmonton. He was still working in his construction business. We started discussing retirement and he promised to pay us a visit when he retired. I could tell he was very dedicated to his work. I thought to myself that he'd never retire and told him what I was thinking. He said, "You watch me. I know I can give up my work for a retirement of leisure." He did retire shortly after we first visited with him and they have visited us several times. He is a man of his word.

Cousin Gerry Cadieux

Gerry and his wife, Mae, live in the Lac LaBiche area on his dad's farm homestead where they have been quite successful in farming and ranching. Grandpa's homestead is across the road. Mae taught school until her retirement. Gerry and Mae have three sons, Darrell, Dean, and Dale

Cousin Jay Cadieux

Jay, Uncle Edward's youngest son, lives with his wife, Josie, in Edmonton where he spent many years of his life in the tow truck business. They have three children, Eddie, Eileen, and Marie.

Aunt Marie Anne Cadieux Perron ~ 1902-1973

The first time I met Aunt Marie Anne I was a teenager still living in ND. She and her husband, Mike Perron, were on vacation from Canada visiting relatives in the area. Mike's brother, Hector Perron, lived in our community and so did Aunt Bertha and her family. The visit was an opportunity for the brothers and sisters to get together. Mike and Marie Anne had farmed in the area before they moved back to Lac La Biche, Alberta, where Aunt Marie Anne was raised. She and Mike had four children, Evelyn, Cecile, Lucille, and Raymond.

Caroleen and I drove up to Alberta in the early 60's and I had the chance to see many of my relatives some of whom I had never met. It was the last time I saw Mike. A few years later we went back to Lac La Biche with a camp trailer and parked it in her yard. Mike had passed away and Aunt Marie Anne was living alone. I think she enjoyed the company. She died of heart disease just months before her 71st birthday.

Cousin Evelyn Perron Clark

Evelyn lived in Edmonton, Alberta, where she raised her family. Her husband, Bob Clark, was in auto sales. We had an opportunity to visit them several times over the years. They were great people. Bob passed away years before Evelyn. She is also deceased after many years of retirement in Edmonton. They have two sons Dennis and William, living in the Edmonton area.

Cousin Lucille Perron Danes

Lucille now lives with her son Terry, and his family near Edmonton. Her husband, Morrie Danes, passed away a few years ago. Lucille is a happy individual with a great sense of humor. They had two sons, Vern and Terry.

Cousin Raymond Perron

We were in close contact with Ray and his wife, Sybil, over the years. Ray, Sybil, and their son, Harvey, lived in Port Angeles, WA. We visited quite often and became close friends. Ray had a rough retirement. He had Lou Gehrig's disease, an extremely disabling condition. It caused considerable suffering for many years prior to his death from effects of the disease. Sybil lived many years after Ray, but is now also deceased. Harvey and his family live in Bremerton, WA.

Cousin Cecile Perron Parker

Cecile lived in Vancouver, BC, where she and her husband, Hal Parker, spent most of their lives working and raising their family. We were within a reasonable driving distance to Vancouver which gave us many opportunities to visit with Cecile and Hal. We really enjoyed our times with them.

Hal passed away a few years ago. He was a great guy who was fun to be with. Cecile passed away in February 2010 near her family in the Vancouver, BC, area. They had one son, Harold (Skip,) and two daughters, Marie Anne and Colette.

Aunt Bertha Cadieux Henrickson ~ 1903-1982

The Henrickson family farmed near Perth, ND, which was about a half hour's drive over gravel roads from our farm in Picton Township.

Aunt Bertha's place was a favorite destination on holidays and many Sunday afternoons. It was always a treat to visit Uncle Carl, Aunt Bertha and cousins, Don, John, Anne, and Carl.

Most farms in those days were grain farms with a few cattle and chickens. Bertha and Carl were also into raising turkeys. Many of those big birds ended up on the table as the main course at holiday meals that Aunt Bertha prepared. She was a great cook.

After Carl passed away, Bertha and John continued to operate the farm until John's untimely death. Aunt Bertha loved to travel and she continued to tour the world after her retirement in Rolla where she lived until her death at age seventy-nine.

Cousin Don Henrickson

Don left the farm as a young man and moved to Fargo, ND, where he attended a trade school. He later got a good job servicing electrical equipment. He also did quite well as a property owner and landlord in Fargo. I had the opportunity to stay with him and his wife, Jean, and their son, Bob, the winter of 1954-55 when I was in school. Don was a great guy and I learned a lot from him that winter. Unfortunately, he died much too young of a heart attack.

Cousin John Henrickson

John was a fun guy who had many friends. He spent a winter with us in Seattle in the 60's. I have fond memories of some of the parties he and I went on. John also died of a heart attack as a very young man. He had one son, Joe, who lives in the Seattle area with his wife, Teri.

Cousin Anne Henrickson Hoesl

Anne is a favorite cousin. In many ways she is like a sister. We were together often when our families lived on farms in ND. She became a dedicated teacher. She taught in Hansboro, but she was never my teacher. She did manage to keep me out of serious trouble from time to time.

After teaching for many years, she married Don Hoesl, an optometrist in Rolla, where they made their home and raised their family. Don and Anne retired to Wenatchee, WA after selling their home and business in Rolla.

They had five children, Steve, John, Pam, Carla, and Linda. Sadly, Steve is no longer with us. He passed away at the very young age of thirteen. Pam and her husband, Joe Altrazan, and Linda and her husband, Tim Lykken, are raising their families in the Wenatchee area. John also lives in Wenatchee. Carla and her husband, Tom Kane, and their family live in the Kent area.

Cousin Carl Henrickson

Cousin Carl and I were close to the same age and we stayed in contact for many years. We had a lot in common after growing up in ND on our families' farms. After completing high school in ND, he went to SD where he got a great education in the medical field. He later became a professor at Towsend University in Baltimore, Maryland. He and his wife, Eileen, raised their family there. He passed away in his late 50's leaving two young daughters, Sheryl and Ellen, and his wife, Eileen.

Aunt Lillian Cadieux Choquette ~ 1906-1980

In the late 1970's on one of our trips to Edmonton, we met Mom's sister, Lillian and her husband, Joe Choquette. We had a great time with them. She reminded me of Mom. They have two daughters, Evelyn and Doreen. Joe insisted that we had to meet Doreen and her husband, Emil Joly. He took us in his car to their home where we quickly became friends. We found that they were both fun people to be with and we stayed in close contact with them over the next several years. They both have a great sense of humor. We had the opportunity to visit them in Edmonton several times and they in turn came to our place in 1987 for a family reunion. They had five children, Joanne, Bryan, Carol, Ginette, and Marilyn who is deceased.

Uncle Emile Cadieux ~ 1909-1981

We had the pleasure of meeting Emile and Ness years ago on one of our trips to Alberta. They lived on a farm near Lac LaBiche. They had five children, Emile (Sonny), Georgina, Emeline, Gaye, and Mary Lou who is deceased. Uncle Emile passed away in 1981 at the age of seventy-two.

Dora Cadieux Jussero—my mother ~ 1910-1983

My mother was born in Canada but migrated to the US as a young woman. She was a great mother. She worked hard everyday of her life. She had dark hair, a slight French accent and a sparkle in her eye. She and Dad raised their three sons Dwight, Duane and David to be honest, hard-working men. I think she would be proud.

Aunt Virginia Cadieux Stephanik ~ 1911-1989

Virginia and my mother were the two youngest girls in the family. Their age differences were less than a year. Their mother, my grandmother, died when they were only nine and ten years old. Grandpa and their older siblings raised the two younger girls. We had the opportunity to visit Aunt Virginia and her husband, Mike Stephanik, years ago when we were on vacation in Alberta. Their daughters, Pauline and Darlene, were a few years older than Charleen. The kids enjoyed riding the two Honda motor bikes we hauled around on the back of our camp trailer.

In the mid 50's Virginia and Mike and their daughters made a trip to ND to visit Mom and Aunt Bertha. This was the first time I met them. We stayed in contact with them for many years. They moved to southern BC where they operated an orchard for a few years. The move was tough on Mike's health. The last time I saw him he was having serious breathing problems almost to the point of being incapacitated. He died from that condition shortly after we saw him. Virginia moved back to the Edmonton area to be near her daughters.

Aunt Virginia died from natural causes. She also suffered from dementia prior to her death.

Uncle Omer Cadieux ~ 1913-1985

Uncle Omer made a serious impression on me and everyone else who knew him. He expected very little in the way of material goods. He lived a very simple, physically demanding life doing everything the old way. He saw no good reason to change and seemed quite happy living alone on his acreage in his little log cabin. Uncle Omer died from a heart attack. He never married.

Uncle Albert Cadieux ~ 1915-1973

Uncle Albert was the youngest of the nine children. He also farmed in the Lac LaBiche area. We were able to spend a short time with him and Aunt Bernadette on a trip to Alberta in the mid 60's.

We did not see him again. He passed away in 1973 of a heart attack at the age of fifty-seven. They had eleven children, Emile, Lawrence, Daniel, Albert, Anna, Louise, Richard, Leo, Harvey, Denise, and Maurice.

Caroleen's Family

Napoleon Messier

I first met Napoleon in about 1949 when he and his wife, Delphine, and their daughters, Caroleen and Joyce, moved to the farm across the road from our farm in ND.

Nap was born in 1911. His father died in the flu epidemic of 1918 and his mother died about two years later leaving Napoleon and his siblings orphans.

According to the recollection of people who lived through the flu, Napoleon also had it. He was about seven years old and his father was desperately ill or maybe already deceased from the flu. The story is that Nap was gravely ill with a high fever and they thought he was terminal. They moved him from the main part of the house and put him in an unheated porch attached to the house. When they checked on him later his temperature had dropped and his condition had improved. He was one of the strong ones who survived the epidemic

In 1918 there were no phones in the country to call 911, no ambulance, and no paramedics. People were pretty much on their own and it was accepted that if a person were critically ill, there was a good chance they would die. A few miles to the hospital in a horse and wagon or in an unreliable Model T Ford was not practical and there was a chance the trip itself would be lethal. If the illness happened in the winter, the chances of survival were slimmer still. During the 1918 epidemic there were people who kept deceased family members frozen in an outbuilding in the winter until it was practical to transport them to a funeral home.

When their mother died, Napoleon and his brother, Frank, and sister, Aldina, needed to find homes because they were much too young to take care of themselves. They moved to the John and Sylvia Guedesse farm near Rolla and the Guedesse family raised them. Nap's brother, Bill, went to live with the Alvin Sutton family. Fred, the youngest, found a home with the Phelps family on a farm near St. John ND.

Even though Fred, who was four or five years old, lived only a few miles away from his siblings, they lost contact with him. He was in a different school district, telephones weren't available and travel was difficult and slow so they didn't communicate. Fred didn't reconnect with his family until years later when they were adults.

I don't know if the kids were formally adopted or not. People did what had to be done to give this young family a home. I'm sure the fact that they would grow up to be a lot of help around the farm was also considered when they were taken in. Napoleon farmed with "Uncle Johnnie" until he and Delphine were married in 1934.

Nap and Delphine continued to farm in the general area before moving to a 320 acre parcel of land across the road from my parents' farm. It was the home he and Delphine would eventually own. The fact that they were our nearest neighbor meant that I was able to spend a lot of time visiting this wonderful family. I enjoyed Nap's company and he seemed to welcome me hanging around. Hanging around meant the opportunity to spend time near his daughter who was my age. I found more and more reasons to drop by their house. Napoleon and I always had a lot in common and became close friends. We were both country boys and his daughter, Caroleen, would be my wife in a few short years.

Unfortunately, Napoleon and his brothers and sister have all passed on but they are missed. We had a great relationship with the family. Nap's siblings all lived in California in later years and we were able to enjoy visiting with them while vacationing in Sacramento and Woodland, CA. Nap's brothers, Fred and his family, Bill and his sister, Aldina, came to WA occasionally and Frank and his wife, Ada, made it out once.

Napoleon

by
Dave Jussero

Born on the plains
Many decades ago
He grew up on the land
That he cherished so.

This strong, gentle man
Who did nobody harm
Went through tough times
On his Dakota farm.

He loved his wife
And anybody could see
That he thought the world
Of his family.

A mild mannered man
Right to the end,
He loved to be surrounded
By family and friends.

As we say goodbye we'll
Shed many tears
For we'll miss our dear friend
Of so many years.

The time has come
For him to go with the Lord.
So go, Napoleon, and
Claim your reward.

His passing on
Will sure leave a scar,
But there's no doubt
He's better off than the rest of us are.

This is the poem I wrote for Napoleon's funeral.

Delphine Ducatt Messier

Gentle, smiling Delphine was Caroleen's mother. She was the daughter of Jules and Katharine Ducatt. She married Napoleon Messier in 1934 and was a devoted and faithful wife to Nap for about sixty years. They had three daughters, Caroleen, Joyce, and Linda. Delphine became the best mother-in-law I could have asked for when Caroleen and I were married in 1956. I pretty much had her convinced that I could do no wrong.

We enjoyed her visits to WA in the early years of our marriage and were happy when she and Nap decided to retire in Bothell, WA, which is near our home. She continued to live in Bothell after Napoleon passed on until she died suddenly in 2004 of a heart attack.

Her siblings Aloyses, Gerald, Joseph, Rosella Charboneau, Lucille Stein, and Mary Deschamps have all passed on. Many members of her family lived in the Seattle area, but Gerald spent many years in Oregon. Mary lived in Fort Frances, Ontario, and Geraldine lives in California. Cathryn Powell, Gretchen and her husband, Ray Engum, still live in the Seattle area.

Everyone who knew Delphine misses that fine lady.

Napoleon and Delphine Messier

The Messier family from l to r Joyce, Napoleon, Delphine, Caroleen, and Linda

Afterword

It has been about two years since I started this project. It was my first attempt at writing and I couldn't imagine coming up with enough material to write an entire book, but once I started to write, it started to grow. The more I wrote, the more I remembered, and the more I remembered, the more Caroleen typed. The idea was to record some of my experiences and add a few pictures that might interest family and friends. The stack of paper kept growing until now it is a book. I also discovered that I enjoyed writing.

It was my goal to introduce my parents and their siblings, and my grandparents to our daughter, Charleen, our grandchildren, and great-grandchildren. I feel it's important that they know a little about the hardy people who paved the way for the rest of us. They were sturdy, remarkable farmers and business people who made our way of life possible.

I was able to semi-retire by the time I was forty years old. That gave me a lot of time to travel and see much of the US and some of the rest of the world. I have been able to do many things that wouldn't have been possible if I had worked 9 to 5 until I was sixty-five years old.

I'm hoping people who are not part of the family find our ancestors and their stories as interesting as I do. I'm also hoping that I've answered some of the questions my grandchildren haven't yet asked.

FAMILY PHOTOS

Our Wedding in 1956

Delores Berube, Caroleen, Dave, Don Coulter

Mike and Joyce

Dwight (Don) and Barb Jussero

Linda and Vic

Duane and Ann Jussero

Charleen, Justin, Harley, and Cassie

On the left Ryleigh and Max, right Caitlyn and Alex

Dave and Caroleen Jussero